Transnational and Comparative Research in Sport

This book sets out to identify, illustrate and evaluate the major approaches to comparative and transnational analysis of sports policy.

In recent years, there has been a growing recognition that comparative and transnational policy analysis is beset by theoretical and methodological constraints. These include acknowledgement of the prevalence of forms of Orientalism inherent in much Western research, the diminished significance of the 'local' within the rhetoric of globalisation and the challenge of post-modern understandings of truth and knowledge. The fields of sport studies and sports policy are not exempt from these claims.

Transnational and Comparative Research in Sport addresses these difficulties and develops a typology of methodologies for conducting meaningful transnational and comparative research in sports policy.

Part I reviews the theoretical and methodological assumptions and introduces the four-fold typology for comparative policy research. Part II provides research studies illustrating each type of approach. Part III focuses on interculturalism, pluralism and ethics in comparative analysis.

Ian Henry is Professor of Leisure Policy and Management and Director of the Centre for Olympic Studies and Research at Loughborough University, Loughborough.

Transnational and Comparative Research in Sport

Globalisation, governance and sport policy

**Ian Henry
and
the Institute of Sport and Leisure Policy**

Routledge
Taylor & Francis Group

LONDON AND NEW YORK

First published 2007
by Routledge
2 Park Square, Milton Park, Abingdon, Oxon OX14 4RN

Simultaneously published in the USA and Canada
by Routledge
270 Madison Ave, New York, NY 10016

Routledge is an imprint of the Taylor & Francis Group, an informa business

© 2007 Ian Henry and the Institute of Sport and Leisure Policy

Typeset in Goudy by Wearset Ltd, Boldon, Tyne and Wear
Printed and bound in Great Britain by TJI Digital, Padstow, Cornwall

British Library Cataloguing in Publication Data
A catalogue record for this book is available from the British Library

Library of Congress Cataloging in Publication Data
A catalog record for this book has been requested

ISBN10: 0-415-40112-7 (hbk)
ISBN10: 0-203-94473-9 (ebk)

ISBN13: 978-0-415-40112-8 (hbk)
ISBN13: 978-0-203-94473-8 (ebk)

For Dominique and Geneviève Plumion and Aldo Maggi (1918–1992) and Renée Maggi (née Clanet, 1932–1985) whose kindness and generosity first taught me the value of interculturalism

Contents

Figures

Tables

Preface

This book is predominantly the product of the opportunity to interact with three groups of people within, or associated with, the Institute of Sport and Leisure Policy at Loughborough University. The first group is my colleagues within the Institute, Mahfoud Amara, Guillaume Bodet, Paul Downward, Mick Green, Barrie Houlihan, Leigh Robinson and Eleni Theodoraki, who have provided a critical and supportive forum for the discussion of ideas developed in this book. I am very grateful for their generosity and collegiality which generates a very positive social, as well as work, environment.

The second group is made up of colleagues who have been visiting scholars or associates at the Institute or who are based at institutions which have received me as a visiting scholar. It is not possible to list all here, but I should mention Professor Kazuo Uchiumi whose long-standing interest in comparative UK–Japanese policy has resulted in our working on a number of fruitful projects and whose academic scholarship is matched only by his sense of humour (he is Japan's self-professed Tom Jones – believe me, it is unusual); Dr Jolanta Zysko who tested the typology employed in this book almost to destruction in her visit to the Institute in 2004–5 while working on a book on comparative policy; Professor Fan Hong, the founding Director of the Irish Institute of Chinese Studies at the University College Cork, for joint research student supervision and cooperation on a number of comparative projects; Jin Liang of Tianjin Institute of Physical Education who worked in Loughborough on comparative analysis of the development of professional football systems in 2002–3; Li Lingwei of Beijing Sports University who worked at the Institute in 2006 on her research on Olympic policy; Dr Anita White whose policy activism and research interests resulted in our undertaking a review for the IOC of its policy for establishing targets for the proportion of women in executive decision-making positions in National Olympic Committees (2002–4); and Dr Christine Dulac with whom I have worked over a number of years on urban sports policy. In recent years, I have been a visiting professor at Hitotsubashi University in Tokyo, l'Université de la Méditerranée, Aix-Marseille II, in Marseille, and at the University of Technology in Sydney. I am pleased to acknowledge my debt to all these colleagues and the many others who have contributed to our work on comparative and transnational policy, working on projects at the Institute and/or participating in our Friday morning sessions for PhD students and staff at the Institute.

The final group is that of our PhD students (past and present). Engagement with this group has provided intellectual stimulation and a critical, multi-cultural set of research interests and colleagues. Most of those who have graduated have gone on to academic careers at other institutions throughout the world (and three, Mahfoud Amara, Mick Green and Eleni Theodoraki, have become permanent members of the Institute). The PhD group has included Mansour Al-Tauqi, Dawn Aquilina, Elesa Argent, Ilona Berry, Moran Betzer-Tayar, Nikolai Böhlke, Dikea Chatziefstathiou, Yi-Wen Chin, Hyun Joo Cho, Ji-Hyun Cho, Shane Collins, Aurelie Cometti, Megat Daud, David Denyer, Laura Fishburn, David Hindley, Eunah Hong, Hsien Che Huang, Chris Kennett, Ling-Mei Ko, Jae Bok Lee, Ping-Chao Lee, Ian Lindsay, Max Malfas, Nic Matthews, Pantelis Nassis, Jimmy O'Gorman, Dave Piggott, Wirdati Radzi, Juan-Luis Paramio Salcines, Tien Chin Tan, Weiming Wang and Jo Welford as well as visiting research students Lionel Arnaud, Nicolas Chanavat, Chunyan Gao and Ameline Gerbel. Pivotal to the activities of the postgraduate group in recent years has been Mayumi (Ya Ya) Yamamoto who, as both part-time administrator/clerical support for the Institute and the Centre for Olympic Studies and Research and part-time research student, has managed to organise both staff and postgraduate groups with apparently inexhaustible supplies of patience and enthusiasm while maintaining admirable momentum with her own research. Working with such a culturally varied group has provided me with a rich learning experience, particularly in relation to the comparative and transnational policy material developed in this book.

All of the material except that for Chapter 4 was developed in the context of work undertaken by research teams or PhD research under my supervision in the Institute. I would, therefore, like to particularly acknowledge the generosity of Simon Shibli (Director of the Sport Industry Research Centre at Sheffield Hallam University) and Jerry Bingham (Head of Strategy, Ethics & Research, UK Sport) for agreeing to provide the material for Chapter 4 and for allowing me to comment briefly within the body of the chapter on the strengths and limitations of Type I studies. This was the only one of the four types of comparative or transnational studies for which we had no example to draw on from the Institute's work. Simon and Jerry's involvement in this project was thus critical if the book was to reflect the full range of types.

I would like also to thank the following publishers for providing permission to draw on, and adapt material from, four of our own previously published articles.

Sage Publications: Henry, I.P. and Pantelis Nassis. 1999. 'Political clientelism and sports policy in Greece'. *International Review for the Sociology of Sport* 34:43–58.

Presses de l'Université de Québec: Dulac, C. and I.P. Henry. 2001. 'Sport and social regulation in the city: the cases of Sheffield and Grenoble'. *Loisir et Societe/Society and Leisure* 24(2):355–379.

Henry, I.P. 1999. 'Globalisation and the governance of leisure: the roles of the nation-state, the European Union, and the city in leisure policy in Britain'. *Loisir et Societe/Society and Leisure* 22(2):355–379.

Human Kinetics: Henry, I.P., M. Al-Tauqi, M. Amara, and P.C. Lee. 2005. 'A typology of approaches to comparative analysis of sports policy'. *Journal of Sport Management* 19(4):ISSN 0888 4773.

Finally, I would like to thank my wife Carol for her wonderful patience and support and Alasdair and James and extended family for putting up with my preoccupation, being 'locked away', particularly during the latter stages of this project.

Having thanked all those who have made this book possible, responsibility for any imperfections in the text is, of course, my own.

Ian Henry
Loughborough

Part I

Theoretical perspectives and methodologies

1   Globalisation, governance and policy

Ian Henry

Introduction

The first question one might ask in embarking on a project such as this is 'why?'. What is sufficiently intrinsically interesting or extrinsically significant about the topic to dedicate resources to the production of an extended argument in the form of a book? That sport itself is regarded by a large proportion of the global population as sufficiently intrinsically interesting is evident from phenomena such as the television viewing figures for the Olympic games – the International Olympic Committee (IOC), for example, claims that:

> The Athens Olympics broke global TV viewing records, with nearly 4 billion people tuning in … 3.9 billion people watched an Olympic broad-cast at least once during the Aug. 13–29 games, beating the previous record of 3.6 billion viewers for the 2000 Sydney Olympics.
>
> (European Tour Operators Association 2006)

Moreover, the Men's Soccer World Cup Federation Internationale de Football Association (FIFA) estimated viewing figures of 28 billion for the 2002 World Cup (Federation Internationale de Football Association 2002). Sport is thus a significant indicator of global *cultural* trends. In *economic* terms, sport is also seen as an important contributor to the GDP of, for example, European economies (Andreff *et al.* 1995; Jones 1989), and it has become increasingly important to, for example, Asian economies with the global outsourcing of much of the physical production of sports goods and clothing to non-Western economies (Donaghu and Barff 1990; Laabs 1998).

In *political* terms, the importance of sport became increasingly evident throughout the twentieth century with, for example, the clamouring for the recognition of the IOC (as well as of the United Nations) by the newly independent states in the post-colonial period of the 1960s and 1970s (Al-Tauqi 1993) and by the post-Soviet Union independent republics in the 1990s (Bowker 1997; Goodbody 1991; McElvoy 1994). The significance of sport for Western hegemony is also evidenced in the effort by the USA to aid the restarting of the Olympic movement in Afghanistan and Iraq.

The USA is spending over $10 million of "coalition forces" and US tax-payer money to create a new Iraqi National Olympic Committee and prepare its athletes for the Olympic Games. Although none have yet to qualify for any Olympic competition, already numerous young Iraqi athletes are training in the USA and are flown, with military escort, all over the world to compete in qualifying events. ... The IOC has already agreed to allow any qualifying Iraqi athlete to compete in the summer games. The question is whether they compete as individuals, under a neutral flag, such as the Olympic flag, or be sponsored by a recognized Iraq National Olympic Committee and participate under the flag of Iraq.

Under what flag Iraqi athletes compete in the 2004 Summer Olympics may seem a trivial matter but it is critical to whether the IOC will allow the Bush Administration to use the Olympics for propaganda purposes. The US-led occupation government is going to great lengths to show a global television audience that, thanks to American intervention, there is now a new "free" Iraq on the world stage. For the IOC, it would be an unprecedented decision to allow a National Olympic Committee to participate without an independent – let alone internationally recognized – government. The Olympic Movement would suffer immeasurable damage as a result.

(Calmes 2004)

However, as the successful bids of Beijing for the hosting of the 2008 Olympics, and of South Africa for the 2010 Men's Soccer World Cup, illustrate, the attraction of sport in political, economic and cultural terms is increasingly difficult to confine to, or explain as, a concern of the 'developed' economies of the West. Thus, a prima facie case can be made that sport is a compelling topic in its own right and an interesting vehicle for discussion of many of the problems and issues affecting societies globally.

Thus, it is evident that sport is a significant phenomenon worthy of serious treatment, but what of the focus on comparative policy? The vogue for comparative analysis has been in decline for some years now – certainly, a literature search employing keywords of 'sport', 'policy', 'comparative' or their equivalents will render a relatively modest return. Indeed, the social analysis of sport (in terms of sociology, economics and politics) has burgeoned in the literature contemporaneously with the decline of comparative analysis. This decline can be ascribed to three key factors. The first is the phenomenon of globalisation, with its emphasis on the interconnectedness of political, economic and social systems, which has led some to question the appropriateness of using the individual nation state as the default unit of analysis, and thus questioned the value of simple comparisons of national policy systems.

The second factor is theoretical pluralism and the associated epistemological difficulties involved in making comparisons. This is not simply a matter of the critique of positivist claims to be able to compare 'social facts' relating to one national system with those relating to a comparator but also the whole panoply of issues associated with post-modernism and the relativist nature of claims made about national systems. This set of issues is addressed in Chapter 2 in which the argument made is that although such a concern does not represent an impasse for comparative studies, it has provided a significant discouragement for those who might otherwise have employed the term 'comparative' to describe their work.

The third factor explaining the paucity of recent comparative material grows out of the first two. It is associated with the general critique of the Western-centred nature of much social analysis. This is given powerful expression in the Orientalist critique initiated in literary and cultural analysis by Edward Said (1991, 1994, 1997) and taken on in political analysis by writers such as Ziaud-din Sardar (1998, 1999). The critiques of such writers underline the fact that the promotion of Western views of the world is often made on the basis of the (implicit or explicit) disparaging of the 'other', the non-West (which increasingly in the post-communist era represents an Arab/Muslim other), such that writers such as Huntington (1996) can allude to the 'clash of civilizations' in ways which suggest irreconcilable differences between Western and non-Western ways of viewing the world.

In summary, this book represents a qualified rejection of each of these arguments. In essence, it will seek to oppose the following claims:

- first, globalisation diminishes the role of the nation state to such an extent that an understanding of the roles and activities of nation state actors is no longer essential to explanations of the determination of policy;
- second, epistemological difficulties have become so intransigent that comparison of policy systems and contexts is no longer feasible; and third, 'Western' ways of viewing the world are incompatible with non-Western perspectives such that comparisons become impossible.

In this chapter, we take on the first of these issues, globalisation, the role of the nation state and transnational bodies in the development of sports policy. In Chapter 2, we address epistemological issues in comparative policy and seek to steer a course between the claims of universal truths of the 'Enlightenment project' and relativism of radical post-modern analysis. This chapter develops a typology of approaches to comparative analysis based on contrasting epistemological and theoretical perspectives. In Chapter 3, the issue of the limitations of Western-based perspectives on non-Western contexts is considered, in particular the issue of linguistic particularism, and the critiques of Orientalism and the 'clash of civilisations' that seek to undermine the potential for cross-cultural analysis are rehearsed. This chapter takes the line adopted by Bassam Tibi (2001) and others that reference to civilisational blocks that are monolithic and coherent in terms of world view, moral position and epistemological approach is mistaken.

Chapters 4–8 deal with case studies of comparative sports policy analysis which fall into the four categories of comparative analysis identified in Chapter

2. The last of these case study chapters deals with discourse analysis approaches to understanding policy which allow us to reconcile Western and non-Western accounts of policy. Finally, the concluding chapter reviews the ethical dimension of policy and, in particular, difficulties associated with establishing moral consensus across different cultural and policy communities.

Globalisation and social analysis

Globalisation as a concept and as a social phenomenon had, by the beginning of the 1990s, become one of the most discussed topics in the social analysis literature in general and in the sociology of sport in particular. It was not that globalisation itself represented a recent phenomenon. Robertson (1992), for example, identified phases of globalisation from as early as the sixteenth century, and other writers have adopted an even longer timeline. However, the pace and spread of change bound up with globalisation processes had accelerated so quickly in the period since the 1960s that, for many, it seemed that globalisation represents not merely *a* major feature of the contemporary world but rather *the* major feature.

The recognition that globalising tendencies impinge on virtually every sphere of economic, cultural and political life has thus become commonplace. Much of the initial work on globalisation reflected the growing economic interdependence of nation states and national economies (Rhodes and vanApeldoorn 1998). Political interdependence was also subject to debate (Casanova 1996; Rosenau 1989), and there was a particular focus on the impact of globalising tendencies on the role of the nation state (Hirst and Thompson 1995; Mann 1997; Morris 1997; Shaw 1997; Smith 1998). This is allied to the apparent growth in importance of the region and the city as the locus of significant political activity (Andrew and Goldsmith 1998; Jones 1998; Keil 1998). In addition, considerable research effort went into identifying ways in which cultural or leisure forms, including sport, have been either, or both, a reflection of such tendencies or a reaction to globalising phenomena (Featherstone 1995; Maguire 1993a,b, 1994, 1995; Negus 1993; Robertson 1992; Stevenson 1997).

Perhaps what have been regarded as the two key characteristics of globalisation are the speed and geographical scope of change in the contemporary world. Giddens (1990) characterises globalisation in terms of *time–space distanciation*, that is, the phenomenon of people's lives being increasingly less tied to local circumstances, while Harvey (1989) focuses on *time–space compression*, the speeding up of processes given the technological and economic change, in particular across the period since the end of the 1960s. Both acknowledge the increasingly evident interdependence between markets, polities and everyday life in formerly spatially, culturally, politically and economically distinct constituencies. The hierarchy of causes of such globalising phenomena is subject to considerable debate, with some authors giving primacy to economic factors (Sklair 1991; Wallerstein 1983) and others to advances in technology (Rosenau 1989) or to culture (Perlmutter 1991) while both Giddens (1990) and Robertson (1992) argue that globalisation represents the results of multiple dimensions of change. Hay and Marsh (2000), in addition, underline the view that globalisation represents a range of processes or flows which are contingent outcomes of related phenomena in a number of different domains They point to a 'first wave' of globalisation studies which they argue was characterised by studies with different disciplines emphasising particular trends or tendencies but with a lack of attention to detailed evidence. Thus, deregulation and financial liberalisation are emphasised by economists; the withering of the state by political economists; the decline of the nation state by political scientists and international relations scholars; Westernisation, McDonaldisation and cultural homogeneity by sociologists; and post-national, post-modern, post-colonial global culture by cultural theorists. They point to a second wave of studies which critically evaluated many of the taken-for-granted claims of the evidence (Busch 2000) and support Taylor's (2000) contention that globalisation should be seen as a set of tendencies to which there are countertendencies.

Appadurai's (1990) characterisation of globalisation as a system of flows – of finance, technology, media images, values and people – highlights the dimensions of the globalised context, but as Robertson argues, such flows are not 'unidirectional' processes. He highlights a series of tensions inherent in the processes of globalisation, underlining the fact that globalisation-related phenomena vary from one context to the next. However, though the causal accounts of different sources may vary, and though there may be disagreement about the significance of, for example, the role of the nation state in a global polity, or the spread of transnational capital, there is a considerable measure of agreement that major change is occurring in many locales in the ways in which economic, political and cultural life is conducted in the contemporary context. Our concern in this chapter is with highlighting some of the key changes which are claimed in relation to policy systems and subsequently evaluating the extent to which these have impacted on sports policy in a particular context, that of the UK.

Concepts of governance and their implications for understanding policy change

The concept of governance is intrinsically bound up with that of globalisation. As Rhodes comments, the term 'governance' is well used in the literature but is imprecise. He identifies six connotations of the term, namely the minimal state, corporate governance, the new public management, 'good governance', socio-cybernetic systems and self-organising networks, and goes on to provide his own stipulative definition of governance as consisting in "self organising, inter-organisational networks" (Rhodes 1996: p. 652).

There are perhaps three particular concepts of governance that pertain to the analysis of policy in general (and therefore to sports policy) (Henry and Lee 2004). The first is systemic governance, which concerns the way that sport is governed, not directly by national and international sports bodies (such as the

FIFA or the IOC) but rather through the interaction between such bodies and other major stakeholders [media companies, governmental organisations, sponsors, athletes' associations and transnational bodies such as the European Union (EU)] in a network of actors involved in competition, cooperation, negotiation and mutual adjustment. Here, the concern with understanding governance is with understanding the relationships between such stakeholders and the processes of their interaction. The second concept of governance which is prevalent in the literature is that of corporate, or good organisational, governance. This relates to a concern with the ethics of management and policy and the prescription of values such as transparency, democracy, equity and accountability. The third concept of governance relates to political governance. This type of analysis focuses on how governments seek to achieve their objectives, not simply by direct provision of sporting facilities or opportunities, or legal controls, but by a mixture of moral and fiscal incentives in addition to sporting provision, prescription and proscription. An analysis of political governance thus seeks to explain and evaluate the means by which policy objectives are formulated, the strategies for realising these objectives and explanations as to whether and why such policy prescriptions have been successful or unsuccessful. Our focus throughout this book will be primarily on aspects of systemic governance (how mutual adjustment between organisations is negotiated and explains policy outcomes) and political governance (how governments use a variety of policy tools in pursuing policy objectives) but will nevertheless include an ethical dimension in terms of the moral appropriateness of particular policy goals or the means of policy implementation.

As notions of systematic and political governance imply, the use of the term 'governance', in place of 'government', reflects a recognition that in contemporary developed economies governing decisions can no longer be taken by governments alone (whether national or local). Rather, effective decision-making in public policy will need to incorporate other stakeholders from the commercial and/or voluntary sectors. This in turn is a reflection of the interconnectedness of change. As economic competition has increasingly globalised, so pressures have induced nation states, in line with *neo-liberal*, free market philosophy, to reduce state expenditures in order to lower taxation and maintain a competitive position in relation to industrial costs. Thus, the notions of the *minimal state*, or the *hollowing out of the state* (Barnett 1999; dellaSala 1997; Patterson and Pinch 1995), are associated with globalisation of the economy and have key significance in terms of issues of governance. The transfer of knowledge and ideas about governance, whether this takes the form of political ideologies or professional/policy approaches, is also accelerated by greater internationalisation of networks, leading to what Dunleavy (1980) has termed, 'ideological corporatism'. These processes, however, should not be exaggerated, or their manifestation taken for granted. Global–local tensions in policy are, for example, evident in many of the case studies which manifest both globalising tendencies and local responses or resistance.

Claims relating to the hollowing out of the state or the minimisation of its activities do not simply imply an overall reduction in state activities but rather a reduction in particular kinds of activities. Thus, as Gamble (1988) illustrates (in relation to 1980s Britain) in his book *The Free Economy and the Strong State*, a reduction in state activity in certain areas may require a strengthening of the state's powers in others. The pressure for the reduction of state activity is predominantly to be felt in the welfare domain (Taylor-Gooby 1991; Wilding 1992), and thus a *restructuring* if not *withering of welfare states* has ensued in many national contexts (Pierson 1991). Indeed, Jessop has characterised the restructuring of welfare policy in the developed economies as a shift from the welfare state to the *Schumpeterian workfare state* (Jessop 1995; Peck and Jones 1995). The state is 'Schumpeterian', in the sense of conforming to the neo-liberal precepts of Joseph Schumpeter, and 'workfare', in the sense of allying social policy to economic development, work-related goals. These claims invite a consideration of whether similar developments have actually taken place across national boundaries in the domain of sport policy.

While the transnational organising of capital has continued to develop (though still accompanied by the importance of local capital), the need for something beyond the national organisation of labour, and of economic policy, has been recognised. The EU, the development of the single market and moves towards political integration reflect such an approach. The increasing significance of transnational governmental activity conflicts with the tendency to reduce governmental activity, and it is at the transnational level that some social legislation is possible if the costs of social policy advances are not simply to be visited on the economies of 'progressive' states. Thus, the EU has, for example, been the site of discussion and legislation for workers' rights, marginal though the gains may have been in most instances (Hyman 2001; Platzer 2002).

The EU provides perhaps the best contemporary example of transnational governmental activity. The activities of the EU are, of course, coordinated by the governments of nation states, though power is shared between the institutions of the European Parliament, the European Commission and the Council of Ministers (which is drawn from national governments). However, direct accountability is perceived as a problem and results in what is described as 'democratic deficit' (Bellamy and Warleigh 1998; MacCormick 1997). In leisure, culture and sport, superficially at least, there would seem to be a strong argument for respecting the principles of *horizontal and vertical subsidiarity*, that is, that decisions relating to these policy areas should be taken at the lowest level possible (vertical subsidiarity) and also, wherever possible, should be taken by non-governmental organisations (NGOs) (horizontal subsidiarity). Proximity of decision-making to the local community is thus seen as an antidote to democratic deficit.

The Europeanisation project itself, which has invoked the deepening and widening of the EU, is as much a cultural and political, as an economic project, as the ongoing debate about a new constitution for the EU illustrates (Lamassoure 2003; Lammer 2003; Maus 2003). Although, for many of the actors initially involved, the European Community may have been seen as wholly or predominantly an economic project, it has become increasingly clear that to achieve economic goals, a strengthening of transnational political activity would be necessary, and that this would imply some degree of compromise of *national sovereignty*. In order to achieve greater political integration, the cultural dimension of commitment to Europe on the part of its 'citizens' would have to be developed. Thus, issues relating to the *development of European identity* have become increasingly significant. However, the development of a European identity is not unproblematic in that it may be seen as in competition with the national identities that have been constructed over time (Bakke 1995; Hardt-mautner 1995; Haynes and Pinnock 1998; Neumann 1998; Shore 1996; Smith 1992). Leisure, culture and sport have traditionally played key roles in the development of national and local identities, and in any attempt to construct or reinforce European identity, one might reasonably expect sporting forms to perform a significant function.

The role of nation states in economic terms has been complemented by not just an increase in economic significance of governance at the transnational level but also a growing role for subnational economies. Cities in particular have come to see themselves as involved in an inter-urban competition which is no longer bounded by the nation state (Barlow 1995; Kantor *et al.* 1997), and city governments have increasingly become involved in economic development activities, focusing more on 'selling' their cities to prospective investors and less on the delivery and management of traditional public sector services. David Harvey's (1987) seminal article, 'From managerialism to entrepreneurialism: the transformation of urban governance', sought to capture the nature of this shift, spawning a burgeoning literature on the character and significance of *urban entrepreneurialism* (Boyle and Hughes 1994; Hubbard 1996; Leitner and Garner 1993; Wood 1998). The shift in focus from traditional service delivery to entrepreneurial activity has also been associated with changing styles of governance at the local level. Emphasis on local coalitions (Harding 1991, 1994; Jonas 1992; Levine 1994; Wood 1996), or on urban regimes (Digaetano and Kleman-ski 1993; Kantor *et al.* 1997; Stoker and Mossberger 1994), highlights the development of partnerships, particularly with business interests, in the formulation and promotion of policy goals.

The final element of the link between globalisation processes and governance which is to be introduced here is the development of *new managerialism* in the public sector, particularly at the local level. Perhaps the major dimensions of this shift are the changes in culture, in organisational structures and in the criteria employed for evaluating policy outcomes. The shift in culture is referred to by commentators as a shift from welfare provider to service enabler, with provision both by public sector employees and by private and voluntary sector bodies being controlled by contract, hence the identification of this as a shift to a contract culture (Leach *et al.* 1994; Parker 1997). Contracts require the specification of outcomes to be achieved, but while financial goals may be readily specified and their achievement evaluated, this is less straightforward in areas of service provision, and social goals will tend to be under-specified compared with financial goals, and hence a tendency to compromise accountability in the pursuit of effectiveness, efficiency and economy has been identified (Farnham and Horton 1993). The shift from government to governance not only incorporates actors from beyond the traditional public sector in service delivery but also embodies a rejection of the traditional bureaucratic structures of the public sector. In their stead, 'flatter', more autonomous, organisational structures are favoured, fostered in particular by the use of contracting out of management responsibilities (Lane 1995). In addition, partnership activity rather than direct provision has proliferated, with governments seeking to influence delivery of outcomes by exertion of influence through mutual adjustment of goals. The spread of ideas about new managerialism is thus attributed by a number of commentators to aspects of globalisation not only because the interconnectedness of global economies presages common solutions to problems of public sector budgets but also because the interconnectedness of policy networks fosters rapid communication of policy goals, styles and approaches (Harvey 1989).

Illustrating the implications of globalisation and governance for sports policy: the recent history of sports policy in the UK[1]

In the brief review above of claims relating to the growing significance of, and relationship between, globalisation and of governance, five sets of factors of generic significance for policy are identified. These are not necessarily exhaustive of the range of such issues but selected as those which carry the most evident and significant implications for sports policy. They are as follows:

1   the growth of neo-liberal ideology and the process of the hollowing out of the state;
2   the restructuring of the welfare state and the growth of new public managerialism;
3   issues of national identity, national sovereignty and European identity;
4   horizontal and vertical subsidiarity and
5   the development of urban entrepreneurialism.

Such factors have clear implications for comparative policy since they represent transversal influences, cutting across national policy boundaries. The commentary that follows will seek to identify and exemplify their impact more specifically on sports policy by reference to the key aspects of the recent history of sports policy in the UK.

The growth of neo-liberal ideology and the process of the hollowing out of the state/the development of the minimal state

At the end of the 1950s, Daniel Bell's book proclaimed in its title *The End of Ideology: the Exhaustion of Political Ideas in the Fifties* (Bell 1960) that the ideology of social democracy and attendant ideas on economic management and the role of the state had become so dominant that ideological debates were dead. Social democracy, with its emphasis on a mixed economy and progressive taxation to fund welfare measures (though with differing complexions in particular states), had become the orthodoxy of the West. In similar vein, at the beginning of the 1990s, some commentators felt able to declare 'the end of history' (Fukuyama 1993), referring to the end of ideological dispute because of the dominance of the neo-liberal model. Thus, by the late 1980s, the political colour of governments of the day seemed increasingly to have only limited impact on the policy direction they felt able to adopt, with a convergence around neo-liberal policy prescriptions on the part of 'socialist', and centre left governments on the one hand and liberal and conservative governments on the other (Bobbio 1997). This shift from welfarism to a more free market-oriented philosophy was as true for sports and for leisure policy as it was for other policy areas (Bramham *et al.* 1993).

What then might be some of the sports policy implications of the growth of neo-liberal ideology and where might one expect to see these in evidence? One would anticipate that Britain in the late twentieth century, with its legacy of more than a decade of Thatcherism, would be among the nation states most likely to exhibit the policy symptoms of neo-liberal thought. Certainly, a reduced role for the state, the promotion of individualist rather than collectivist policy goals and the shift away from universal provision of welfare services (including sport for all) have all been evident in policy in Britain in the 1980s and 1990s (Henry 2001a; Ravenscroft 1994).

State expenditures on public services were a prime target for Conservative Government cuts in the 1980s and 1990s, and since the delivery of many such services had traditionally taken place through local government, this implied a concerted attempt to reduce the expenditure of local authorities. Such a reduc-tion was indeed achieved, with leisure revenue expenditure by local authorities (a category which incorporates expenditure on sports services) falling by almost 20 per cent in cash terms in the period 1992–3 and 1997–8 alone (CIPFA 1997b). Furthermore, while most of this reduction occurred under Conservative administrations, the incoming Labour Government elected in 1997 accepted the spending limits projected by its Conservative predecessor up to 2000, reflecting a continuity across Conservatives and Labour governments, encapsu-lated in the term 'Blaijorism', signifying a more socially responsive rhetoric than Thatcherism but a shared commitment to reduction of the size of the public sector (Hay 1997). The control of local government expenditure has, however, failed to achieve significant reductions over time, though the growth rate of expenditure has slowed considerably (Treasury 2006).

Neo-liberal policy is not simply a matter of instituting cuts to reduce the level of activity of government, it also implies promotion of market approaches in the services which remain in the public sector and of an individualist self-help philosophy and a denial of collective interests. The partial replacement of state expenditure on sport by funding from the National Lottery reflects the impact of neo-liberal thinking. The National Lottery was launched in the UK in 1994 with a considerable proportion of the proceeds being made available to five 'good causes', including sport and the arts. These were not insignificant sums. In the first 42 months of operation for England and Wales alone, £755 million of grant was awarded for sport, considerably more than that granted by the Sports Council and its successor bodies over the same period. Thus, the rational planning of sport and funding on the basis of need (welfare planning under the welfare state) were partially replaced by a system where bidding for funding is dominant. Central planning of funding for elite sport through UK Sport (one of the successor bodies to the Sports Council) was increasingly evident, but community sport funding was bidding led. In terms of community sports provision, the Lottery funding system rewarded those most able to bid effectively for funds, rather than those most in need. Furthermore, funding from the Lottery was largely for capital projects (and for the revenue support of individual elite sports competitors), so that where revenue funding for repairs to a publicly owned facility had been lost because of reduced public sector budgets, Lottery funds could not be used in their stead. A key difference between a system based on bidding and one founded on needs-based social planning is that the former can compound problems of need since the neediest groups include those with the fewest resources with which to construct bids for funding. The shifting emphasis from treasury and local authority funding support for community sport to Lottery funding thus reinforced this problem.

The rise of neo-liberal thought has implications for all spheres of policy, but in particular it implied a radically altered relationship to welfare policy and the notion of the welfare state and thus to the social goals of sports policy.

The restructuring of the welfare state and the growth of new public managerialism

The decline of the welfare philosophy of universal rights led to a de-emphasising of the notions of sport for all and culture for all. Indeed, in the mid-1990s, the Conservative government in a major policy paper on sport, *Sport: Raising the Game* (Department of National Heritage 1995), confirmed the refocusing of policy at the national level on sporting excellence and national performance, and on youth, and the delegating of responsibility for sport for all to local government. However, this delegation of responsibility to local government was accompanied by a continuing squeeze on local government expenditure, so that concentration of responsibilities in local government was accompanied by a reduction in financial resources. Although under New Labour there has been considerable emphasis placed on the rhetoric of challenging social exclusion in and through sport (Banks 1998; Collins *et al.* 1999; Labour Party 1997), the steps to be taken to achieve this have often been ineffectual (Collins 2002).

Thus, the emphasis in sports policy on universal *rights of citizenship* (neatly encapsulated in the policy slogan 'sport for all', which signified an extension of more basic welfare rights such as education or housing for all) by the mid-1990s had given way to an emphasis on *consumer rights*, the right to meet one's needs through the market without due let or hindrance by the state. However, the decline of social democracy was not associated in Britain with a dismantling of the welfare state, but rather with its significant restructuring. A preoccupation of the Labour Government of the late 1970s and of the Conservative Governments of the early 1980s was with urban social disorders, and this ensured that sports policy priorities were for inner-city schemes which targeted disadvantaged areas and potentially volatile groups. Sports Council schemes such as 'Urban Deprivation Grants', 'Areas of Special Need' and 'Action Sport' were accompanied by general Urban Programme funding direct from central government for sport and recreation (Henry and Bramham 1986). However, when it became clear that urban disorders, though serious, were only sporadic phenomena, Mrs Thatcher declared economic development to be her priority for inner-city action after winning the 1987 election (Deakin and Edwards 1993). There ensued a marked shift away from the social targeting of inner-city expenditure (using sport in particular to 'integrate' socially disaffected youth) towards expenditure on sport as a tool of economic development, involving the use of sport for purposes such as city marketing or forms of revenue generation (Henry 1993). Social service-oriented sporting provision in inner-city areas was thus subordinated to the goals of direct or indirect income generation, an approach most evident in the forms of urban entrepreneurialism discussed in the next section.

The restructuring of the welfare state not only implied changes in the nature of the services provided by the state, it also implied the development of new approaches to the management of public sector service delivery. The term 'new managerialism' reflects change along three principle dimensions: those of organisational structures, of organisational cultures and of accepted measures of output or policy evaluation criteria. In the contemporary context, criteria of organisational performance in sport and leisure services often tend to be couched in market-oriented terms, with an emphasis on economy and efficiency rather than on social criteria of effectiveness (Coalter 1995b). The culture of the public sector organisation has been subtly changed such that service beneficiaries are deemed to be customers or consumers, rather than clients or citizens (Coalter 1990; Ravenscroft 1993), and the professional identity of sports policy professionals is framed less in terms of the notion of a liberal welfare semi-profession and more in terms of an industrial semi-profession – a transformation from social worker to marketeer (Farnham and Horton 1993).

The introduction of market forces in public sector management of sports facilities in particular through the introduction of compulsory competitive tendering (CCT) for the management of publicly owned facilities tended to produce a set of public sector facilities which were often driven by the need to maximise revenue, and which therefore sought to attract high-value market segments, at the cost of low-income groups within the general population (Aitchison 1997; Centre for Leisure and Tourism Studies 1992, 1993; Centre for Leisure Research 1993; Coalter 1995a). Thus, in addition to the privatisation of aspects of the public sphere and/or its management, even where service delivery remained in public sector hands, pressures to become more market-like undermined the traditional public service orientation of those services.

At the end of its first term in 2000, New Labour replaced the requirement to subject local government services to CCT with its own broader initiative of 'Best Value' which placed a requirement on local government among other things, to consult local communities about priorities, to compare performance (against benchmarking data) (English Sports Council 2000) and to subject services to competition. This was part of a wider modernisation programme which incorporated the promotion of business models of management in the public sector and which to a degree also fostered other forms of outsourcing of publicly provided services. The Best Value initiative clearly grew out of the earlier value for money philosophy pursued with CCT and the Citizens' Charter in the UK and other similar initiatives in Europe, Australia and New Zealand and represented a confluence of the streams of thinking associated with new public managerialism, and community and local governance, with Best Value representing a softening of the contract culture involved in new public managerialism (Bovaird and Halachmi 2001). While social goals may be more evident in the rhetoric surrounding the imposition of the Best Value system (English Sports Council 1999), they remain in tension with other aspects of performance (Pratchett 2002), and business excellence is still for many local authorities the core of what New Labour's Modernisation programme is intended to promote (Ball *et al.* 2002). The continued presence and growth of initiatives in the externalisation of provision such as the proliferation of trusts and the continued presence of private contractors in the management of sports facilities, together with the pressure to achieve commercial goals under value for money evaluations, ensure that the state's role in sport represents a continuation of key aspects of the new public managerialist approach

Issues of national identity, national sovereignty and European identity

The discussion to date has highlighted the impact of global forces on domestic sport and leisure politics, arguing that globalisation tendencies in the economy have to a degree fostered neo-liberal philosophy, which encompasses the view that the welfare state should be restructured along lines which would render the national economy less tax ridden and therefore more competitive. The room for manoeuvre in social policy terms on the part of national governments in such circumstances has become reduced (though not eliminated). Indeed, the area of sports policy is one in which there may ironically be greater room for autonomy than others for a number of reasons: its political salience may be perceived as lower than other policy areas such as education or health and therefore less subject to ideological attack and more prone to political consensus; it may be seen as a relatively cheap means of alleviating some of the social costs of economic restructuring; the costs of policy modifications may be small in relative terms since sport does not constitute an area of high direct spend by government; marginal funding is available from non-governmental sources (the National Lottery); and finally, sport has value in economic as well as social terms. In addition, culture in general, and sport in particular, is of real significance in promoting notions of national identity. This means that the attention of those whose political interests are linked to the nation state, in particular national governments, is likely to be drawn to aspects of sports policy. This characteristic is well illustrated in the British case by the circumstances surrounding the publication of the governmental statement *Sport: Raising the Game* (Department of National Heritage 1995) in the run up to the general election of 1997.

Raising the Game was the first major policy statement on sport in Britain for 22 years. The significance of sport for key actors in the government is underlined by the fact that though the document was published under the auspices of the Department of National Heritage, the Prime Minister himself chose to write a preface to the document outlining the significance of sport. The document and, in particular, the preface are fairly unequivocally nationalistic. John Major, for example, writes:

> Some people say that sport is a peripheral and minor concern. I profoundly disagree .... Sport is a central part of Britain's National Heritage. We invented the majority of the world's great sports and most of those we did not invent, we codified and helped to popularise throughout the world. It could be argued that nineteenth century Britain was the cradle of the leisure revolution every bit as significant as the industrial and agricultural revolutions we launched in the centuries before. ... Sport is ... one of the defining characteristics of nationhood and of local pride.
>
> (Department of National Heritage 1995: p. 2)

The document focuses policy interest in sport on two areas, that of youth and of national performance, and indicates the government's intention of investing £100 million in the establishment of a National Academy of Sport. The policy statement came at a time when the Conservative Party had reached a low ebb of public support and when the Party itself was manifesting deep and electorally damaging divisions on the issue of Europe and the erosion of national sovereignty by the growing power of the European (Black 1992). Sport was one policy area in which the Government could demonstrate, at least in symbolic terms, its affiliation to the protection of national identity in a way which was likely to have a wide appeal. Attempts to rectify the decline of Britain's national performance would almost invariably attract cross-party support from among the electorate.

However, if the construction of *national* identity through sport was implicitly recognised in the policy moves of the Conservative government of the mid-1990s, the role of sport (and that of other cultural forms) in helping to construct a *European* identity had been recognised by the EU explicitly in the

1980s (Shore 1993). The process of European integration since the signing of the Treaty of Rome has proceeded sometimes fitfully, with hiatuses such as that during the 1960s when De Gaulle pursued an 'empty chair' policy, refusing to attend meetings in order to frustrate plans for widening the then European Community. Nevertheless, it came to be widely recognised that progress in European market integration, which started as a predominantly economic endeavour for some, was likely to be impossible without a strong element of political integration. Political integration itself could not be achieved without winning over the consent and the commitment of European citizens, that is, citizens of the member states would have to come to relate to a European identity. This concern exercised the minds of the European Community Council of Ministers when they received the Adonino Report *A People's Europe*, in 1985. The report highlighted ways in which a cultural identity for European citizens might be developed. Some of its recommendations such as the adoption of a European anthem and an EU flag and the promotion of EU policy in the cultural sphere have been adopted. In the Treaty on European Union agreed at Maastricht in 1994, a competence in the field of culture was adopted for the first time, and the revision of that Treaty at Amsterdam in 1997, although stopping short of adding an article on sport giving the EU definitive powers in the field of sports policy, incorporated a declaration on sport for the first time (Henry and Matthews 1998). This did not go as far as some parties in the sports world had wished since it did not give the EU the authority to intervene in sports policy for its own sake, but it did reflect the acceptance that this was a policy area of significance for the EU as well as for the nation states.

Among some of the ideas rehearsed in the Adonino Report were the establishing of a pan-European Games, the entering of a European Olympic team and the provision of support for sporting events which promoted European identity. Some of the more radical ideas have not been acted upon, but others found their way into EU policy. For example, the EU has funded the establishment of sporting events such as a European Clubs Swimming Championship and supported the (already existing) European Ryder Cup team (even though that represents more than simply the EU states). It also supported during the 1990s developments such as the European Yacht Race, a race which was routed to join various European ports and the extension of the Tour de France into other countries (Netherlands, Belgium, Germany, UK, etc.). This symbolic use of sport to 'unite' the territory has precursors in the pre-modern and the modern eras, at the levels of the local and the nation state, respectively. In the pre-modern era, marching or riding the bounds, for example in Scottish towns, was a means of reasserting annually the extent of the boundaries of the township; similarly, in Brittany, the tradition in catholic parishes of the *pardon*, or procession round the boundaries of the parish, on the feast day of the saint after whom the parish church had been named, reaffirmed the sense of religious and political community of the parish. Phillip Dine (1997) has illustrated how in the modern era in the early twentieth century, the Tour de France was inaugurated in part as a means of asserting the unity of the French nation, and formed as it had been out of diverse regions, sometimes with aspirations for separate identity. In the late modern or high modern period of the late twentieth century, it may be argued that the EU support for the European Yacht Race seeks to perform in symbolic terms much the same function, of publicly asserting a symbolic unity of a political entity. Whether one accepts this assertion or not, it is difficult to deny that culture, sport and identity politics are intrinsically bound up and that there is a tension in the period of late modernity between their use in promoting national, supra-national or local identities (Roche 1998).

Horizontal and vertical subsidiarity

The principle of subsidiarity is one which is central to the policy philosophy of the EU. Vertical subsidiarity is the principle that any decision which is taken by government should be taken at the lowest level possible. Thus, environmental policy is taken at transnational level in relation to, for example, global warming, but decisions about management of schools may be a purely local matter. Horizontal subsidiarity is the principle by which decisions should not be made by governmental bodies if non-governmental bodies can efficiently and fairly undertake responsibility. Culture and sport might be said to be archetypal policy areas where the involvement of government, and of transnational government in particular, might be minimised. The governance of sport, for example, is a matter largely for NGOs such as the national and international sports federations and bodies such as the IOC or FIFA, and local decisions about sporting competitions, eligibility of individuals to play and to coach sport, would be taken by local bodies within the framework of decisions by governing bodies.

The principle of subsidiarity is, however, harder to defend in the context of sport than might first appear to be the case. This is in part because sport is a cultural phenomenon, access to which is regarded by many as a democratic right. Sport is part of the cultural heritage of a nation or a community. Thus, for example in the broadcasting of sports events of national or European significance, the EU has sanctioned exemptions to competition policy to allow national governments to restrict broadcasting of certain events to free-to-air television (Billingham 1996).

Sport is also a major area of economic activity such that legislation on freedom of movement of persons, capital and services in sport may be protected. As the Bosman case has so graphically illustrated, the decisions of sporting bodies are subject to legal challenge if they do not conform to required EU employment or contract practices (Morris et al. 1996; Silvestro and Silvestro 1996; Urbain 1996). The Bosman ruling established that the Union of European Football Associations (UEFA) and other sporting bodies had no right to restrict the numbers of European players playing in a club side within a member state of the EU, and that when professional sportspersons reached the end of their contract period, they were free agents whose movements could not be constrained by the transfer fee demands of former employers. This ruling, particularly in relation to the freedom of movement of European citizens within the EU, has led to the radical internationalisation of the playing rosters of club sides. Chelsea or Arsenal in the English Football Premiership, for example, have regularly fielded teams with few or no British players in their starting line-up. This clearly has implications for the domestic production of players. The logic of the end of tariff barriers is that production of goods, services or personnel in the EU takes place in those regions where it is most efficient and that there is a clear degree therefore of regional specialisation anticipated in production terms. However, this logic applied to the production of footballers is likely to result in the worrying phenomenon of poor national sporting performance where locally produced players cannot develop because they cannot get access to playing positions in their country's own domestic professional competition.

Other rulings of the European Court in relation to sport have also had far-reaching implications. The Heylens case in 1986 is one such example, where a Belgian football coach appealed successfully to the European Court against his prosecution by the French state for coaching professionally without a French coaching qualification. Heylens' case established the principle that EU member states could not exclude from employment any citizen of a member state who had undertaken qualifications equivalent in level and duration to those required of its own citizens (Seary 1992).

What is clear from these brief examples is that the locus of decision-making in relation to sport does not necessarily lie in the voluntary or private sectors with the sports' governing bodies nor are decisions necessarily taken at local or national levels. Sport is therefore not a classic case of either horizontal or vertical subsidiarity, and if globalised sport-media production continues to grow in prominence, the inter-linking which is implied in the globalised context of sport seems likely to further implicate transnational government in sports policy decision-making.

The debate about whether the EU should adopt an article on sport in the amended Treaty on European Union continued to develop after the signing of the Treaty of Maastricht. The Nice Treaty in 2000 produced a protocol appended to the main body of the document underlining the role of the EU in safeguarding current sports structures and maintaining the social function of sport within the EU. This protocol included sections on amateur sport and sport for all – the role of sports federations; sports training policies; protection of young sportsmen and sportswomen and the economic context of sport and solidarity – and on player transfers. This was subsequently reflected in the draft Constitution for Europe which in 2003 proposed the adoption of the following elements of Article III which would provide a legal competence for EU intervention in the field of sport.

> The Union shall contribute to the promotion of European sporting issues, given the social and educational function of sport ... developing the European dimension in sport, by promoting fairness in competitions and cooperation between sporting bodies and by protecting the physical and moral

integrity of sportsmen and sportswomen, especially young sportsmen and sportswomen.

Article III-182 of the Draft Treaty Establishing a Constitution for Europe
(Europa 2003)

Though the Constitution currently lies moribund following the failure of refer-enda in 2005 in France and the Netherlands to support ratification, the Council of Ministers and UEFA together promoted an *Independent European Sport Review* (Arnaut 2006) which explored alternative means of legitimating EU action in sport.

The development of urban entrepreneurialism

If the hollowing out of the state refers to displacement of policy concerns upwards to the supra-national level, it also implies displacement downwards in the direction of the region and/or the city. In Britain, in the period of welfare state growth and consolidation of the 1960s and 1970s, in relation to sport as with other forms of social provision, cities were charged with the detailed implementation of policy, promoting the consumption of social services. By the early 1980s, priorities had changed. Many local economies had been restruc-tured following deindustrialisation, and the emphasis on sport and leisure as a social service (with 'sport for all' delivered via local government) gave way to the use of leisure as a tool of economic development (sport and culture for city marketing). This shift in emphasis implied very different forms of leisure provi-sion. A review of sports policy in major cities such as Sheffield, Birmingham, Manchester or Edinburgh will reflect this shift.

The major feature of sports policy in Sheffield in the last two decades was the attraction and staging of the World Student Games in 1991, which left a legacy of excellent facilities but also of debt. In the post-Games period, the City Council adopted the structural strategy of managing the new facilities through a trust, allowing more freedom, for example to raise capital, but placing the running of the facilities at arm's length from the Council. Traditional sporting services were, however, retained under the umbrella of direct municipal provi-sion. Each year, subsequent to establishment of the trust, pressures to improve financial performance have grown such that management has had to become increasingly entrepreneurial in order to meet income targets. The structural change has thus also meant a change in organisational culture, and the local authority (or its trust) has found itself, for example, competing with the com-mercial health and fitness sector in the city in terms of price and quality (Henry and Paramio Salcines 1999a).

The overall outcome in terms of sports policy might be characterised there-fore as a two-tier policy, with an increase in consumer rights for those who can afford to pay private sector or near private sector rates, with some lower level welfare rights (subsidised sports development) for others who do not have the financial resources to benefit from consumer choice. Sheffield in attempting to enter the transnational inter-city competition for attracting inward investment has sacrificed in part its commitment to retaining local social service aspects of policy. Of course, not all shifts in sport and leisure policy are unidirectional and market oriented; welfare items do receive consideration. However, the story of the development of leisure policy in the city of Sheffield highlights the increasing pressures on local goals of inter-urban competition which sucks cities in to the approaches involved in urban entrepreneurialism.

Conclusions

In this chapter, we have sought to address ways in which globalisation processes have impacted on policy, illustrating with examples from a UK and European context. However, globalisation processes are both multifaceted and contingent in their manifestation (Hay and Marsh 2000). Global structures are the product as well as the context of human agency, and in any given locale or policy area, the influence of global phenomena may (consciously or unconsciously) be embraced, adapted or rejected. Thus, this introduction invites a number of questions in relation to policy at a number of levels, specifically at the level of the nation state, of international/transnational policy and of the city. It is the addressing of these questions and the identification of methodologies which are employed in these contexts which constitutes a target for the book (rather than, for example, a systematic attempt to describe sports policy systems in any representative fashion).

The case study material incorporated in this book seeks to illustrate and evaluate analysis at these various levels. Chapters 4, 5 and 8, for example, consider policy developments at the national level. While Chapter 4 addresses questions of comparative measures of performance in the context of the intensification of international Olympic competition, Chapters 5 and 8 specifically address the tensions between global and local factors impacting on sports policy in the context of the 'local' phenomenon of clientelism. Chapter 6 seeks to identify different national sports policy responses to the global phenomenon of cultural heterogeneity. At the city level, Chapter 7 focuses on the explanation of policy congruence in two very different urban/national contexts. At the international/transnational level, Chapter 3 rehearses the history of the (re)construction of the Olympic movement in the 1960s and 1970s, while the final chapter provides an analysis of the difficulties in agreeing global policy goals in a culturally differentiated world. In each of these studies which incorporate a wide range of contexts (Algeria, France, Greece, Taiwan, UK, Africa and Asia, the EU member states and the global context of the Olympic family), an explanation is sought within particular theoretical frameworks which allow for the contingent evaluation of global structures and processes and for local historical, cultural and political specificity. In Hay and Marsh's terms, we are as concerned to demonstrate how local practices construct or reform global practices as we are with the impact of the global on the local (Hay and Marsh 2000).

2 Methodologies in comparative and transnational sports policy research

Ian Henry, Mansour Al-Tauqi, Mahfoud Amara and Ping-Chao Lee

In the previous chapter, we noted three core sets of difficulties which to some extent explain the decline in comparative policy studies generally and in relation to sport in particular. The first set of factors, that of globalisation and associated phenomena which cut across nation state and policy boundaries, was the subject of discussion in Chapter 1. In the commentary which follows, we focus on the second set of factors associated with the epistemological and ontological implications of the methodological pluralism which has been increasingly evident in the social sciences over the last two decades, in particular with the onset of post-modern critiques of traditional methods. The certainties of modernity – of rationality, progress, scientific method, universal knowledge and objective truth – have come under increasing attack from advocates of post-modern, relativist, locally specific, discourse-produced knowledge, the truth value of which is local, subjective and limited. Such a set of claims renders comparison problematic, even within cultures and at the local level, let alone comparison on a cross-national basis. However, while these methodological problems are real and significant for comparative policy analysis, little reference is made to such issues within the comparative sports policy literature.

What this chapter therefore intends to provide is a conceptual ground-clearing exercise, relating to work in this field. Specifically, the chapter has three aims. The first is to characterise the changing nature of comparative policy analysis in the field of sport. The second is to outline a framework for conceptualising the nature of comparative and transnational studies and to apply this to the field of sports policy. The third is to highlight the methodological and epistemological foundations of the approaches to comparative policy analysis identified.

Commentary will be structured around a typology of approaches to comparative analysis, two of which represent somewhat traditional approaches to comparative studies, the third of which is associated with the body of work which might loosely be described as globalisation studies and the final is one which specifically relates to analysis of policy as discourse.

Traditional approaches to comparative sports policy analysis

Type I: seeking similarities

The first of the approaches involves those studies which operationalise some measures of participation/policy commitment to allow comparison along the multiple cases of policy systems. In classic studies of this type, 'objective' data are subject to analysis to identify forms of statistical association between social, political, economic and cultural conditions or context on the one hand (e.g. levels of GDP across comparator countries) and policy outcomes on the other (e.g. size of sports club or association membership). Typical dependent variables in such studies might be frequency of participation in sport, levels of government expenditure in sport, number of hours spent on physical education in schools, time allocation to sport in time-budget studies or media data in respect of hours of sport broadcast.

The approach adopted in this type of research can be characterised as nomothetic, since it seeks to establish law-like generalisations. There may be an element of providing support for a particular theoretical base or position; for example, the modernisation thesis might be supported where measures of increased bureaucratisation of sporting organisations provide evidence of an increasingly rational design set for sporting organisations in a diverse range of national contexts. In other instances, however, the statistical associations generated may simply provide the basis for qualitative exploration of associations discovered.

The strength of this Type I approach is to be found in its ability to accommodate and summarise large numbers of cases, although operationalising the concepts one might wish to measure, such as 'sports equity', and the quality, availability and comparability of data in such studies, will present significant difficulties [indeed, classic criticisms of, for example, Durkheim's (1952) study of suicide alert us to such difficulties]. The approach of 'seeking similarities' thus tends to ignore cultural specificities in the search for universalisation or generalisation. The social meaning of an activity or of a definition of an expenditure category is sacrificed for the purposes of cross-case comparison.

We will discuss four studies here as exemplars (Table 2.1) since each of these illustrates in different ways the contribution and limitations of the Type I approach. These are Szalai's (1972) study of time use in different national contexts, Jones' (1989) review of the expenditure patterns on sport in selected Council of Europe member states, Gratton's (1999) analysis of sports participation in European states and Rodgers' (1978) review of sports policy systems in European states. In addition, Chapter 4 in this book provides an example of Type I study of indicators of Olympic success across nation states.

The first two studies to be discussed illustrate the difficulties of operationalisation of concepts in simple, quantifiable, comparable units. Szalai's multinational study sought to compare the uses of time across different national cultures and was focused on (among other uses of time) leisure rather than sport. The

Table 2.1 Four types of comparative analysis of sports policy

Types of approach to comparative sports policy analysis	Nature of approach	Strengths	Weakness	Core problem	Examples of policy studies approximating to type
Type 1: seeking similarities	Nomothetic – seeking law-like generalisations, e.g. modernisation theory and structural Marxism	Large numbers of cases accommodated once concepts are operationalised	Identifies statistical or other forms of association without explaining why these occur by reference to agents' accounts	Defining and operationalising concepts in widely different contexts	• Szalai, Alexander (ed.) *The Use of Time* The Hague: Mouton, 1972; Jones, H. (ed.) *The economic impact and importance of sport: a European study*, Strasbourg: Council of Europe, 1989 • Rodgers, B. *Rationalising Sports Policies: Sport in its Social Context: International Comparisons*, Strasbourg: Council of Europe, 1978 • Gratton, C. (ed.) COMPASS 1999, London: UK Sport, 1999 *See also Chapter 4*
Type 2: describing differences	Ideographic – emphasis on historical specificity of cases, often middle range theory, e.g. policy networks	Accounts for how and why societies differ	Danger of explaining everything by reference to historical contingency	Validation of interpretation and moving beyond the descriptive	• Houlihan, B. (1997). *Sport, policy, and politics: comparative analysis*. London: Routledge, 1997 • Henry, I. and Paramio-Salcines, J. (1999). 'Sport and the Analysis of Symbolic Regimes: an Illustrative Case Study of the City of Sheffield', *Urban Affairs Review* 34(5). *See also Chapters 5 and 6*

Type 3: Theorising the transnational	Glocalisation – Intra, inter, and trans-state analysis	Considers both global and structural context and local and agency responses	Complexity – e.g. evaluating not simply impacts of structure but actors' perceptions of such impacts	How to balance explanation between global and local factors – and between structure and agency	• Henry, I.P., Liang, J., Uchiumi, K. and Amara, M., 'The governance of professional soccer: Five case studies - Algeria, China, England, France and Japan', *European Journal of Sports Science*, 5(4), December 2005, 189–206. • Henry, I.P. and Uchiumi, K. (2001). 'Political Ideology, Modernity and Sports Policy: A Comparative Analysis of Sports Policy in Britain and Japan'. *Hitotsubashi Journal of Social Sciences* 33(2):161–185. *See also Chapter 7*
Type 4: Defining discourse	Seeks to clarify how the conceptualisation of the policy issue is defined by the discursive process – discourse analysis	Focuses on the social construction/ definition of policy problems, and the power of discourse to frame the possible	Relativism – claims that 'real' problems do not exist independently of their discursive construction	Issues of validity/ reliability, and the privileging of one account over another	• Amara, M. (2003). *Global sport and local modernity: the case of professionalisation of football in Algeria*. Unpublished PhD thesis, Loughborough University, Loughborough *See also Chapter 8*

use of time might be thought to provide one of the simplest and most 'culturally independent' units of analysis. Its use as a measure is presumably intended to get round difficulties such as how leisure is to be defined. It might seem at first sight to obviate the need to measure 'leisure' or 'sport'; one simply has to measure amounts of time used for particular purposes. However, this is an oversimplification, since what constitutes 'sport' or 'leisure' has to be defined before quantification can take place. Produced as the Szalai studies were at a time which predates much of the feminist literature on the different relationships to time of men and women, what had appeared to be relatively value-free notions of time accounting have been subjected to considerable debate in the light of feminist critiques (Green et al. 1990). Such critiques have argued that, given the traditional divisions of labour, time use will be experienced, and described, differently by men and women and that in particular the notion of free time will be problematic for many women for whom domestic labour is not characterised as 'work'.

Similarly, the Council of Europe's study of the economic importance of sport, which is reported in Jones (1989), is limited in value (as the authors clearly acknowledge) by the lack of comparability in the ways in which sports expenditure had been measured across the countries involved. Thus, evaluations of which countries spend higher proportions of their GDP on sport are made in the most tentative of ways, hedged by caveats concerning the accuracy and comparability of the data used, reducing confidence in the significance of claims made.

While Brian Rodgers' (1978) comparative analysis of the sports policy systems of Western Europe also acknowledges the difficulties of operating in a field in which available data were non-comparable, Gratton (1999) COMPASS study seeks to address the difficulties of non-comparability by both reporting existing data and influencing the collection of data in future national sports participation surveys within the Council of Europe. Despite problems with the existing data, on the basis of seven countries, the authors do seek to make some general claims, identifying a North-South 'split' with higher levels of participation and greater penetration of sports participation in difficult target groups (women and the elderly) in the two Scandinavian countries in their sample (Finland and Sweden) when compared with the two Southern European countries (Italy and Spain). In addition, they are able to point tentatively towards evidence of increased sports 'literacy' in Europe since Rodgers' earlier policy review.

Although the COMPASS study certainly addresses the key issue of comparability, it makes certain assumptions (about translatability of concepts) in relation to transnational surveys or comparable national surveys. However, even where statistical patterns are identified, such as similarities between Northern or Southern European participation rates, one cannot assume common cause or causes of similar outcomes. Such claims can only be developed on the basis of detailed qualitative analysis which is absent from this approach of 'seeking similarities' through statistical association.

Thus, to summarise, the exemplar studies for this approach cited earlier provide illustrations of difficulties of operationalisation (Szalai) and comparability of data (Jones), of measurement (Rodgers) and of explanations of causality (Gratton), weaknesses which, in effect, promote qualitative analysis to evaluate and explain associations between social, political, economic and cultural conditions and policy outcomes. Indeed, the study reported in Chapter 4 of this book also illustrates the need to complement quantitative analysis with broader qualitative explanations, a point which the authors acknowledge in their reflexive account.

Type II: describing difference

The second approach to comparative analysis involves considering policy not as a set of statistically operationalised concepts but rather as detailed qualitative accounts of individual policy systems and perhaps the interactions between those systems. Thus, this approach is not nomothetic but ideographic in nature, since it lays emphasis on capturing the specific policy history and context rather than searching for general laws. This approach is premised on the argument that what is distinctive about a society is important, and the goal of social explanation should therefore be to account for how and why societies differ. The danger of this approach, however, is the tendency to explain everything in terms of historical contingency. Comparison of a large number of exemplar states, or policy systems, is not possible because of the complexity of detailed analysis and description, and thus the core problem for the 'describing differences' approach is that of validation of interpretation and moving beyond the descriptive. This approach generally is associated with theoretical accounts of a middle range nature, often relying on 'ideal type' concepts to capture the essence of the national systems to be described.

We consider here two exemplar studies in addition to the two case study chapters (Chapters 5 and 6) which adopt a Type II approach (Table 2.1). In Barrie Houlihan's (1997) account of the sports policy systems of five countries, he chooses two policy areas (drugs in sport and physical education policy) to evaluate the nature of the policy process in each country. The approach he adopts is to use Downs' (1972) sequential model of the policy process arguing that 'a sequential model ... not only provides a framework for organising the material but also provides an ideal type against which the actual development of policy may be measured' (Houlihan 1997: p. 257). In effect, he is able to demonstrate that while one policy area, drugs in sport, has become an international issue and has developed a relatively clear policy community, the physical education and sport grouping represents a weak policy network with only marginal impacts on wider policy debates.

The selection of the second exemplar study might appear to be an odd choice since it involves a single case. However, we would concur with Durkheim's (1982) claim that all theoretically informed social analysis is held to be comparative since it addresses the question of typicality or uniqueness.

This second Type II study (Henry and Paramio-Salcines 1999) focuses on urban regeneration in Sheffield. Here, the nature of the exercise was to evaluate whether what Stoker and Mossberger (1994) term 'symbolic urban regimes' were evident in European cities. The urban regime concept, which originated in the USA, is based on case studies of urban policy-making, and its use in policy contexts outside of the North American context has been contentious. A regime is defined as 'an informal yet stable group with access to institutional resources that enable it to have a sustained role in making governing decisions' (Stone 1989: p. 4), and although regimes are constituted of formal and informal networks from the private, voluntary and public sectors, they are seen in the US context as led by private sector interests and actors. Regimes bridge the divide between popular control of government and private control of economic resources; in effect, they are public–private collaborations. Distinctive policy agendas can be identified, e.g. development regimes, middle class progressive regimes, symbolic regimes (Stone 1993). A regime may not feature complete agreement among its members over beliefs and values, but a history of collaboration would tend to produce consensus over policy. Sports policy, in this urban context, may play one or both of the two predominant roles, the role of socially progressive policy (sport for all or sport for disadvantaged groups) and of economic development policy (sport as a symbolic tool in place marketing, for example). In the case of the latter role, symbolic regimes are said to be those groupings or regimes, which mobilise around a shared vision using sport to promote a new image of the city. Thus, the aim of comparative studies of urban regimes is to identify the circumstances under which such regimes emerge and are sustained, and the case study by Henry and Paramio Salcines (1999b) evaluates such circumstances in the context of an English city.

The two chapters which constitute Type II case studies deal with a bilateral case (Chapter 5) and a multilateral case (Chapter 6). The first deals with the emergence and influence of political clientelism in sports policy in two very different national contexts and seeks to identify the conditions under which clientelism develops in each case and the differing forms it takes. The second of these chapters seeks to identify the nature of the use of sport as a vehicle for promoting intercultural or multicultural or assimilationist policy in the 25 member states of the European Union.

All four Type II studies (Henry and Paramio Salcines 1999b; Houlihan 1997; and Chapters 5 and 6) employ a core concept or concepts in the process of developing comparison – 'policy networks', 'urban regimes', 'political clientelism' and 'inter/multiculturalism', respectively. Such concepts should, of course, be subject to evaluation in terms of their utility and robustness. Potential conceptual weaknesses in this approach are highlighted by Sartori (1991) who identifies four types of mistakes in the logic of comparison which may be evident. These he terms: *parochialism* – a tendency of comparativists to continually invent new terms or use old ones in unintended ways; *misclassification* – ignoring important differences and the clustering together of unlike phenomena; *degreeism* – to represent all differences as a matter of degree rather than qualitative difference; and *concept stretching* – removing aspects of the original meaning of the concept so that it can accommodate more cases.

The answers to whether such 'sins' have been committed in the adoption of a particular concept may not be absolute but rather a matter for debate and empirical demonstration. There is no reason why, for example, urban regimes or policy networks might be found in every city or every policy system. On the other hand, political clientelism, which tends to be assumed to be prevalent in certain types of society, may be more widespread than is often assumed, and policies of integration/assimilation may be more evident in what governments do not do than in their conscious pursuit of particular goals. Thus, Sartori's catalogue of potential errors provides a useful checklist against which the concepts employed in characterising the policy system may be evaluated.

The difficulties associated with this Type II approach therefore relate predominantly to the validation and interpretation of concepts to summarise complex qualitative data relating to what may be remarkably diverse policy systems.

Type III: theorising the transnational: transnational rather than cross-national comparison

The third approach to comparative analysis is what we term 'theorising the transnational', and here the global context is the constraining/enabling frame of policy action within which the local/national context is produced and mediated. One of the problems of the first two types of comparative analysis is that both take as their unit of analysis nation states as unique and bounded cases. They fail to take account of the increasing interlinkages/interactions between nation states and the shared global context. Studies of globalisation, for example, have tended to evaluate intra-state, interstate and trans-state phenomena. They seek to take account of both transnational (global) pressures and intra-national (local) context; hence, the coining of the term 'glocalisation' by Robertson (1992).

The case studies cited here and in Chapter 7 to illustrate Type III approaches (Amara *et al.* 2005; Henry and Uchiumi 2001) draw on two theoretical traditions, those of globalisation theory(ies) and of regulation theory. We have already alluded to the approach that we wish to adopt in relation to globalisation theory (i.e. one which avoids a simplistic or even structuralist account in which global structures 'impose' cultural homogeneity). A similar caveat has to be placed over the use of regulation theory as an explanatory framework. Early forms of regulation theory tended to attribute social consequences to structural economic change and were thus subject to critiques of structural determinism (Henry 2001a) (Chapter 8). Although regulation theory has its roots in Marxist analysis, its application in the context of this study (Chapter 7) is essentially neo-pluralist. Thus, Fordist, neo-Fordist and post-Fordist systems are treated not as functional requirements of an accumulation regime but as rather ideal and typical descriptions of the sets of social relations which have accompanied particular changes in the economic structures of a society. Such sets of social relations and economic structures are the outcomes of the interaction of agency and structure. In this study of policy in Grenoble and Sheffield, the argument made is that the structural context of decision-making in both cities limits the freedom of operation of policy in two very different cities.

The strength of the Type III form of comparative analysis is that it seeks to accommodate the global and local *structural* context (as with the Type I, 'seeking similarities', approach) and the local nature of *agency* within this structural context (as with the Type II, 'describing difference', approach). The two theoretical perspectives cited here (regulation and globalisation theories) share core characteristics, at least in the way they are applied in the three studies cited. The explanations contained in these examples

- are macro-theory oriented (though not meta-narratives);
- adopt strategies that link concerns with structure and agency;
- adopt neo-realist assumptions that social structures are socially constructed, but exist independently of the individual, and may have impacts which are not necessarily directly observable; and imply that since such structures are socially constructed they will be culturally relative.

Policy is thus explained by reference to actors' reactions to/reinforcement of global interdependencies existing in the cultural, political and economic domains.

The comparative analysis of Grenoble and Sheffield related in Chapter 7 seeks to compare urban policy for sport in terms of ideology and objectives in Grenoble and Sheffield, which reflect two very different national and local contexts. However, in spite of these contrasting profiles, sports policy in both cities was moving in very similar directions, namely the use of sport for economic development rather than social purposes, centralised decision-making involving local elites and an emphasis on elite sport rather than sport for all. The direction of policy change described here is consistent with features of a shift away from traditional, Fordist modes of social regulation. However, these shifts in policy are not to be seen as the result of some functionalist requirement. Rather, we seek to tease out how the local political, institutional and structural contexts in each case, although very different, made the development of sports policy in similar directions attractive to policy makers.

The study by Amara *et al.* (2005) illustrates the opposite tendency, that is, the nature of local difference in what might be mistakenly seen as a globally homogenising process, the professionalisation of football in five countries (England, France, Algeria, Japan and China). There is, of course, evidence of the more or less conscious adoption of modernising approaches, but these forms of modernity are locally specific [what Göle (1997) terms local modernity].

The third study used for exemplification is a comparative analysis of the development of sports policy in Britain and Japan by Henry and Uchiumi (2001). If the comparative study of urban policy in Sheffield and Grenoble warns us of the dangers of reading off similarities in policy as consequences of similar structural change in spatially and culturally adjacent societies, then the comparative study of policy in Britain and Japan should be undertaken with care not to read off differences in policy as determined by political and economic differences or the cultural specificity of Japanese or British society. From an occidental standpoint, the dangers of Orientalism and the 'exoticisation' of the other (Said 1991; Sardar 1998, 1999) are evident problems to avoid.

Preston (2000) warns against the tendency evident in many policy accounts of Japan that promote 'particularistic' accounts which focus on the 'uniqueness' of the Japanese context. These accounts argue that Japan is 'just different' because of its geography, ethnic make-up, psychological or cultural and linguistic character. Such arguments, Preston warns us, promulgate determinist fallacies in one of the following forms:

- geographical determinism – the argument that Japan is a different society because of its geographical isolation as an island;
- ethnic determinism – that Japanese are a homogeneous people, unlike others;
- psychological determinism – that the psychology of the Japanese people is a group (rather than individualist) psychology, thus favouring consensual approaches to social decisions;
- eugenic determinism – that Japanese society is meritocratic, and that reward is thus a matter of natural difference and effort, and that such factors lead to fairness in social arrangements; and
- linguistic and cultural determinism – that the Japanese language has a uniqueness which means that Japanese culture (ways of viewing the world) is unique.

Of course, Japanese society is in many ways different from Western societies, but there are also contrasts within and between such societies as well as similarities between them. The particularities of Japanese society cannot be assumed but rather should be argued for on the basis of specific evidence.

Despite the very different forms of economic organisations (corporate capitalism in Japan and welfare capitalism in Britain) and of political ideological context in both cases, Henry and Uchiumi highlight ways in which the responses of Japanese government and British government, to the experience of extended recession in the UK in the 1980s and in Japan in the 1990s, engendered strong policy similarities. These include the commercialisation of sport; increasing privatisation of provision; the growing 'mediatisation' of sport, which is also reflected in the growth of sports spectating through commercial television channels; and increasing individualisation in patterns of participation. However, these broad similarities do not support any crude notion of policy convergence. Global trends and conditions have had an impact on sport and policy in Britain and Japan, but they have been experienced differently, and though there are some similarities in terms of policy response, there are also important differences.

In summary, for each of these three studies, though exhibiting significant contrasts in theoretical basis or in the policy systems being compared, there is a shared logic of comparison

- that refers to the need to focus on structural context and local interpretation of that context by policy actors;
- that looks to factors (and groups of actors) which operate across the boundaries of nation states; and
- that looks to identify whether there are any 'interaction effects' between policy systems such as one group of policy actors learning from another.

However, while such studies differ significantly from Types I and II, they share with those earlier types the conception of policy as being used to address problems and issues in the wider context. Type IV studies, which we label as 'defining discourse', seek to understand the ways in which policy discourse defines the policy world and the problems it seeks to address.

Type IV: defining discourse

While studies of policy as discourse have grown over the last decade (Chalip 1996; Marshall 2000; Richardson and Jensen 2003), relatively little work has been undertaken in relation to sports policy in this domain. It is perhaps worth distinguishing between discourse in policy and policy as discourse here. The former is concerned with evaluating language to identify an underlying reality (and tends therefore to be linked with a critical realist or a neo-realist ontology) while the latter is concerned with the construction of realities through language (and is thus related to post-modern relativist ontological position). Examples of the former would include Chalip's (1996) critical theory-based analysis of policy discourse and McKay's (1994) analysis of the ways in which the Australian Sports Commission has framed its gender equity policy in the mutually reinforcing hegemonic discourses of masculinity and corporate managerialism.

A policy as discourse approach rejects the notion of an underlying reality and argues instead for the notion of socially constructed realities (Wood and Kroger 2000), constructed in this context through the discourse implicated in the development and articulation of policy. For example, policies dealing with urban poverty and deprivation which focus on addressing problems at the level of the individual (e.g. re-education and training projects, programmes developing social capital) define urban problems as being a matter of individual or group pathology, while policies which focus on improving the operational effectiveness of public or private sector bureaucracies in this field might be said to define the problem in terms of organisational failure. Policy discourse is thus seen as defining, rather than simply responding to, a problem.

It is claimed by advocates such as Schram (1993) that post-modern enquiry into the discursive construction of policy has the potential to make a distinctive, democratizing contribution to public policy analysis. Such an approach is adopted in Chapter 8 in a review of how the policy of the 'professionalisation of sport' launched by the Algerian Government in 1998 is interpreted and expressed in the Algerian context and how its expression in policy documents and policy action defines the nature of the construction of the social world of sport. The strengths of this approach include the highlighting of the exercising of power in the development of policy discourse. Such analysis is bound up with Foucauldian notions of power (Foucault 1986), and as Schram suggests, this holds out the possibility of emancipatory outcomes:

> More so than conventional approaches, a postmodern policy analysis offers the opportunity to interrogate assumptions about identity embedded in the analysis and making of public policy, thereby enabling us to rethink and resist questionable distinctions that privilege some identities at the expense of others.
>
> (Schram 1993: p. 249)

However, this approach also opens itself to the consequences of a relativist epistemology in which it might be argued that policy problems only exist insofar as they are discursively constructed and that issues of reliability and validity and the privileging of one account over another are similarly problematic.

Conclusions: the ontological and theoretical orientations of the four types of comparative sports policy research

The aim of this chapter has been to identify the logic of comparison evident in different types of comparative policy analysis. More specifically, this chapter has sought to characterise and exemplify different approaches to sports policy analysis and to highlight strengths and weaknesses of such approaches. Type I, 'seeking similarities', allows identification of some trends for further exploration but is dogged by problems of operationalisation of key measures to make them amenable to statistical analysis. Type II, 'describing differences', provides detailed description of individual policy systems and perhaps even of interaction between policy systems or policy actors from different systems but generally fails to take account of the wider structural context of international or global change. It has the benefit of using middle range theory to explain policy phenomena in a restricted sphere but by definition provides limited explanation. Type III, 'theorising the transnational', is one in which the global structure is seen as (re)produced by, and forming the context of, social action. It considers internation, intra-nation and global interaction. While all-embracing as a form of social analysis, it suffers from the problems of complexity associated with developing both micro (local) and macro (global) levels of analysis at the same time. Type IV, 'defining discourse', acknowledges the power of discourse in defining the nature of policy problems and solutions and sees the role of policy analysis as one of deconstructing such meaning systems to identify whose interests are served by the nature of the particular policy formulation under review.

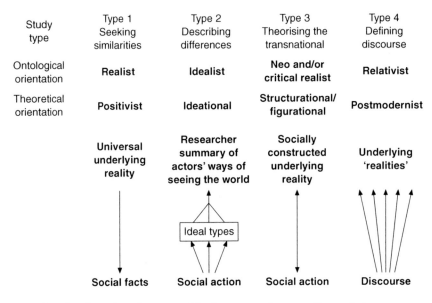

Study type	Type 1 Seeking similarities	Type 2 Describing differences	Type 3 Theorising the transnational	Type 4 Defining discourse
Ontological orientation	**Realist**	**Idealist**	**Neo and/or critical realist**	**Relativist**
Theoretical orientation	**Positivist**	**Ideational**	**Structurational/ figurational**	**Postmodernist**

Figure 2.1 Ontological implications of the four types of sports policy analysis.

There are, of course, difficulties associated with this approach which are associated with the relativist nature of this exercise.

Figure 2.1 underlines the point that different theoretical orientations associated with each of the four types are premised on very different ontological assumptions. Type I is associated with a positivist orientation which assumes a single external reality and an external world of facts to be discovered by an admixture of inductive empiricism and deduction. Type II studies suggest, by contrast, that while there may be a single external world, there is no possibility of comprehending it in an holistic manner; that middle range theories which have a restricted ambit are thus more useful; and that human action is to be explained by reference to actors' own world views rather than by reference to attempts to capture an external reality. Thus, while Type I is structure oriented, Type II might be regarded as more agency oriented. Type III emphasises that while there is an external reality, it is largely socially constructed and that underlying structures which exist in a society (such as race, class and patriarchy) and which provide the context for human actions are both the product of previous social action and can be modified by current and future social action. For this reason, we describe this as a structurationalist perspective. Type IV accounts, however, argue that the only way we can know and express reality is through language and that different discourses therefore constitute different realities. Such an approach in its radical form suffers from major epistemological difficulties, since if discourse systems reflect different realities, none of which may be logically privileged over another, then arguing in favour of one interpretation over another is problematic, and indeed it is not clear how communication across discourses would be possible at all.

This latter problem is particularly significant where discourse analysis is being undertaken across linguistic divisions as is the case for the study reported in Chapter 8 which incorporates analysis of the material in French and Arabic as well as English. Foucauldian notions of discursive power exercised by those who control the means of policy expression and discussion are difficult to accommodate in comparative analysis if one holds the hard-line view that discourse is language specific. However, though advocates of a radical form of the Sapir–Whorf hypothesis (linguistic relativity theory) (Davies and Corbett 1997; Hill and Mannheim 1992; Lucy 1997) might wish to claim that languages are separate meaning systems, in effect 'hermeneutically sealed', and that therefore translation in the literal sense is not feasible, this seems inconsistent with our daily experience. Language systems are not totally sealed off; otherwise, there would be no means of communication across language communities. In fact, though 'perfect' one-to-one translation of terms may rarely be possible, we do work across language communities on the notion of nearest approximations most of the time. Thus, even though a language may express aspects of a world view which is simply not expressible in another (one can cite here the much used example that Inuit languages have a plethora of words for snow, indicating different grades and types, but have no direct one-to-one translation in English), this does not mean that translation across the Inuit–English divide is impossible, but rather that approximate understandings are achieved in translation. Thus, comparing policy discourses or epistemic communities across language boundaries may be difficult and imperfect but not impossible and represents a potentially fruitful area for further comparative analysis.

In highlighting the ontological and epistemological bases for the development of each of the four types of comparative policy study, we aim to have identified more clearly what each of these types of research sets out to achieve, the nature of the analysis they promote and therefore the nature of the answers they may provide. The case study chapters which follow illustrate these processes in practical, applied contexts.

3 Evaluating alternative theoretical perspectives on sports policy

Ian Henry and Mansour Al-Tauqi

Introduction: modernity, postmodernity and sports policy studies

This chapter has two aims. The first is to provide a practical example of the evaluation of theoretical perspectives on sports policy through their application to explain the initiation and development of a particular transnational policy initiative, the emergence of Olympic Solidarity. The second aim is to address the third of the core difficulties which were identified in Chapter 1 as a key to understanding the limitations affecting the development of comparative sports policy analysis, that is, the growing recognition of the significance of the western, and therefore partial, origins of sport as a phenomenon and also of sports policy studies as an academic domain. The advent of post-colonial and postmodern theories in particular has underlined the peculiarly partial view of what constitutes the truth or adequacy of an account and therefore of which statements about sports policy systems might be claimed to be 'true' or to provide an adequate basis for explanation of such systems.

The debate around postmodernity implies assumptions about the condition of modernity. Modernity has been construed as an epistemic condition as much as an historical period, one which is founded on rationality in the form of deductive logic and inductive empiricist reasoning. The fundamental assumptions about this rationalist world view include that (a) it was regarded as the dominant world view, (b) it was developed (if not born) in the West from the European Enlightenment of the eighteenth century and (c) it was subject to global convergence with traditional, 'pre-modern' societies adopting this world view in order to benefit from 'progress'. However, each of these three features of modernity, or the modern world view, represent challengeable claims.

In respect of the first of these assumptions, the rationalist world view which was taken to be the dominant perspective in technologically advanced societies is not necessarily the dominant world view in terms of numbers of adherents in such societies. In political terms for example, (unenlightened) self-interest rather than rational calculation may be characteristic of individualistic, neo-liberal approaches to politics. And in relation to religion, despite various Enlightenment-inspired attempts to construct 'rational religions' or rational proof of the existence of a higher being (Descartes 1881; Paley 1807), rational, modern societies incorporate their fair share of religious believers whose adherence is based on faith as well as reason, in addition to atheists and agnostics (whose lack of belief in a higher being may also be based on faith rather than reason). The failure of Thorstein Veblen's (1912) prediction of the development of the 'rational technocrat' as the ideal typical product of an increasingly technologically driven set of societies bears witness to the failings of modernisation-type arguments at the beginning of the century, as do Bell's (1960) and Fukuyama's (1992) accounts, which represent aspects of the convergence thesis in their mid- and late-twentieth century forms, respectively. History has largely subsequently significantly undermined such theoretical claims.

With regard to the second claim, many of the major advances in science were based on the work of 'pre-modern' thinkers. In the natural sciences, in relation to advances in medical science, we can cite Ibn Sinna (or, in the westernised form, Avicenna, 980–1037), in terms of logic and mathematics, Ibn Raschid (or Averroes, 1126–1198), and in the social sciences, Ibn Khaldun (1332–1406), whose work on the state and on the stresses experienced in societies growing out of smaller kinship-based communities provides material for a strong claim to be among the founders of modern social analysis, if not sociology as a discipline. Thus, the portrayal of the Western Enlightenment as uniquely 'unlocking the door' to a rational world view is one which is difficult to sustain.

The final claim of convergence around a dominant model of society is based on science and technology as an engine of economic growth, with pluralist politics, and a pluralist state. This claim is one which is also inconsistent with the evidence. Some of the new states, to emerge throughout the twentieth century, were based on dynasties (e.g. Saudi Arabia) or religion (e.g. Israel, Iran) or on a mixture of political ideology and charismatic political leadership (e.g. Cuba) as well as on 'rational' ideologies, and they remain features of the contemporary political scene. Notwithstanding these problems for claims relating to 'modernity', notions of 'progress' and teleological accounts, whether liberal pluralist or Marxist, have exercised considerable influence.

If we look to trace the development of theoretical perspectives in western social analysis in the last two decades or so, in relation to the comparative analysis of sport in a range of societies, we can identify four significant groups of theories. The modernisation thesis and convergence theories tend to describe the development of sport and therefore sports policy in functionalist terms, reinforcing a rational, Darwinian, performance-oriented world view which will foster the adoption of a 'single best model' of society. Cultural imperialism, dependency and hegemony theories characterise sport as a cultural vehicle of the reinforcement of political and economic dominance within and between societies. Globalisation theories (as we noted in Chapter 1) have tended to locate explanation of change in the inextricable interplay of global and local phenomena, with both 'unicausal' accounts (emphasising the singular importance of economic, political or cultural factors) and multi-causal accounts (arguing for a more complex multi-layered explanation of social change) as well as accounts which deal with globalisation as a set of historically contingent tendencies. More recently, postmodernism and Orientalism have characterised sport (or other cultural forms such as literature or film) as discursive resources used to define reality in particular ways, privileging the power of the West. While there are ontological and epistemological differences between (and in some instances, within) such theoretical traditions, and such approaches may be regarded as conceptually distinct at one level, in substantive terms, one may find that individual authors range across these perspectives and, in some instances, may seek to fuse elements of different approaches in a single account.

Before we go on to consider the implications of the last of these approaches for understanding comparative sports policy in the final section of this chapter, we want to illustrate the ways in which accounts of policy development at the transnational level can both draw on and be used to evaluate the evidence for particular perspectives, using the first three types of theories highlighted earlier. This will be done by reference to an evaluation of different perspectives on the process of development of Olympic Solidarity and its forerunner the Committee for International Olympic Aid (CIOA), which have continued to represent a key element in the Olympic movement since the 1960s.

The historical development of Olympic Solidarity: evaluating alternative perspectives

The historical and geo-political context

The Olympic movement has, from its earliest articulations in the form of Coubertin's writings on the revival of the Games, represented itself as a 'universal' movement. However, the history of the Modern Games across the twentieth century has been one of the initial exclusion of certain groups by the International Olympic Committee (IOC), subsequent challenge by these excluded parties and eventual incorporation into an expanded Olympic movement, on terms negotiated in ways which reflected the power and influence of the respective parties during the process of incorporation. The emergence of Olympic Solidarity took place in response to one such challenge that was experienced by the Olympic movement in dealing with the aftermath of European (and Japanese) empire with the emergence of newly independent states in the 1950s and 1960s. Other major challenges came from the women's athletic movement and workers' and communist games in the early twentieth century and from professional sport and the Paralympic movement in the latter half of the twentieth century. While each of these challenges was largely defused by the incorporation of these 'movements' into the body of the Olympic family, such a process involved modification of the interpretation of Olympic values and, in particular, modification of just how 'universal' or inclusive the Olympic movement was going to be.

The rapid growth of newly independent states took place at the period of the onset of the Cold War, and from the beginning, that war was waged as a series of battles for hearts and minds (as well as for economic and cultural dependency) through the development of international aid. Those forms of aid included international sports aid, which both the USSR and the USA were using as vehicles for promoting their cultural and economic as well as political interests (Peppard and Riordan 1993). The IOC, anxious to avoid any 'separate development' of sport in the newly independent states analogous to what had been experienced with the separate women's, workers' and communist championships or major events, determined to ensure the adherence of the new states to the Olympic movement. The principal mechanism for achieving integration was initially the CIOA, the forerunner of Olympic Solidarity, which was founded in 1961, and Olympic Solidarity itself from 1971. The background to the development of these two organisations will unfold as the story is told, but Olympic Solidarity has subsequently become the means for distributing the income from media rights to National Olympic Committees (NOCs) and has, therefore, taken on a key redistributive role.

The nature and purposes of Olympic Solidarity are defined in Rule 8 of the Olympic Charter in the following terms:

> The aim of Olympic Solidarity is to organise aid to NOCs recognised by the International Olympic Committee (IOC), in particular those which have the greatest need of it. This aid takes the form of programmes elaborated jointly by the IOC and the NOCs, with the technical assistance of the International Federations (IFs), if necessary.

While Olympic Solidarity has gone through major changes in its form and philosophy since its inception, an analysis of the period of its conception, birth and early existence provides a useful insight into the ways in which the Olympic movement adapted to a radically changing international context.

The rapid growth of independent states is evident in the post-war recognition of Asian and African NOCs (Figure 3.1). While only one African and five Asian NOCs were recognised before the 1940s, 56 new NOCs were recognised in Africa and Asia from the 1940s to the 1970s (representing 28 per cent of the total number of all NOCs). There had been some early Asian and African participation in the Games. Japan, for example, participated in the Summer Games from 1912, and the Winter Games from 1928, winning its first medal in the 1920 Summer Games; and in 1920, Egypt participated (reaching semi-finals of football in 1928), while in 1932, India won a gold medal for hockey. However, most African participation and much Asian participation in the Olympic Games prior to the Second World War generally took the form of participants competing for colonial powers. A poignant example is that of the two Korean athletes Sohn Kee-chung and Nam Sung-yong who competed as Japanese athletes, provided with Japanese names, in the men's marathon at the Berlin Olympics of 1936, winning gold and bronze, respectively.

Attitudes in sport as in other spheres were dominated by colonial and often racist thinking. For example, proposals for *Jeux Africains* for non-Europeans

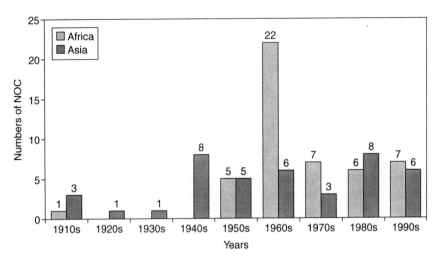

Figure 3.1 National Olympic Committee (NOC) recognition by the Olympic movement.

were accepted in principle in 1925 by the IOC, though plans to stage these Games were frustrated partly by economic problems and partly by the opposition of the French and the British who feared that such games might fuel the demands of the incipient independence movements (Benzerti 2002). Thus, although plans to stage such events remained unfulfilled until the *Jeux d'Amitié*, was organised in the early 1960s (for French-speaking nations), and the first African Games in 1965 in Brazzaville, the initial proposals constituted one of the many forms of early sporting apartheid.

In 1948, the IOC refined the definition of the status of NOCs to ensure that they were to be viewed as subordinate to the IOC. At its meeting in 1948 in London, the IOC modified its charter to specify that, to be recognised, NOCs must be based in independent states (rather than colonies or in protectorates) and that NOCs should be autonomous (that is, they should be free from government control). This latter requirement was aimed at two groups. The first was the NOCs of the communist bloc, which had been admitted following the Second World War, to nullify the threat to the Olympic movement of the Worker Games and the Spartakiads which had been a feature of the inter-war years. Membership of the NOCs of the communist states was manifested by government appointment. The second group targeted by this measure was that of newly independent states who were seeking to develop a voice and political presence independent of the East–West Cold War parties. Just as there were tensions between former colonies and the western powers, generally in politics [for example, in the United Nations (UN), the emerging opposition to the G7 group by the 'third world' lobby Group 77], so also in sports, such tensions would be evident in, for example, the struggles between the IOC and the non-aligned movement in the organising of the Games of the Newly Emerging Forces (GANEFO) in 1963.

Evaluating alternative explanations: the research approach

In considering alternative theoretical perspectives explaining the development of Olympic Solidarity, three key research questions need to be addressed:

1 Who was responsible for the initiation and development of the Olympic Solidarity initiative and what were their specific goals? Who were the individuals or groups concerned and what were the types of 'constituency' they represented?
2 How was the incorporation of the newly independent states managed? What types of strategies or tactics were employed and which were effective?
3 How might the processes of dialogue and incorporation be explained in theoretical terms?

The primary data sources through which answers to these questions were developed were largely accessed through the Olympic Museum in Lausanne, where 247 pieces of correspondence, reports and minutes of meetings in English and French were identified as relevant to the development of Olympic Solidarity and its forerunner, the CIOA, from the period 1960 to 1971 (Al-Tauqi 1993). These items were scanned into text files and analysed with the aid of NUD*IST (Non-numerical Unstructured Data Indexing Searching and Theorising) software. The items were then subjected to analysis using protocols drawing on Altheide's (1996) approach to ethnographic content analysis, which allowed the development of inductive and deductive categorisation of the data, facilitating the emergence of categories and concepts which aided the evaluation of competing theoretical perspectives. In addition, secondary literature relating to the communication and transmission of Olympic knowledge, practices and values was reviewed.

The evaluation of the data principally, therefore, concerned the analysis of communications between various parties involved in initiating, developing, receiving or resisting what was initially referred to as Olympic aid. In order to evaluate the nature and direction of communication, geo-political constituencies were broadly conceptualised in three groups – the 'core' capitalist economies of Western Europe, the United States, Canada and Australia; the 'semi-periphery' of the Eastern bloc and the 'periphery' of, largely, Asian, African and Latin American states. These divisions, reflecting relative economic wealth and influence, on the whole, represent a reasonable fit with the system of Olympic influence. The presidents of the IOC have all come from the core, and with one or two exceptions (Tokyo in 1964 being the first) the Summer Games have taken place in the core, while Olympic performance by athletes from states in the semi-periphery has been exceptionally strong, due in large part to the nature of state support in a command economy. There are exceptions in terms both of countries and individuals. For example, Japan might actually be regarded as part of the core. Indeed, it had won the right to host the Games in 1940. Cuba in the 1960s, though part of the periphery, had begun to develop a sporting system which belied its size and wealth as a nation. Individuals in 'peripheral' nations (e.g. former colonies) often had more in common with the former colonial power than with the politics and culture of the newly independent entities. Nevertheless, the distinction between core, semi-periphery and periphery is one which provides a useful starting point for analysis.

The theoretical approaches identified

One of the aims of this analysis was, as we have noted, to reflect on the relationship between the data generated to answer the research questions identified earlier and three major theoretical traditions rehearsed in the literature. It is worth revisiting each of these three theoretical approaches briefly here before considering the data relating to the development of Olympic Solidarity itself.

The modernisation thesis, societal convergence and sports policy

Alan Guttmann's (1978) ground-breaking book, *From Ritual to Record: the nature of modern sports*, represents an appropriate point of departure in relation to modernisation arguments. At its core, it seeks to identify the key characteristics of 'modern' sport, which it defines as secularisation, rationalisation, bureaucratisation, equality of the opportunity to compete and in the conditions of competition, specialisation of roles, quantification and the quest for records. Guttmann's (1994) account (*Games and Empires: modern sports and cultural imperialism*) and subsequent commentaries reflect the 'slippage' between the modernisation thesis and Marxist and neo-Marxist accounts. In the cases of both the modernisation thesis and traditional Marxist explanations, these are distinctively teleological accounts. Societies are depicted as moving inexorably along a given trajectory, in the former case to a liberal pluralist, capitalist end-state and in the latter to a communist end. In terms of neo-Marxism, sport is a contested terrain, reflecting the struggle for hegemonic leadership with sport legitimating (largely implicitly) the claims about nation states or social groups, or fostering notions of (imagined) community, or simply distracting potentially disaffected groups from expressing political discord.

Roger Caillois' (1961) classic study *Man, Play and Games*, in so far as it promotes a functionalist view of sport, identifies the characteristics of dominant sport forms in competitive capitalist economies, which reinforce the competitive ethos, through forms of *agon*, or competitive sport. As such, it might be said to provide one of the classic expressions of the functionalist thinking underpinning much of the modernisation thesis. In pre-modern societies, games of chance (what Caillois terms *alea*) associated with superstition and the vulnerability of outcomes to 'fate' or the 'whim of the gods' will thus be the dominant form. While the concept of *agon* (competition, a feature of 'modern' societies) invests the individual (through talent or effort) with responsibility for success and promotes values of competitive meritocracy, in games of *alea* (luck, chance or superstition, a feature of 'traditional' societies), stoicism in accepting outcomes which are the product of external forces, is the value implicitly transmitted. While such functionalist accounts are able to highlight the consonance between game forms and some sets of values, they fail to take account of the fact that such game forms often form contested terrain, with different groups of values evident among different sets of participants in the same activity, and indeed, such accounts fail to develop convincing arguments about how social change comes about and how some leisure pursuits including sports can be used to challenge, rather than reinforce, hegemonic values.

Marxist and neo-Marxist perspectives on sports policy: hegemony theory, dependency theory and cultural imperialism

The modernisation thesis suggests that homogenisation of sport forms reflects a process of the homogenisation of world societies (Wagner 1990). The concept of cultural imperialism also promotes a notion of dominant groups or societies employing cultural/sporting forms which engender appropriate values to 'incorporate' outsider groups. However, there is a distinction to be made between Marxist and neo-Marxist uses of the term 'cultural imperialism'. Traditional Marxism tends to focus on the imposition of an ideology which fosters homogeneity and conformity, disciplining the workforce to conform to values consistent with the promotion of capitalist forms of economic order (Brohm 1978), while neo-Marxists appeal to the concept of hegemony and see dominance as contested, never wholly accomplished, and subject to continual struggle (Hargreaves 1992; Tomlinson 2001).

The diffusion of sport is a much debated phenomenon, characterised differently by the competing perspectives. However, while modernisation/convergence theories share with Marxist accounts the implication of the homogenisation of sport forms, neo-Marxism focuses on the pervasive influence of dominant groups, but also on the resistance of local subordinates, such that the pattern of sport which emerges is contingent and therefore may be varied and heterogeneous. Guttmann (1978) cites examples such as that of the introduction of cricket into the Trobriand Islands by British missionaries in the early twentieth century. The game which survived into the later part of the century was substantially adapted to the local context such that it became virtually unrecognisable as a reflection of the modern sport. The form which the game took owed more to the local need for ritual and celebration of community than to modern sporting forms.

What we see then is a move away from functionalist and Marxist teleology in modernisation and traditional Marxist forms, towards more nuanced accounts of cultural contestation in neo-Marxist critiques (and subsequently also to Orientalist, post-colonial approaches, to which we will return in the final sections of this chapter).

The cultural imperialism approach to theorising the globalisation phenomenon involves investigating cross-cultural processes. The cultural flow is identified with activities undertaken by the nation state and/or multinational corporations, whether governmental or non-governmental. These activities entail a form of domination of one culture over another or the increasing hegemony of a particular central culture. Issues of control, power and the ability of indigenous people to understand, interpret and resist cultural manipulation and domination arise in evaluating these types of studies. The idea of the replacement of an indigenous culture by a foreign one is central to an understanding of the processes involved. The main emphasis in the cultural imperialism approach is placed on the notion that the globe is made up of a collection of nation states in competition with each other: it views the world as an integrated political and economic system of global capitalism.

Guttmann (1994), whose work had shifted from its original emphasis on a modernisation perspective, went on to argue that the intense ritualism associated with the Olympic Games has emphasised the European origins of the Games and has made it necessary for non-western nations to participate in the Olympic movement on western terms. Guttmann reviews the activities of the IOC from 1954 to 1990. He traces the process of recruitment of IOC members, the origins of sport that constitute the Olympic Games programmes, the managerial structure in which sport is organised and the geographical location of countries that have hosted the Games. His work illustrates the domination and the control of western culture in the body of the Olympic movement. Similarly, Thoma and Chalip (1996) conclude that the majority of world sports, particularly those sports whose origins were not European, are excluded from the Olympic Games (see also Seppanen 1989). Darby (1997) also seeks to illustrate how Federation Internationale de Football Association (FIFA) featured in the post-colonial era, promoting forms of exploitation of the emergent nations by elites from European and South American countries, providing thereby support for claims concerning the existence of economic and cultural imperialism.

In developing explanations of the relationship between rich and poor countries, dependency theory has contributed significantly to the shedding of light on the phenomenon of 'core'/'periphery' relations. While classical Marxist theories of cultural imperialism were interested in explaining the causes of imperialism and how capitalism had expanded geographically out of its own borders, they ignored the effects of capitalist expansion in peripheral areas. These theories assumed that the struggle between social classes in Europe within capitalist societies would be reproduced elsewhere. Thus, dependency theory is concerned with the uneven way in which global society has developed. It sets out specifically to analyse the nature of this unevenness, its causes and the form which dependency between states has assumed during the twentieth century.

The central argument of dependency theory is that, over time, three different forms of dependency have developed and have characterised the economic relations between the countries of the core and the periphery (Hoogvelt 1997; Prebisch 1998). The first is colonial dependency, which emerged during the period of imperialism when land, raw material and labour were monopolised by colonial 'masters'. The second, financial–industrial dependence, gained importance towards the end of the nineteenth century when the first world undertook heavy investment in the developing world. The third form manifested itself in a technological–industrial dependency which emerged after the Second World War. This work is important in the sense that it helps us to view dependency as a historically dynamic process in which the imperialist/dependence relationships between the rich and poor countries have been expressed in different forms and are likely to continue to be so in the future.

Work in the field of the diffusion of sport has also helped to address the issue of a fourth dimension of dependency, namely cultural dependency, addressing the question of the flow of cultural activities in the world system and whether this follows the same forms and patterns of economic and political expansion. Stoddart's (1988a,b) work on cricket, Klein's (1991) on baseball, Darby's (2002) on football and Bale and Sang's (1996) on athletics represent work of this genre.

Perhaps the most critical difficulty for dependency theory in economic terms is the fact that it is unable to explain, and therefore does not fully recognise, the economic growth, and social and industrial development that has clearly occurred in some countries of the periphery. The theory utilises a dominantly economic framework of analysis in explaining development and underdevelopment within the global system. Indeed, the emergence of newly industrial, and to some degree post-industrial, countries in East Asia represents a serious challenge to the adequacy of the development and underdevelopment version of dependency. However, others argue that most of the development and achievements in the 'peripheral' countries represent versions of development that serve the interests of the 'core' countries and ensure the continuation of dependency structures (Hoogvelt 1997).

In cultural terms, specifically in international sport, dependency might be questioned because some peripheral countries manage to achieve a strong position in sport activities. Nigeria and Cameroon have managed to win gold medals in recent Olympic Games and in the Youth Football World Cup (Darby 2002). Senegal and South Korea achieved remarkable results in the 2002 World Cup. India, Pakistan and the West Indies are highly respectable performers in professional cricket. Algeria, Ethiopia, Kenya and Morocco dominate the long-distance events in track and field. Latin American footballers dominate the world ranking of the best teams and players in the world. It could be argued that despite peripheral athletes' achievements in western sport, the periphery is still dependent on the West for providing coaches, equipment, knowledge and even the administration of high-level competition. In addition, financial revenue for athletes depends on their ability to compete in core countries' national leagues. Currently, the success of African countries in world sport events depends on the success of African athletes in their journey to Europe and America. In common with other Marxist-related approaches, the claims of dependency theory have thus been subject to the criticism of espousing an economic determinism which is not wholly supported by the data.

Globalisation theories

As we have reviewed aspects of globalisation theories in the two previous chapters, comment here is limited to a number of summary points. Globalisation processes involve speed, scope and span (Giddens and Lash 1994; Harvey 1989), and as Robertson (1992: p. 8) argues, globalisation reflects not only material change but also changing thought patterns in terms of the 'intensification of consciousness of the world as a whole'. Globalising flows are pluridimensional. In addition, globalising tendencies may be embraced, accepted reluctantly, adapted to local circumstances or rejected, and the reach and scope of globalising tendencies will vary from one location and/or one social domain to another. Sport, it is argued, is one of the cultural and economic forms of activity which manifest considerable scope and reach (Houlihan 2003) though it may be experienced differently in different contexts (Maguire 1999).

Having reviewed these three traditions in social analysis, we might ask the question of what could be sought in the historical data to be reviewed which might constitute support for one rather than another perspective. Crudely, one might argue that in relation to the modernisation thesis we can look for evidence of greater rationalisation, bureaucratisation and scientisation of sports systems. In neo-Marxist terms, one might look for aspects of centralised control and peripheral resistance in the imposition of policy, or in terms of cultural imperialism or dependency approaches, evidence of ways in which cultural dominance reinforces economic exploitation of the periphery by the core. In respect of globalisation theories, one might identify evidence of ways in which centrally derived policy is interpreted, responded and resisted differently in different contexts, with the global core of the Olympic movement reacting to and perhaps accommodating, to some degree, such local differences. However, such claims are crude because the same piece of evidence may be employed in support of more than one such perspective. For example, where Olympic Solidarity activity results in greater bureaucratisation of local NOCs, this might be taken as evidence in support of a modernisation perspective. If 'imposed' by the centre with or without local resistance, this same phenomenon of bureaucratisation might be said to illustrate neo-Marxist claims, and where it is resisted or interpreted locally (so that local versions of centrally promoted bureaucracy are developed), this might be cited as evidence of 'glocalisation'. This rather simplistic example is given to underline the fact that the relationship between evidence and theory is not a simple matter, either of 'correspondence' with the 'facts' or of 'coherence' with the theoretical account. As the discussion of ontological and epistemological underpinnings in Chapter 2 has suggested, the adequacy of a theoretical account cannot simply be evaluated by reference to 'neutral' data. What counts as data and how data are conceptualised are, in part, determined by the theoretical frameworks we use to describe those data. Nevertheless, the 'warrantability', or theoretical adequacy, of the account may be assessed by reference to the network of relations between the internal coherence of the theory, the ability of the theory to accommodate observations/data and the acceptability of the (explicit or implicit) ontological and epistemological premises on which the theory relies.

The emergence of Olympic Solidarity: reviewing the evidence

The introduction of sports aid in the Olympic movement was a product of pressure from the Soviet Union in the late 1950s and took place in the context of the competition between the West and the USSR in aid terms. In a draft resolution proposed to the 58th Session of the IOC in 1961 in Athens on Aid to Africa and Asia,[1] Adrianov, the Soviet IOC member, and his fellow countryman Romanov suggested the following:

> The International Olympic Committee, solemnly [declares] thereby, that one of its important tasks of the present time shall be to draw sportsmen from countries of Africa and Asia into the world Olympic movement without any discrimination on the ground of politics, religion, or race, to render every aid and assistance at its disposal to the Olympic movement and amateur sport in these countries, and feels confident that such an aid shall make a great contribution towards further development of world sport and the Olympic movement and strengthening the friendship between the youth and sportsmen of all countries.

The USSR was apparently keen to be seen as championing the notion of aid to the newly independent states, as part of what was seen in the West as an attempt to enhance its sphere of influence in Africa. The struggle over how the Olympic movement is controlled, and by whom, might be said to lend itself readily to a cultural imperialism perspective.

The USSR's reference to the need to decolonise was seen by some commentators in the West as unwarranted preaching to the established colonial powers, and the response by the French IOC member Comte Jean de Beaumont (who was to become the first Chair of the Committee) to the proposal by the USSR is interesting.

> In the note sent by USSR to all the NOCs and the IFs, we are told of decolonisation. I must say, France did not wait for external intervention in order to carry out decolonisation in every field, especially in the field of sport when France developed sport in French speaking African territories.
>
> (Jean de Beaumont 1961: undated letter to Avery Brundage)

The tone of the response is interesting since it came at a time immediately before Algerian independence, which was gained through particularly bloody resistance. Indeed, sport had played a key role both in the French project to resist Algerian pressure for independence and in the Algerian *Front de Libération Nationale* (FLN) response (Amara and Henry 2004).

It is also clear that, for some at least, the USSR's support for the incorporation of the new states into the Olympic movement, and the rapid recognition of their NOCs, was motivated by the USSR's wish to change the balance of power in the IOC (even though NOC membership and the appointment of members to the IOC itself were entirely separate matters). Nevertheless, the IOC agreed at its meeting in Athens in 1961 to the establishment of the CIOA which was the forerunner of what would become Olympic Solidarity.

A common theme throughout the correspondence in the archives is a concern by the IOC President, Avery Brundage, in particular to ensure that state nomination of candidates should not predominate. The notion of political interference is one about which he was particularly sensitive. This involvement of governments in Olympic matters was an ongoing concern, and there was a distinct contrast between French and Anglo-Saxon interests. For the French, with a strong tradition of a *dirigiste* state and with the approach of the former French colonies to state construction, the involvement of state actors in Olympic activity was regarded as the norm. This was anathema to Brundage whose neo-liberal, individualist approach to such matters manifested itself in a vehement, and occasionally almost pathological, distrust of state intervention. Nevertheless, we note that in the selection of African representatives to attend the IOC Session scheduled for Nairobi (which was subsequently relocated to Baden-Baden) in 1963, Brundage thought it preferable to accept the nomination of the French colonial power rather than to trust the nomination of local bodies.

> Concerning the choice of African observers that will be present at this session, Mr. Brundage is in favour of the original idea, in other words to await the suggestions of the High Commissioner for Youth and Sports. These suggestions will have the advantage of providing a maximum of guarantees concerning the recommended personalities.
>
> (M. Muewly, 11 February 1963: report to Jean de Beaumont)

de Beaumont, as the first Chairperson of the CIOA, took the initiative to develop its activities. The motives of the IOC for establishing the sports aid system are expressed in correspondence to the external world outside the Olympic family in terms of the need for efficiency and altruism, as this letter to UNESCO indicates.

> Now, the world has seen itself enlarged by a new dimension: that of developing countries. The I.O.C. would like to offer these countries some tangible evidence of brotherliness in sports through practical, technical and financial aid.... It would appear that many countries in Europe and America operate individually insofar as Aid to sports is concerned, both for Africa and Asia. It will therefore be necessary to make a list of all these

activities with a view to coordinating them, in order to avoid losses of time, energy and money; they would be overseen by an international and a political organization

(Jean de Beaumont, 4 October 1962: letter to Mr Mehau, UNESCO)

However, internally, the western-dominated group within the IOC was concerned about being upstaged by the USSR, as we see from the following two extracts: the first letter from Lord Luke, a British Olympian, IOC member and President of the International Amateur Athletics Federation (IAAF), to de Beaumont in August 1962; and the second from Otto Mayer, the IOC Chancellor, to the editor of the French sports newspaper, *L'Equipe*.

There is another confidential point, which needs to be watched (but not mentioned in public) – it is my private opinion that the U.S.S.R. are only keen about this effort in so far as it is part of their political objective of extending their influence in Africa, and they see in the I.O.C. a means to that end. We must not forget that the overwhelming influence of the U.S.S.R. in the United Nations affairs has been accentuated by their support of the African states, and we have to beware that too much influence on the I.O.C. of increased African membership could have the same effect. In the same way the U.S.S.R. is jealous of the effort the U.S.A. is making in Africa through various forms of aid. Therefore, to sum up, we are fairly close to political issues in our new-found African venture and we must therefore treat them carefully.

(Lord Luke, 28 August 1962: letter to Jean de Beaumont)

I would also like to emphasise the fact that the French were the first to encourage sports in 'Black Africa' particularly in the newly independent countries, and thus avoid that others might claim those laurels. I am thinking of the Russian member of the I.O.C. who is in de Beaumont's commission, who did not even deign to answer any of the 3 letters that De Beaumont sent to him.

(Otto Mayer, 6 January 1962: letter to Gaston Meyer, editor of *L'Equipe*)

As Luke's letter points out, the USSR's tactics in the UN involved fostering support from the newly independent states, and members of the IOC hierarchy were concerned that the same tactics were being employed in sport. It was feared that the USSR was garnering support to oppose western conservative domination of the IOC.

There was, however, evidence of more worrying rationales. Racist attitudes are clearly evinced in this letter from Otto Mayer, the then Chancellor of the IOC, to Avery Brundage.

One thing I regret not to agree is, when Jean de Beaumont intends to get money to send to those people what are they going to do with that money?

Can you imagine non-organized people, knowing practically nothing – or not much – about sport, receiving suddenly money for what? What those people should receive...are: educators in sport, trainers and material.... That money should be used for that only: material sent from Europe and Instructors sent from Europe or USA, but certainly not cash money which will disappear in the pocket of some clever negroes! The first thing is to find intelligent people there who would listen FIRST to what Count de Beaumont tells them.

(Otto Mayer, 25 January 1962: letter to Avery Brundage)

A further letter from Mayer to Brundage in August of the same year indicates clearly, in the context of a discussion about seeking funds from NOCs for Olympic aid purposes, that his sympathies lie with the colonial powers fighting against liberation movements in Africa.

Personally I must confess that I did not like to send that circular letter as we always said that we were not going to ask money from the NOC's. I met a friend of mine the other day, a member of the Portuguese O.C. who said to me that they decided never to send a cent for African countries! I can understand it after the political trouble they have down there.

(Otto Mayer, August 1962: letter to Avery Brundage)

Given the opprobrium that had been expressed in relation to Brundage's role in supporting the Berlin Olympics, the fact that Mayer (the Chancellor, as the post holder of Chief Executive, was then called) felt secure in communicating his thoughts in this manner (to the IOC President) suggests that there may have been a common set of assumptions about Black Africa within the network of IOC members from the core countries. Of course, such racist stereotypes would probably not have been unusual in any number of western-dominated organisations of the time. It would perhaps be naïve to expect the IOC to be exceptional in this respect, but it is still somewhat shocking to see these views being aired at a senior level.

Avery Brundage's own comments, though rather more circumspect, reflect something of a similar mindset. In the context of discussions relating to the action to be taken against South Africa and Zimbabwe following Kenya's refusal to allow visas to representatives from those countries to attend the Nairobi Session of the IOC (which was subsequently moved to Baden-Baden, as a consequence), the prejudicial treatment of black South Africa was ignored, and the implication was that black (or 'coloured') sportspeople were complaining without due cause. Brundage stated that, 'From the evidence submitted, it seems that as much or more is being done for the coloured sportsmen in South Africa as in any other African country' (Avery Brundage, 22 November 1963: letter to Alexander). In terms of dependency theory, there is ample evidence of the sustained promotion of cultural dependence. NOCs were, in particular, dependent on the IOC for admission to the Olympic sports domain and had to conform to certain requirements. Dependency was reinforced by the provision of technical assistance with coaching and administration in particular but which was provided 'with strings'. Assistance was invariably provided without financial aid so that the beneficiaries could not simply buy assistance in an open market but rather were tied to the forms of assistance and the providers of assistance, nominated by the CIOA. This format is illustrated by the response to the following request from Morocco, in the early stages of the CIOA's work: '...Concerning any financial aid from the I.O.C. that might be available, we place our trust in the hands of the I.O.C. to secure as much funding as possible for the Moroccan Sports Federations or Associations' (Lahoucine M'sika, 25 May 1962: letter to de Beaumont). This letter was met with the approval to provide coaching and technical training, but no money was to be paid to the recipient country. The benefits did not straightforwardly flow from core to periphery. Only relatively small amounts of money were available, but such payments as there were went to *donor* countries for the purchasing of equipment or the payment of experts to visit the applicant country. In addition, when elite athletes from developing nations were relocated for training purposes, they also served to enhance the pool of talented athletes competing in the receiving country's system, potentially forcing up local standards of performance. Thus, as with economic dependence, cultural dependence provided a flow of benefits to the western donor states. In addition to aid which was directly related to sport, sports also formed part of some general aid agreements which were part of wider economic deals often benefiting core states themselves or multinational companies based in core states.

However, if there was evidence to support the adoption of a dependency perspective, there was also evidence which can be construed as support for aspects of the modernisation thesis. The aims of the CIOA itself suggest the notion of the convergence of political and societal development around a unitary rational, 'scientised', bureaucratic model of social organisation, as in this extract from a speech by de Beaumont in Dakar in 1963.

> The aims of Olympic aid are '...to further the moral action of the IOC in a more practical and direct manner by offering help to all the countries who need help; to explain *how one gets organised, how one trains, how one follows the rules and by-laws of the IOC.* Particularly *how one helps oneself,* and also *how one enters into the large family of amateur Olympic sport,* by avoiding any discrimination on racial, religious or political grounds, aiming only (at) the development of the human being towards a harmonious accomplishment of the individual, being quite understood that it is the best man (sic) who wins and who gets applauded.'
>
> (de Beaumont, 5 April 1963: speech in Dakar: emphases added)

de Beaumont's speech in Dakar in 1963 reinforces the notion that Olympic aid is about showing the new nations the 'single best way' to organise themselves to produce elite athletes. Universal humanism is also emphasised. The means of delivery of these ideas included

- Information dissemination (about Olympic rules, Olympic philosophy and history);
- Scientific courses (sending experts in sports science and administration; qualifying sport leaders; courses in sports medicine and sports training);
- Technical assistance (scholarships for athletes, sending coaches, equipment, establishing national competitions);
- Promotion of Olympic activities (Olympic week, promotional visits from famous teams or athletes).

Thus, the forces of what organisational theorists term 'institutional isomorphism', providing a blueprint for developing a sporting culture, were built into the programme of Olympic aid.

The third group of theoretical perspectives, which relates to globalisation theories, is that which acknowledges the nature and force of transnational pressures, but which also seeks to identify the ability of local groups to respond, to resist and even to reshape those global forces. The first point to make here is that the IOC itself was not unanimously in favour of the activities of the CIOA. There was resistance in the form of a struggle within the Olympic movement between those who founded the CIOA (led by Comte Jean de Beaumont) and those who opposed it (led principally by Avery Brundage), which is very evident in the correspondence.

The reasons for the concern expressed by those within the IOC (and Brundage in particular) relating to the activities of the CIOA fell into essentially three categories: concern that the CIOA was too closely involved in politics, fear that it was fostering financial demands from new states which at that stage the IOC could not meet; and concern that CIOA would simply duplicate other sports aid schemes provided by entities such as the Commonwealth, International Federations (IFs) and UNESCO. To avoid such difficulties, de Beaumont was asked to remove the word 'Olympic' from its title, changing it to *Comité D'Aid Financier Sportif International*, and the Commission was instructed not to use the IOC letterhead in its correspondence (Brundage, 1963: letter to Jean de Beaumont). In addition, the IOC Executive demanded that the CIOA must not accept financial support from states or cities and must not itself grant financial aid. Thus, in effect, the activities of the CIOA were quietly sidelined from 1963.

However, over the period, the new and peripheral states had been gaining strength. Continental Games were organised in the periphery (the Pan American and the Asian Games from 1951 and the African Games from 1965, with the Pan Arab Games inaugurated in 1953), and the nations of the periphery flexed their political muscles, for example, in terms of opposition to apartheid, when Kenya refused to allow visas for the South African representatives to attend the Nairobi IOC meeting in 1963 and when South Africa and Rhodesia were not invited to the first African Games in Brazzaville in 1965. This prompted Brundage's response in a letter to IOC members and to NOCs arguing that, 'The International Olympic Committee will, we trust, never permit anyone to decide who will or will not attend its meetings' (Brundage, 23 August 1963: letter to IOC members and NOCs). This tension had even led de Beaumont, in a letter of 2 October 1965, to propose the merging of white-governed South Africa and Rhodesia with Oceania in an Olympic region which he termed 'Australafrica', a form of Olympic apartheid which fortunately found little support.

Perhaps the major turning point in terms of IOC relations with the peripheral nations was the struggle over the GANEFO in 1963. Indonesia's refusal to provide visas for Israeli and Taiwanese representatives to compete in the Fourth Asian Games had led to a confrontation between the Indonesian NOC and the IOC which culminated in Indonesia's organising of the GANEFO. The games which incorporated countries from Asia, Africa, Latin America and socialist countries were planned to be a forerunner of a parallel alliance in the political arena. The IOC and Fédération Internationale de Natation (FINA) threatened to ban athletes who participated in the event, and further difficulties were probably only ultimately avoided because GANEFO itself ran into political difficulties, when President Sukarno was ousted in a coup in 1965 (Sie 1978).

With the onset of the GANEFO crisis, the IOC establishment clearly recognised that there would be a need to bring the NOCs more closely into the core activities of the Olympic movement, but this did not necessarily mean increasing their numbers in the membership of the IOC itself. The great fear of the IOC members was the swamping of the membership by the new nations which would have radically affected the balance of power in the Olympic movement. This is evident in, for example, comments by Brundage himself in a letter to de Beaumont, who stresses that entry into the movement means entry into the Games and not into decision-making, and by Alexander, a white Kenyan businessman, and IOC member, expressing concerns about excessive nationalism on the part of the representatives of the new nations.

> Another point that must be explained [to the new nations] is the organization of International sport and that the countries will not participate in the I.O.C. itself, but that their National Olympic Committees will be recognized so that they may participate in the Olympic Games.
> (Brundage, 16 April 1963: letter to de Beaumont)

> I earnestly believe that members of the International Olympic Committee must in their attitude be truly international and that we must get away from this identification with specific countries. One danger facing the Olympic Movement is an excessiveness of nationalism and this certainly should not be allowed to appear in the governing body itself. A mass of nations, each represented on the IOC will, I am sure, produce the same result as is happening in the United Nations with power blocks forming in order to press a certain philosophy.
> (Alexander, 7 January 1969: letter to Brundage)

By the later 1960s, the NOCs (both from the core countries and from the Olympic political periphery) and the IFs, whose sports made up the diet of the Games, were becoming frustrated with a lack of power and influence and began to press for a greater say in the Olympic movement. Both groups established bodies through which to represent their collective interests, in the form of the Permanent General Assembly (PGA) of NOCs in parallel with the General Assembly of International Federations (GAIF).

As de Beaumont suggests in a letter of 1969 to the IOC Executive Office, the issue of international aid to NOCs was central to the concerns which led to the establishing of the PGA of NOCs.

> The Aid Commission as it was planned when created in 1961, was intended to support the action of the IOC in the field of expansion and promotion of the Olympic ideal and movement. The setting up of this commission, if we look at its extremely promising beginning, it certainly dealt with the needs of the time. It was only after its dissolution[2] which was a mistake, that various National Olympic Committees palliated its disappearance by trying to find solutions, which could meet with their needs. This was how the Permanent General Assembly of National Olympic Committees came to be founded.
>
> (Jean de Beaumont, March 1969: letter to IOC Executive Office)

Thus, it is not surprising that one of the first issues to concern the PGA was to establish an Olympic Solidarity fund and to formally request from the IOC that television rights' income be allocated through the PGA to aid NOC work. In a formal resolution, it argued that the IOC should:

> Accept the responsibility of financing in part the assistance actions realised by the PGA of NOCs within the framework of 'Olympic Solidarity', by attributing to this programme yearly subsidies deriving from the quota accruing to the IOC on behalf of the NOCs from television rights on the Olympic Games.
>
> (PGA of NOCs resolution, 1971)

The IOC accepted most of the PGA of NOCs requests and formally incorporated it and the GAIF into the organisational infrastructure known as the Olympic family. By doing so, the IOC was able to unite the movement, coordinating the interests of different forces within it, protecting against both political interference and commercialism/professionalism, while also still effectively holding the new NOCs at arm's length. The adoption of Olympic Solidarity which was formally established in 1972 at Sapporo was in effect the price to be paid for ensuring the compliance of the NOCs.

However, although it accepted the idea of Olympic Solidarity, the IOC still initially resisted the provision of financial aid through this vehicle. Control over funding was still effectively vested in the IOC since it insisted that aid takes the form of training and other such services. This was in part an attempt to reinforce a form of financial dependency in terms of the core–periphery relations which restricted the financial flow from the core to the periphery as far as sports aid was concerned (though financial aid could be used for the staging of the Continental Games).

> In this connection (re the Olympic Solidarity schemes) it should of course be born in mind that although there will be naturally be some funds, originating from the proceeds of TV, made available for conducting NOC's activities. Such funds will have to spread out over a period of four years. There will be consequently be no room for fancy schemes, etc., nor can the NOC's count on any in the form of actual cash to be handed out, as decided some time ago.
>
> (van Karnebeek, 2 August 1972: letter to IOC technical director)

This position, however, became more and more difficult to sustain, and with the onset of major revenue streams from television rights and sponsorship in the post-1984 era, and the introduction of increasing decentralisation of fund allocations (albeit for programmes centrally decided) in the 1990s, the NOCs of the peripheral nations appeared to have, in many respects, achieved their goals.

Evaluating alternative explanations of transnational policy

In introducing this case, the review of the early history of the Olympic Solidarity and its forerunner was intended to illustrate ways in which evidence for particular perspectives may be rehearsed and evaluated. The evidence reviewed allows us to draw a number of conclusions. It is clear, for example, that the origins of Olympic Solidarity, or at least its subsequent incorporation into the IOC's formal activities, performed the function of unifying the Olympic Movement by neutralizing the pressure exerted by the IFs and NOCs for a greater say in the running of the Olympic system. Furthermore, the establishing of Olympic Solidarity did indeed foster the development of the global network of the Olympic family. In addition, the activities of the CIOA and of Olympic Solidarity did facilitate the flow of western culture to non-western societies but in terms which were increasingly contested/negotiated rather than imposed. The increasing ability of the peripheral NOCs to exert influence is clearly evident by the beginning of the 1970s. This is particularly evident in the forcing of the IOC's hand in terms of banning South Africa from the Games and the movement.

Finally, the unravelling of the story of its development provides us with elements of evidence for each of the perspectives cited – but the top-down elements of cultural imperialism, dependency and modernisation theory are most relevant to the processes in the early period, the 1960s, while more multi-directional accounts of influence appear more appropriate to the period of the early 1970s. As the newly independent states developed, so too their ability to assert their own wishes and views became increasingly apparent, and what had been an evidently top-down imposition of policies could not be sustained in the longer term. This is not to argue that there were no hierarchies of power, but globalisation theories and multi-causal approaches to explanation of the phenomena under consideration thus appear to offer a more satisfactory account in the longer term. Certainly, there are elements of rationalisation of culture and its delivery in the development of the Olympics in the newly independent states, as there is evidence of cultural imperialism (it is essentially western culture which is being promoted, with little reference to indigenous sports and games). Similarly, there are aspects of cultural dependency as the newly independent states seek entry to this world cultural club, the Olympic movement, with almost as much assiduousness as they seek entry to the (western-dominated) political club, that is, the UN. However, the outcomes in policy terms cannot be explained by reference to these factors alone. The interplay of political, economic and cultural factors supports the notion of both core and periphery being able to exert influence. One cannot, for instance, imagine a 'world' event in track and field having any credibility without central participation by Kenyan, Ethiopian, Moroccan and Algerian athletes. Power imbalances exist of course, but they are not all unidirectional.

Orientalism and postmodernism

In the foregoing discussion of the development of Olympic Solidarity, the discussion is rather more concerned with access to and control over western sport forms and political processes of domination via cultural forms more broadly. However, there is very little discussion of the 'textual nature' of sport, the kinds of values and meanings promoted through sport forms, and by implication of the kinds of values that are 'demoted' or ignored, for example, in the subversion of traditional sports and games. A concern with this type of 'textuality', which is evident to some degree in aspects of ethnography and anthropology, is more central to the traditions of postmodern and poststructuralist accounts, in particular those associated with the critique of Orientalism.

The term 'Orientalism' has multiple meanings. It refers to the study of the Orient (students/scholars may be called Orientalists), but the study of the Orient implies discursive construction of its object (Foucault 1972) and as Edward Said claims:

> My contention is that without examining Orientalism as a discourse one cannot possibly understand the enormously systematic discipline by which European culture was able to manage – and even produce – the Orient, politically, sociologically, militarily, ideologically, scientifically and imaginatively in the post-Enlightenment period.
>
> (Said 1991: p. 10)

The process of construction of the Orient is necessarily accomplished by the antinomic construction of the West by western commentators. The Orient is the other by which 'we' (the West) know ourselves. The description of the Orient as manifesting despotism, splendour, cruelty, sensuality, etc., is in implicit contrast to the measured, objective, rational characteristics of the West. Said, in his book *Orientalism: western conceptions of the Orient*, teases out how representations of the Oriental have been developed by western artists, writers, journalists and poets, tacitly legitimating the dominance of the West over the East.

> One must repeatedly ask oneself whether what matters in Orientalism is the general group of ideas overriding the mass of material…. Shot through with doctrines of European superiority, various kinds of racism, imperialism, and the like, dogmatic values of the 'Oriental' as a kind of ideal and unchanging abstraction.
>
> (Said 1991: p. 12)

Knowledge, Said and others wish to argue, is never pure and unadulterated by politics – it is inherently political. Thus, the deconstruction of such linguistically constructed views provides a form of knowledge which is itself political, about how the Orient has been constructed, the 'other' defined and the position of the western self-reproduced. Imperialism, political dominance and marginalisation of the non-West are thus explained with reference to this 'us–them', 'superior–inferior' dichotomous construct. The Orient is not necessarily the East (it can include Africa for example) since it is not intended to define a spatial relationship with the West but rather a political process. It defines difference and legitimates subordination in conjoint processes.

Since its inception, Islam has constituted Christianity's principal 'other', though it is not the West's only other. The communist bloc and, to a lesser extent, Judaism have provided contrasts which define the West, but it is from the Crusades of the eleventh century to debates about *The Clash of Civilizations* (Huntington 1996) that the Christian–Muslim relationship has provided a set of defining processes.

Orientalism is clearly of significance for comparative studies in general and comparative policy studies in particular. There is also a clear link between the concept and approach of Orientalist critique and that of postmodernism. Both tend to be interested in discursive construction. Both acknowledge problems with absolute, universal judgements viewing reality as relationally constructed. Both tend to employ forms of deconstruction to generate insights, while both deny the possibility of making universal claims to truth.

While Said's arguments are primarily concerned with western education, literature and art, sport as a cultural form can be subjected to such a critique. Orientalist discourse denigrates the non-West by implicit comparison. The Orient is implicitly or explicitly characterised as governed by a range of 'failed', 'flawed', 'dominated' polities, reliant on 'ethnic and kinship links', and deviant political arrangements such as 'political clientelism', and the cultural and social forms, including sport forms, which complement this political set of arrangements are also similarly 'inferior' when compared with the western tradition.

The rationally constructed 'egalitarian' universalist nature of western sport is thus to be compared with the crude, often cruel, nature of traditional sports, with restricted access (by class or gender) with functions of reinforcing kinship networks and association with superstition. It does not require the most subtle deconstructive analysis to be able to recognise that forms of cruelty, crudeness, tribal behaviour, inegalitarian organisation and restricted access are evident in modern western sport. The (re) emergence of bare knuckle fighting and 'absolute combat' (forms of combat with virtually no holds barred) in countries such as the United Kingdom in recent years and the death of horses in races such as the Grand National undermine claims about the 'civilised' nature of modern sport in the West. A cursory glance at the western sports which involve technology such as the 'swiftsuit', carbon fibre cycle frames, state-of-the-art rowing boats, water-based artificial turf international hockey pitches and the like, undermines the myth of egalitarian competition in western sport. The England soccer team manager, Glen Hoddle's use of a faith healer with the England squad (British Broadcasting Corporation 1999), parallels the alleged use of 'magic' (*The Guardian* 2002). The roles of sport and other 'modern' western cultural forms in reinforcing 'tribal' identities (Maffesoli 1996) also belie the notion of rational individualism. Orientalist analysis thus involves a deconstruction of the definition of western culture which is shared by many of those living in the West but also shared by political, social and economic elites in the non-West and is made more acute by the demands of those of the non-West (including those living in western nation states) for a recognition of their right to assert non-western values.

Thus, while our critique of the development of Olympic Solidarity in this chapter is intended to be critically reflexive, in the sense that is subjecting a western-originated phenomenon to critical scrutiny, the theoretical tools adopted to conduct this critique are derived from a western epistemological tradition which tends to take as 'given' the language and thus the 'epistemic frame' within which this policy is developed and discussed. Types I–III of the approaches to comparative policy analysis exemplified in the chapters which follow reflect this limitation, and we thus return to postmodern/post-colonial approaches (which have their own limitations) in the final case study chapter of this book (which deals with Type IV studies) in order to illustrate the nature of the contribution which postmodernist/post-colonial approaches can bring to our understanding of the policy process and outcomes but more importantly the framing of policy debates.

Part II

Case studies of comparative and transnational analysis of sports policy

4 Measuring the sporting success of nations

Simon Shibli and Jerry Bingham with Ian Henry

Introduction

This chapter reviews the measures developed to address comparative analysis of Olympic performance in the Summer Games and, in particular, considers the uses and limitations of a range of comparative measures of performance. Such measures are important if meaningful comparisons are to be made between national sports performance production systems, and by implication, the most successful systems identified. The arguments rehearsed in this chapter were developed in the context of a wider study of the factors associated with success in elite sport – the SPLISS project (an International Comparative Study of Sports Policy Factors Leading to International Sporting Success) directed by Veerle de Bosscher and Paul De Knop of the Vrije Universiteit Brussel, Belgium; Maarten van Bottenburg and Bas Rijnen of the Mulier Institute, the Netherlands; Simon Shibli and Chris Gratton of Sheffield Hallam University, UK; and Jerry Bingham of UK Sport, UK. The study is a useful vehicle for illustrating some of the strengths and weaknesses of the Type 1 – seeking similarities – approach to comparative analysis identified in Chapter 2.

One way of characterising the process of elite athlete development is to adopt a simplified model of the policy process, identifying policy inputs, policy process and policy outputs in the manner illustrated in Figure 4.1. This has the benefit of highlighting, and to some extent isolating, for the purpose of comparison, operational measures of resources allocated, means of processing such inputs and policy outputs. At one level at least, this allows for direct comparison with the implicit assumption that enhancement of the efficiency of converting inputs to outputs (classical example, money into medals) can be readily measured. Such claims will be the subject of evaluation in the concluding section of this chapter.

Increasingly, as sports performance production systems have developed in recent years, the 'production' of successful elite athletes by nations has been (implicitly or explicitly) treated as an output from a strategic planning process. Nations for whom sporting success is important commit to strategic planning processes such as the World Class Performance Programme in the UK or Performance 2008 in the Netherlands. The components of these and similar

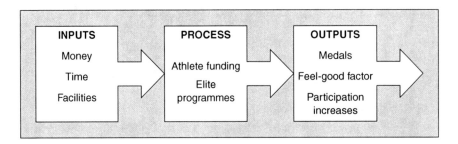

Figure 4.1 Elite athlete production as a process model.

programmes across the world are becoming increasingly familiar and are documented in the emerging body of literature. Oakley and Green (2001) and
Green and Houlihan (2005) argue, along with Clumpner (1994), that the elite
sports development systems of the UK, France, Spain, Canada, USA and Australia are becoming increasingly homogenous to the extent that they are based
around a single model of elite sports development but each with slight variations on that model. It follows that if nations are adopting a strategic approach
to the production of elite athletes, then part of that process must be to evaluate the results achieved (outputs), relative to the resources invested (inputs).
The notion of the 'process' approach to the production of medal-winning elites
and the implied imperative of measuring performance is illustrated in
Figure 4.1.

A core focus of this chapter is thus to examine various methods by which the
outputs of an elite athlete production system can be measured using the
Summer Olympic Games (28 sports) as a case study. In addition, the limitations
of the analysis are examined, and some alternative measures for future development proposed. The wider study, of elite sports policy production systems, to
which this analysis is a contribution seeks to examine the effectiveness and efficiency of systems in order to identify *who* is performing well and *why* they are
performing well, and in order to answer these questions, a clearer indication of
how to measure performance is required.

However, before examining performance measurement methods in more
detail, we present a brief overview of the nature of the Summer Olympic
Games.

The nature of the Summer Olympic Games

Along with the FIFA World Cup, the Summer Olympic Games is the event
with the highest profile in the global sporting calendar. In recent editions of the
Games, the International Olympic Committee (IOC) has sought to make the
event truly global. This point can in part be appreciated by reviewing the
growing number of nations taking part as reported in Table 4.1.

Table 4.1 Olympic Summer Games data 1896–2004

Date of Summer Olympic Games	Number of national teams	Number of athletes	Number of sports contested	Number of events contested
1896	14	245	9	43
1900	24	1,225	18	87
1904	13	689	17	94
1908	22	2,035	22	109
1912	28	2,547	14	102
1920	29	2,669	22	154
1924	44	3,092	17	126
1928	46	3,014	14	119
1932	37	1,408	14	116
1936	49	4,066	19	129
1948	59	4,099	17	136
1952	69	4,925	17	149
1956	67	3,184	17	145
1960	83	5,346	17	150
1964	93	5,140	19	163
1968	112	5,530	20	172
1972	121	7,123	23	195
1976	92	6,028	21	198
1980	80	5,217	21	203
1984	140	6,797	23	221
1988	159	8,465	25	237
1992	169	9,367	28	257
1996	197	10,320	26	271
2000	199	10,651	28	300
2004	201	11,059	28	301

Table 4.1 also illustrates the long-term trend of increasing numbers of national teams taking part in the Olympic Games in the modern era. The only noticeable breaks in the series reflect the African nation-led boycott of 1976 and the American nation-led boycott of 1980. Although the 1984 Games were boycotted by the then 'Eastern bloc' countries, there have been increases in the number of nations taking part in every edition since 1980. Thus, the Olympic Games has become increasingly more global in its reach. In addition, as the number of nations taking part has increased, so too has the number of athletes and the number of events.

The data in Table 4.1 indicate that the number of athletes taking part in the Olympic Games more than doubled in the period 1980 (5,217 competitors) to 2004 (11,059 competitors. In addition to increases in the number of nations and athletes, there have also been increases in the number of sports contested and the number of events.

The number of sports contested at each Olympic Games has risen from 17 in 1948 to 28 in 1992, 2000 and 2004. The number of events peaked in 2004 at 301, and the long-term growth trend in the number of events can in part be explained by two factors. First, the increase in the number of sports contested, and second, an expansion of the programmes for selected sports, notably an increase in the number of events contested by women. An interesting finding from the data relating to increased numbers of nations, athletes, sports and events is that the number of nations which have developed medal-winning capability has also increased as shown in Figure 4.2.

In 2004, a record 56 nations won at least one gold medal, and in 2000, the number of nations winning a medal of any hue increased to a peak of 80.

It is clear that if more nations are developing medal-winning capability, then medals are becoming even harder to win and competition to win them must therefore be increasing. We have tested this relationship by plotting the number of nations winning any medal against the number of nations taking part. The results of this analysis are shown in Figure 4.3.

There appears to be a strong correlation ($r^2 = 0.88$) between the number of nations taking part in the Olympic Games and the number of nations winning a medal of any type. It is our view that the increase in medal-winning capability illustrated in Figure 4.3 is explained by an increasing number of nations taking a strategic approach to the development of medal-winning elites. If this point is accepted, then there are two implications. First, competition for medals is increasing, and second, 'standing still' (i.e. not continuing to increase investment in elite sport programmes) will result in a degradation of performance because other nations continue to develop competitive advantage.

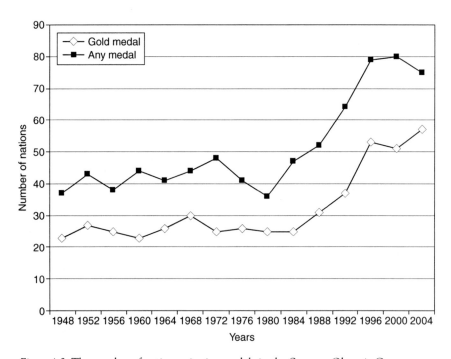

Figure 4.2 The number of nations winning medals in the Summer Olympic Games.

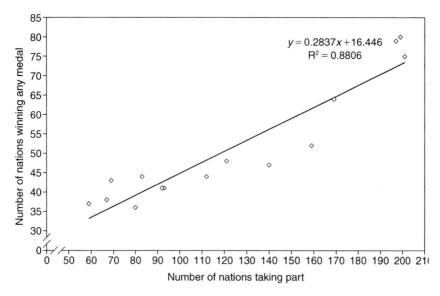

Figure 4.3 Evidence of increasing competition for medals.

As the supply of medals (success) remains essentially fixed (the IOC has indicated that it would like the number of events to be capped at around 300), and demand for success is increasing (more nations taking part and more nations winning medals), then the 'market' adjusts by raising the price of 'success'. In practice, an increase in the 'price of success' means that even more resources need to be invested in order for a nation to retain its medal-winning capability.

As a consequence of investing increasing resources in pursuit of elite sport success, the need for performance appraisal increases so that those providing the resources to fund success can derive some feedback on their return on investment.

Measuring performance in the Olympic Games

The following data are drawn from a research project carried out for UK Sport by the Sport Industry Research Centre at Sheffield Hallam University (Sports Industries Research Centre 2003). The original research focused on performance in the Summer Olympic Games 1948–2000 and has been updated to include the additional findings of Athens 2004. Although the examples used throughout this chapter relate predominantly to the UK, we would suggest that the basic principles are applicable to all nations that take a strategic approach to the development of elite athletes. Thus, although it would have been relatively straightforward to include the same analysis for other nations, in the interests of brevity, we focus primarily on the UK.

The IOC does not recognise the Olympic medal table as an order of merit. Nonetheless, it is widely accepted in the sporting world that the final medal table for each games is an order of merit. This finding is perhaps best demonstrated by the fact that many nations invest heavily in sport precisely to climb the unofficial order of merit. Despite the medal table's simplicity of being a list in descending order of gold, silver and bronze medals, it is not an effective measure of performance for a number of reasons. To illustrate these reasons, an excerpt from the table of results for the Athens 2004 Games is reproduced in Table 4.2.

The first key weakness with the medal table is that it is a measure of relative rather than absolute achievement. In other words, it is possible for countries to improve their position in the ranking table simply by other countries performing less well. When taken to its logical conclusion, it would be possible for Great Britain to improve its medal table standing by maintaining current performance (nine gold medals) so long as the countries at the very top became even more dominant at the expense of those immediately above Great Britain. Thus, for example, if the USA had improved its position by depriving Korea of a gold medal, Great Britain would automatically have moved from tenth to ninth place.

When analysing position in the medal table on a time series basis, it can be difficult to assess actual performance between one edition and another of the Games. For example, in Sydney 2000, Great Britain achieved tenth place by virtue of winning 11 gold medals. In Athens 2004 also, Great Britain achieved tenth place, but on this occasion, by winning only nine gold medals. If position in the medal table was the only measure of performance, then tenth place in two consecutive editions of the Olympic Games would be said to have been a performance of identical value. As will be shown later in this chapter when using alternative measures of performance, Great Britain's success in 2000 and 2004 was not the result of identical performance.

The second key weakness with the medal table is that it ignores the totality of achievement in much the same way that assessing capital investment projects

Table 4.2 Excerpt from Athens 2004 medal table (a)

Nation	Gold	Silver	Bronze	Total medals
1 United States of America (USA)	35	39	29	103
2 People's Republic of China (CHN)	32	17	14	63
3 Russian Federation (RUS)	27	27	38	92
4 Australia (AUS)	17	16	16	49
5 Japan (JAP)	16	9	12	37
6 Germany (GER)	14	16	18	48
7 France (FRA)	11	9	13	33
8 Italy (ITA)	10	11	11	32
9 Korea (KOR)	9	12	9	30
10 Great Britain (GBR)	9	9	12	30

using payback methods ignores the lifetime of a project. To illustrate this point, a second excerpt from the Athens 2004 medal table is reproduced in Table 4.3.

In the Athens medal table, China was ranked above Russia as a result of having won 32 gold medals compared with Russia's 27 gold medals. However, this ranking ignores the fact that Russia won 92 medals overall compared with China's 63.

Various methods have been used to analyse the Olympic medal tables to allow for the totality of achievement. The most basic of these is to list countries according to the total number of medals won. Using this method on Tables 4.2 and 4.3 would place Russia ahead of China. The total medals system can also be used to a limited extent on time series data. Figure 4.4 illustrates the performance of Great Britain in the Summer Olympic Games 1948–2004.

If we ignore the boycotted Olympics between 1976 and 1984 (when fewer nations took part in the events, and therefore, competition for medals was reduced), there has been only one instance in which the number of medals won by Great Britain has increased in two consecutive editions of the Olympic Games, that is, 1996–2004. This period coincides with the worst performance since 1952 (Atlanta 1996) and the introduction of the World Class Performance Programme in 1997 which is widely credited for the significantly improved performances of 2000 and 2004. In short, Great Britain has never won more medals in non-boycotted Olympic Games than it has since the introduction of the World Class Performance Programme.

However, the total medals system itself is limited because it does not take into account the relative value of medals. Taken to its logical conclusion, one gold medal under the total medals system would be equal to one silver medal or one bronze medal. Thus, in Figure 4.4, if the total medals method is adopted, Great Britain's performance appears to have been better in 2004 (30 medals) than 2000 (28 medals). There is a strong argument to suggest that the 'quality' of medals won in 2000 (more gold, more silver and less bronze) was higher than that in 2004. For this reason, we discount total medals as a measure of performance in favour of a system that discriminates between the quality of medals won.

One method which allows for the relative values of gold, silver and bronze medals is a 'points' system which recognises the relative value of medals and makes use of a weighting system to convert a nation's medal haul into a points equivalent. The most simple points system is to award three points for a gold medal, two for a silver medal and one for a bronze medal. Applying this points system to the Athens 2004 medal table (Tables 4.3 and 4.4) would elevate

Table 4.3 Excerpt from Athens 2004 medal table (b)

Nation	Gold	Silver	Bronze	Medals
2 People's Republic of China (CHN)	32	17	14	63
3 Russian Federation (RUS)	27	27	38	92

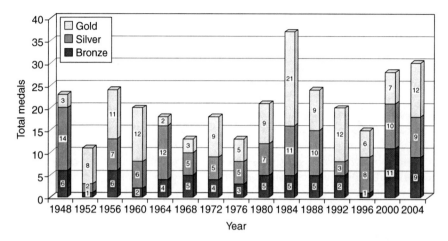

Figure 4.4 Great Britain – total medals in the Summer Olympic Games 1948–2004.

Russia to second place (173 points) at the expense of China (144 points) who would slip to third place. Table 4.4 illustrates this point.

The advantage of the points system is that it moves beyond according the same value to a silver or bronze as to a gold medal. Thus, it is a more useful measure of the performance of an elite athlete production system for strategic planning and decision-making purposes than the official Olympic Games medal table. Applying the points system described here to the case of Great Britain gives the time series analysis shown in Figure 4.5.

Figure 4.5 shows a random pattern of performance between 1948 and 1976, growth during the boycotted Games of 1980 and 1984, a period of constant decline between 1984 and 1996 and considerable recovery and stabilisation in 2000 and 2004. It is worth noting that the points system confirms Sydney 2000 (60 points) was a greater level of achievement than Athens 2004 (57 points) because the points value of the medals won in Sydney was higher.

Although the points system is a more useful measure of performance than position in the medal table or total medals won, it has one major limitation. As the number of events contested at each Games has varied considerably over

Table 4.4 Performance of People's Republic of China and Russian Federation weighted by value of medals won.

Nation	Gold	Silver	Bronze	Medals	Points
2 People's Republic of China (CHN)	32	17	14	53	144
3 Russian Federation (RUS)	27	27	38	92	173

Note
China points = $((32 \times 3) + (17 \times 2) + (14 \times 1)) = 144$.

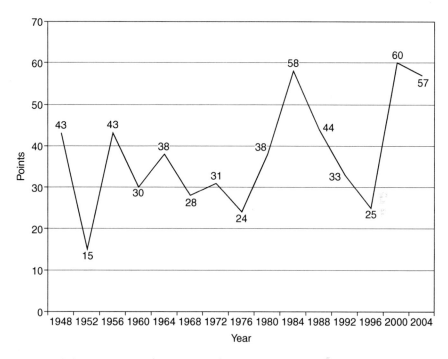

Figure 4.5 Great Britain in the Summer Olympic Games 1948–2004 – total points (3 for Gold, 2 for Silver, 1 for Bronze).

time (Table 4.1) and to a lesser extent the number of points per event has also varied (for example, two or more nations 'tying' for the same medal), the number of points available at each Olympic Games has also varied.

In order to convert points won into a standardised measure, it is necessary to compute market share, that is, points won as a proportion of points available to win. Using market share, it is possible to make a more accurate diagnosis as to whether the 58 points won in 1984, the 60 points won in 2000 or the 57 points won in 2004 was the best performance in standardised terms. The results of this analysis are reported in Table 4.5.

In the 300 events contested in Sydney, a total of 1,829 points was awarded, of which Great Britain and Northern Ireland won 60. This is a market share of 3.28 per cent, which in turn is slightly better than the 57 points won out of 1,832 (301 events) in Athens 2004, a market share of 3.11 per cent. In other words, on a standardised basis, the performance of Great Britain in Sydney 2000 was slightly better than the performance achieved in Athens 2004. However, the performance in Los Angeles is the best of the three performances because the 58 points won from 1,359 (221 events) gives a market share of 4.27 per cent.

Market share analysis can be used to compare standardised performance by

Table 4.5 Great Britain's standardised performance using market share

Edition	Gold	Silver	Bronze	Medals	Points	Points available	Market share (%)
1984	5	11	21	37	58	1,359	4.27
2000	11	10	7	28	60	1,829	3.28
2004	9	9	12	30	57	1,832	3.11

gender. Men and women have to date contested a different number of events in the Olympic Games, and thus, to compare how a nation's male athletes perform relative to their female counterparts, it is necessary to compute market share by gender. This type of analysis confirms that in the case of Great Britain men consistently outperform women in standardised terms, whereas for the Netherlands, the reverse is true.

Furthermore, market share analysis can be applied at individual sport level as an indicator of the effect of given performance programmes and the systems responsible for delivering them. In the case of the Netherlands, the nation has enjoyed considerable success in swimming in the Olympic Games and World Championships, shown by the trend lines in Figure 4.6.

In Figure 4.6, it can be seen that between 1986 and 1996, all of the Netherlands' success in swimming was attributable to women swimmers. The World Swimming Championships of 1998 heralded a new era in elite swimming with the emergence of Pieter van den Hoogenband. This success was built upon in the Sydney Olympic Games in 2000 when van den Hoogenband and Inge de Bruijn won five gold medals between them. Although not quite as successful in

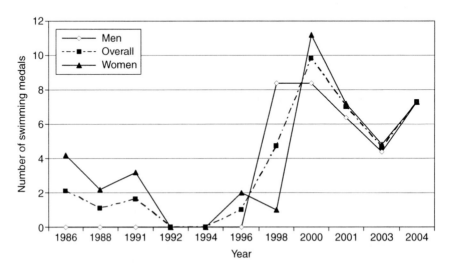

Figure 4.6 Market share of swimming medals for the Netherlands (Olympics and World Championships).

Athens 2004 as in Sydney 2000, it can still be seen that there has been a sustained increase in performance by swimmers representing the Netherlands from 1996 to 2004 compared with performance from 1986 to 1996. In addition, Figure 4.6 confirms that the Netherlands' best performance in standardised terms was at the Sydney Olympics in 2000 when it achieved a market share of 9.8 per cent in swimming – its highest market share in all world and Olympic events during the period 1986–2004.

The limitation of the portfolio of analysis techniques reviewed thus far is that it is possible that conflicting messages can given about performance. This point is perhaps best illustrated by examining the case of Great Britain in the two most recent editions of the Summer Olympic Games. A full breakdown of performance using four different measures is reported in Table 4.6.

Depending on the performance measure adopted, Table 4.6 illustrates that it is possible for a reasonable argument to be made that Great Britain's performance has remained the same, improved or deteriorated. This has implications for UK Sport when trying to justify its investment in elite athlete development during the Athens Olympiad. However, of the four measures outlined in Table 4.6, it is our view that market share is the best indicator of a nation's performance.

The justification of this view is twofold. First, market share is the only standardised measure of the four performance indicators reported in Table 4.6. Second, market share can be increased in one of the three ways:

1   an increase in the number of medals won;
2   an increase in the quality of medals won; or
3   maintaining absolute performance when the number of events has declined.

These are much more robust and controllable measures of success than moving up the medal table simply because superior nations have become even more dominant. The basic point about the value of market share as a measure holds true whether we are examining an aggregate of sports, as in the Olympic Games, or an individual sport in isolation.

It is not only the performance of the UK that fluctuates according to the type of measure used. For the remaining five nations in the sample, we have replicated the analysis reported in Table 4.6. A full breakdown of the change in performance by measurement type is reported in Table 4.7.

Table 4.6 Conflicting measures of performance for the GB Olympic Team

Method	2000	2004	Performance
Position in medal table	10th	10th	Same
Total medals	28	30	Better
Points	60	57	Worse
Market share (%)	3.28	3.11	Worse

Table 4.7 Change in performance 2000–4 by measure type

Nation	Medal Table Position	Total Medals	Points (3,2,1)	Market Share (%)
Great Britain	Same	Better	Worse	Worse
Canada	Better	Worse	Better	Better
Italy	Worse	Worse	Worse	Worse
Norway	Better	Worse	Worse	Worse
The Netherlands	Worse	Worse	Worse	Worse
Belgium	Better	Worse	Worse	Worse

With the exception of Italy and the Netherlands, who both performed worse according to every measure in Table 4.7, there are differing diagnoses for the remaining nations depending on the measure selected. Canada performed better on three of the four measures and was the only nation to have increased its market share. As Canada experienced a decrease in the total number of medals won, it shows that market share must have been increased by an improvement in the quality of the medals won. This point is evident in the fact that Canada's performance was three gold, six silver and three bronze (24 points) medals in 2004 compared with three gold, three silver and eight bronze (23 points) medals in 2000. By contrast, Belgium improved its ranking in the medal table by winning a gold medal in 2004, thereby ranking it ahead of all other nations that won any medal other than a gold medal. By every other measure used in Table 4.7, Belgium's performance in 2004 was worse than that in 2000.

It is as a consequence of the conflicting nature of measures such as those reported in Tables 4.6 and 4.7 that alternative measures of performance are required to measure the effectiveness of investments.

Alternative measures of performance

Although medal-based measures of performance are easily understood measures of success, they still ignore the totality of achievement of an elite sport programme. As has already been demonstrated, competition for medals is increasing as more nations take part in the Olympic Games (Figure 4.3). It is quite possible for Performance Directors in individual sports to make considerable progress in developing a sport without this progress being recognised by medals in elite competition. Some of these alternative measures of success are outlined as the following.

The number of athletes qualifying to take part in elite championships

The global nature of the Olympic Games is such that for some nations and individual sports, the number of athletes who qualify to contest an event at the

Games is a valid measure of performance. In Athens 2004, only one boxer qualified to represent Great Britain in the boxing tournament. In theory, therefore, a successful output for 2008 from the World Class Programme for British boxing might be the qualification of two or more boxers to take part in the event – regardless of their ultimate performance.

The number of athletes qualifying to contest the final of an event

In high-profile sports such as swimming or athletics, in which finals are often contested by eight (and sometimes more) athletes, simply qualifying for the final may well be a considerable achievement. This point is particularly true for smaller nations which have fewer athletes and resources to draw upon than larger more affluent nations. As an example, it might be more of an achievement for a Belgian sprinter to reach the final of the men's athletics 100m than for an athlete representing the USA to win the bronze medal. The threshold of performance can be lowered to recognise achievement in any of the various rounds between basic qualifying and the final. For example, it would be a great achievement for a sprinter from the Cayman Islands to qualify for the Olympic Games and to proceed beyond the first round. It is this more comprehensive view of 'performance' that will help with the broad aim of this analysis to identify over- and underachieving nations in a systematic manner.

The number of athletes posting season's best performances

In an environment of increasing competition globally, the best that might reasonably be expected of an athlete would be for them to achieve a season's best performance in their event. This type of measure can be used as a good indicator of Performance Directors delivering athletes in peak condition for a major championship.

The number of athletes achieving personal bests or breaking national records

As a logical extension of season's best times being a valid measure of performance, it follows that more demanding measures such as lifetime (personal) best performances and all-time national best performances are also valid measures of performance. It is less easy to be critical about an athlete who was eliminated in the semi-final of an Olympic final and who in so doing broke a national record. This type of performance indicates positive 'distance travelled' in terms of the achievement of a given nation while at the same time acknowledging that standards have improved globally. Thus, the narrowing of the gap between a national record and the level of performance required to achieve medal-winning success in a major championship is also a valid measure of success.

One of the reasons why interim measures of success such as those listed earlier are particularly valid is that one of the contributory factors in a successful elite sports development programme is time. Australia performed exceptionally well in the Olympic Games in 2000 and 2004, and this success is widely attributed to the establishment of the Australian Institute of Sport in the late 1970s following a poor showing in Montreal 1976. More recently, France has also performed well in the Olympic Games since implementing various initiatives in the mid-1980s.

In Italy, there has been a strategic approach to the development of elite sport since 1942 when the Italian National Olympic Committee [Comitato Olimpico Nazionale Italiano (CONI)] was given the rights to sports-related gambling profits. These monies have been used to support state, regional and local level networks of elite athlete development. A simple measure of the system's success can be appreciated by comparing Italy's performance in the Summer Olympic Games with that of Great Britain, as shown in Figure 4.7.

In 15 editions of the Olympic Games between 1948 and 2004, Italy has been ranked ahead of Great Britain on 13 of the 15 occasions. Italy has been investing in elite sports development systems since 1942, whereas in Great Britain, the systematic programme of investment did not begin until 1997. Thus, it is reasonable to conclude that time can be considered to be a factor in determining the success of an elite sports development system.

Measuring the efficiency of success

The measures discussed thus far, whether they be the four indicators of success reviewed in Tables 4.6 and 4.7 or the interim measures of success discussed in the earlier sections of this chapter, are all measures of effectiveness, that is, measures of the extent to which pre-determined goals have been achieved. In a world in which resources are limited, a further measure is efficiency in terms of examining the amount of resource used to deliver a specified level of success.

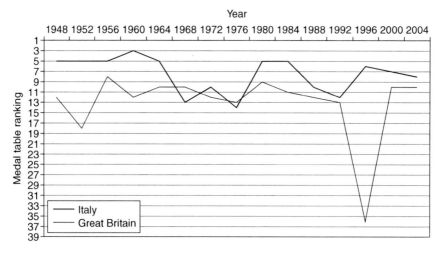

Figure 4.7 Italy versus Great Britain – place in the Olympic medal table 1948–2004.

In the UK, there has been a National Audit Office review of UK Sport's World Class Performance Programme following the Olympic Games of Athens 2004 (Comptroller and Auditor General 2005). Part of this review has led to the compilation of a table of inputs (money invested in given sports), outputs (medals won in Athens 2004) and efficiency (cost per medal won). An adapted version of this data is reported in Table 4.8.

The average 'cost' of medals won by Great Britain in 2004 was £2.4m, a statistic which varied in cost from £0.9m for a bronze medal (Archery) in those sports categorised by UK Sport in the pre-Athens period as its 'Priority 4' sports to £8.2m for a silver medal (Diving) in its 'Priority 3' sports. Assuming that the process for allocating resources towards medal-winning success is rational, Table 4.8 enables informed decisions to be made as to the acceptability of cost or value for money of investments.

Value for money assessments can be made in advance of events by linking the level of investment required to the targeted cost of medals. Thus, although Table 4.8 reveals that the actual cost of medals in Priority 4 sports was £0.9m, the budgeted cost was £0.15m. Therefore, the single medal won in Priority 4 sports cost six times as much as the budgeted cost. This sort of analysis complements the portfolio of effectiveness measures reviewed earlier in this chapter and confirms that medal-based measures are but limited measures of the rounded performance of an elite athlete production system.

An arguably more useful application of the analysis in Table 4.8 is transnational comparison, that is, how much are other nations investing to achieve a given level of success? It follows that if certain nations are using essentially the same elite athlete production system, then, in addition to looking at the effectiveness of a system, we also need to consider efficiency at the same time.

Table 4.8 The efficiency of investments: UK cost per medal, 2004 Olympic Games

Sport Priority	Sport	Investment (£m)	Medals targeted	Medals won	Cost per medal (£m)
1	Athletics, sailing, rowing, cycling	37.2	18	17	**2.188**
2	Swimming, canoeing, judo, equestrian, pentathlon, shooting	21.4	12	9	**2.378**
3	Gymnastics, triathlon, diving	8.2	7	1	**8.200**
4	Taekwondo, archery, weightlifting	0.9	6	1	**0.900**
	Totals	**67.7**	**43**	**28**	**2.418**

Further applications of the analytical framework

The discussion thus far has focused on performance in the Summer Olympic Games which, although a truly global event, is not a measure of success in all sports. Some 28 sports and 35 disciplines are contested at the Olympic Games, and in the UK, over 100 sports are formally recognised by the national agencies of sport (i.e. the Sports Councils). Therefore, the Olympics represent only a subset of all sports, and inevitably for some nations, culturally important sports do not figure in the Olympic programme, for example, cricket and rugby in the case of Great Britain. Furthermore, in some sports, success in the Olympic Games is not recognised as the pinnacle of achievement, notably tennis (Grand Slam tournaments) and football (FIFA World Cup). Therefore, for nations which view themselves as 'sporting' nations, there needs to be another measure to contextualise overall sporting achievement.

In the UK, UK Sport has developed a Sporting Index to derive an overall measure of success in a basket of 60 different sports. In essence, the UK Sport Sporting Index is an adaptation of market share, and the system is used in two ways: first, to compute market share in individual sports, and second, to derive an overall sporting index for 60 sports.

In individual sports, points are awarded to the top eight places where a gold medal is worth ten points, silver eight, bronze six and eighth place one. For every event where there are eight finalists, there are 39 points which, when multiplied by the number of events, gives total points available from which market share calculations can be computed. It is possible to weight different events according to their perceived importance, for example, in athletics, the World Indoor Championships might be weighted one, the World Outdoor Championships two and the Olympic Games three.

Table 4.9 illustrates the application of the UK Sport Sporting Index model to tennis, assessing performance in the 2004 Olympics (weight one), the 2004 Davis/Federation Cups (weight two) and the 2004 Grand Slam events (weight three). The top ten nations are listed in Table 4.9.

Table 4.9 UK Sport Sporting Index applied to tennis

	Country	Market share (%)
1	USA	19.0
2	Russia	17.1
3	Argentina	10.1
4	Switzerland	9.0
5	France	8.6
6	Belgium	5.6
7	Spain	5.3
8	Australia	3.9
9	Great Britain	3.3
10	Croatia	2.4

The same basic approach (i.e. the awarding of points and the weighting of events) is also applied to 60 major sports to derive a World Sporting Index. For the sake of simplicity, the points awarded for first, second and third are only used to produce the World Sporting Index. The scores for top 60 sports are computed to give a market share which in turn can be weighted in one of the two ways: first, on the basis of treating all sports as equal (in effect no weighting); and second, on the basis of public preferences (i.e. sports in which the UK public would like to have success are weighted most heavily, for example, football). At the end of 2004 (i.e. following the Athens Olympics), the top ten nations in the World Sporting Index were as listed in Table 4.10.

All the top seven nations in Table 4.10 finished in the top ten of the final Athens 2004 Olympic medal table. Canada makes the list primarily because of its success in Winter sports, and New Zealand makes the list mainly for its prowess in team sports such as the two codes of rugby, cricket and netball. Between December 2003 and December 2004, the following top ten countries, in ranked order, all increased their market share: Italy, UK, New Zealand, Japan, France, Germany and China. USA, though starting from a high base, saw its market share fall by the greatest amount, followed by Australia, Canada and Russia.

As World Sporting Index results are compiled on the basis of all eligible events within a four-year Olympic cycle, consideration is now being given to reducing the weighting given to the value of points gained by 25 per cent per year so that recent performance is accorded greater significance than more distant performance. This possible development reflects the desire to make the model a more comprehensive measure of performance than simply medals won. The model already makes a distinction between the 'quality' of events. In future, it may also incorporate an element of 'the time-weighted value of success'. The UK Sport Sporting Index can be used for time series analysis so that performance over the period of an Olympiad can be assessed. To illustrate the point, Table 4.11 reports the changes in points won and market share for the six sample nations.

Table 4.10 The top ten nations in the World Index 2004

	Country	Market share (%)
1	USA	11.2
2	Germany	8.1
3	Australia	7.5
4	Russia	7.1
5	Great Britain	6.5
6	France	5.3
7	China	5.1
8	New Zealand	4.0
9	Italy	3.7
10	Canada	3.2

Table 4.11 The sample nations 2000–4

Nation	2000 Points	2000 Market share (%)	2004 Points	2004 Market share (%)	Change in Market share* (%)
Great Britain	431	7.18	387	6.47	−10
Canada	211	3.51	220	3.67	+5
Italy	189	3.14	191	3.19	+1
Norway	167	2.78	163	2.72	−2
Netherlands	123	2.05	95	1.59	−22
Belgium	15	0.25	22	0.37	+46

Note
*Change in Market Share = ((2004 MS − 2000 MS)/(2000 MS)) × 100.

As discussed in the context of Table 4.6, an increase in market share is arguably the most robust and controllable measure of overall performance. If this point is accepted, it can be seen that Belgium, Italy and Canada have improved their performance, whereas the UK, the Netherlands and Norway have all experienced reduced performance. The performance of Belgium (+46 per cent) over the four-year period is largely attributable to the success of tennis players Kim Clijsters and Justine Henin. The decline of the Netherlands (−22 per cent) is largely attributable to a relatively poor Olympic Games performance in 2004 compared with that in 2000 (four versus 12 gold medals) and relative underachievement in the World Swimming Championships of 2001 and 2003. Like Belgium whose success has been driven by two tennis players, the Netherlands appears to have been heavily reliant on the performance of the swimmers Inge de Bruijn and Pieter van den Hoogenband.

In short, the application of market share analysis modified for the importance of a given event, down-weighted by time factors, and up-weighted by public perception, can give a reasonable indication of performance in a single sport or a basket of numerous sports. In the absence of any alternative measures of all-round performance in sport, the UK Sport Sporting Index is a useful barometer of the balance of power within world sport. Inevitably, there will be accusations that the weighting systems used introduce a degree of subjectivity to the process; nevertheless, the criteria employed are both transparent and credible.

Conclusions

If elite sport development systems are viewed as a strategic management process (Figure 4.1), then integral components of the process must be monitoring and control. The importance of monitoring and control can be appreciated by two key points. First, competition for success in elite sport is increasing. More nations are adopting strategic approaches towards the development of elite athletes, and as a result, an increasing number of nations have developed genuine medal-winning capability. Second, the resource implication for elite sport is considerable. In the UK, UK Sport is committed to a total investment of some £270m in the World Class Pathway (incorporating Paralympic and talented young athletes) during the Beijing Olympiad. When such large sums of money are involved, there will be a natural desire – if not a requirement – to measure how actual performance compares with planned performance.

Traditional measures such as medal tables have a function in terms of being easily understood rankings of actual performance. However, as indicated in Table 4.6, it is possible for medal-based measures of performance to give conflicting results concerning a nation's performance. This type of ambiguity does not necessarily help Performance Directors whose future funding and jobs may well be dependent on delivering a specified level success.

Time is identified as an important ingredient in an elite sports development system. Those nations which have been investing in elite sport for the longest tend to be more successful than those nations whose engagement with the process is more recent. For this reason, and the reason that medals won cannot always serve as a measure of distance travelled, it is important that the elite sport programme of given sports is evaluated using more comprehensive measures of success. These might include measures ranging from the number of athletes qualifying to take part in an event to the narrowing of the gap between national records and medal-winning performance.

As more nations adopt essentially the same methods of elite athlete development, a further measure of performance is the efficiency of the production process. As has been shown in the case of Great Britain, it is possible to attach costs to outputs so that calculations such as 'cost per medal' can be computed. Thus, it is possible to assess not only the efficacy of investment decisions but also the efficiency. Although the use of economics and management accounting to evaluate performance in elite sport may be anathema to sports purists, the reality is that increasing competition for medals and increased investment requirements for elite sport programmes will lead to greater scrutiny in the future.

Notwithstanding our argument that the approaches outlined represent an improvement in terms of assessing performance measures and evaluation, this form of comparison still has significant limitations in terms of measurement of policy outputs, inputs and throughputs. The measures outlined do reflect considerable refinement, particularly of the output measures employed providing a more adequate basis for comparison, but further refinements might be anticipated. For example, medals in certain events may be easier to come by since some sports (such as three-day eventing, sailing and rowing) have fewer countries participating and have fewer participants worldwide; one could conceive of further adjustments or weighting of output measures to take account of this. Thus, market share as a measure might be weighted according to some measure of market size or intensity of competition (for example, total number of participants worldwide, or for a given Olympic event, numbers of teams participating in that event rather than in the Games per se).

However, the operationalisation of input measures is perhaps rather more problematic. While one might have inputs such as expenditure readily employ-ing a simple measure (money), accounting procedures vary so widely that trying to compare the level of financial investment across countries is likely to be a very difficult task. In addition, when it comes to measuring other inputs such as the level and quality of coaches available, this may prove simply too hard to handle given an absence of reliable data.

However, the most stubbornly difficult problem to deal with is not in mea-suring input or output but in evaluating throughput as process. We may be able to develop measures of statistical association between certain types of input and of output, but if we cannot explain the mechanisms of turning inputs into outputs, we may not be much further forward in terms of explaining how success is generated. Critics of the input–output model of policy analysis point to the problem of the 'black box' in which inputs are processed to produce outputs. The policy mechanisms are hidden from view within this black box, and thus, the understanding gained is limited. If the evaluation of the model is under-taken in order to inform the adoption of policy, the ratio of operational meas-ures of inputs to those of outputs actually tells us relatively little about why success has or has not been attained. Accounts highlight statistical association but have an explanation deficit. An example of the limitations of this kind of analysis is provided by the debate surrounding the introduction of a national 'Academy of Sport' (subsequently to become Institute(s) of Sport) in the UK. This policy idea was first officially espoused by the Conservative government of John Major in its policy paper *Sport: raising the game* (Department of National Heritage 1995B) and was directly inspired by the successful Australian Institute of Sport, following a visit to Australia by the then Minister of Sport, Ian Sproat. However, the particular model of the Australian Institute delivering elite sport development services which was initially advocated in the UK was a highly centralised model in which centralised provision was imposed on a quasi-federal political structure and on the national federations. By the time this system was being advocated in the late 1990s in Britain, it was under attack in Australia where decentralisation measures have subsequently been introduced. When the 'Academy' proposal was introduced, the UK implemented a decentralised model of elite provision with separate home nation Institutes of Sport and associated regional centres, largely because the sporting world subsequently (and perhaps fortuitously) resisted the centralised model initially proposed (Theodoraki 1999).

The second element of the limitations of this model which the history of the UK Institutes sensitises us to is the failure of the simple policy process model to take account of the broader social, cultural, organisational, political and eco-nomic context. While Australia is a federal state with its own inter-state/territory rivalries, the UK is in essence a more complex system in political, cul-tural and sporting terms. Debates about rationalising the sporting governance system will therefore be almost invariably bound up with discussions of national identity for the Home Nations as well as for Britain.

The difficulties of implementing a UK system illustrate the need therefore not simply to look at inputs, outputs and activities within the policy black box but to consider the wider context (in political, cultural, organisational and economic terms) of the policy system. Whether one is concerned with analysis for policy (generating normative, prescriptive measures of how policy should be developed) or analysis of policy (explaining in analytic or heuristic accounts how and why particular policy approaches have been developed in given situations) taking account of this wider context is absolutely essential.

Chapter 5 of this book, for example, goes on to review political clientelism in sport policy and argues that an understanding of wider context is crucial to an understanding of how such a phenomenon has developed (analysis of policy) as well as of what might be done to counter this (analysis for policy).

While in these concluding comments we have focused to a large extent on the limitations of this Type 1 approach to comparisons of performance, it is worth underlining the contribution which this approach can make. Performance measures are absolutely essential to the political and organisational decision-making process. To be able to benchmark performance of a system against itself (in performance over time) will be just as significant as benchmarking against other systems, since self-benchmarks highlight trends in performance. Refining and enhancing measures of performance are important contributors to any explanation of success. Notwithstanding this, such measures at best indicate trends in success/failure relative to one's competitors, but cannot explain how or why particular interventions have or have not been, or are likely to be successful. To develop this aspect of comparative policy, we are required to open up and examine the internal workings of the policy black box and to consider the relationship of those internal, structurational workings to the specifics of the broader environment.

5   Political clientelism and sports policy systems – case studies of Greece and Taiwan

Ian Henry, Ping-Chao Lee and Pantelis Nassis

Introduction

In this chapter, we focus on the strategic relations at play in two sports policy systems in politically 'turbulent' periods and, in particular, on the phenomenon of clientelism in sporting politics. The first example is that of Greece where our concern is specifically with the funding of national governing bodies of sport (NGBs) during the period 1980–93 in which the political control of central government shifted between the two major political parties in the Greek system. The second example is that of Taiwan also during a period of political change (1995–2002) in which the government had to deal with the development and aftermath of a major corruption scandal concerning gambling and the fixing of matches in the country's major sporting obsession, baseball. The core aim of this chapter is to examine the forms that clientelism takes in these contrasting sporting systems and to identify the conditions under which clientelistic relations come to the fore.

Clientelism as an aspect of strategic relations in the state's role in sport

Clientelism or political patronage involves 'strategies for the acquisition, maintenance and aggrandisement of political power on the part of patrons, and strategies for the protection and promotion of their interests on the part of the clients' (Piattoni 2001). Such strategies are possible in part because of the structural context of politics in given societies and thus can be regarded as a specific form of strategic relations (Henry 1993; Jessop 1990; Lee 2005; Nassis 1994).

Clientelistic relations between political parties and organisational forms in civil society, in certain contexts, perform a strategic function in mediating the state's role. Both the national systems on which we focus this chapter have culturally specific histories and also share particular features. Given the historical context of Greek politics, with deep divisions which were, in living memory, reflected in internecine civil war (in which individuals were sometimes killed simply because of their political affiliation) and with a polity which during the period we investigate (1980–93) had only relatively recently been restored to democracy, it is hardly surprising that clientelistic relations should have remained a significant feature of contemporary politics. Mistrust of the other is as important as commitment to one's own, in such contexts. Thus, replacing reliance on party support, with reliance on the impartiality of those in power, whatever their political persuasion, continued to be problematic. Similarly, the political system in Taiwan has grown out of the context of the imposition of what was essentially a one-party state by the Chinese nationalist forces headed by Chiang Kai-Shek and his political party the Kuomintang (KMT), with opposition in the early stages of the establishment of the nationalists on Taiwan being brutally suppressed (Roy 2003).

Clientelism, or relations of patronage, involves direct and indirect support of 'one's own people' (e.g. family friends, ethnic group). The two principal forms which clientelism takes are those of traditional, dyadic relationships between individuals (Cheng 1988; Lande 1977) and 'modern', political party-directed clientelism, and it is the latter form which concerns us in this chapter. Explanations of political clientelism have tended to fall under two headings. The first is that of 'culturalist' accounts. In such accounts, clientelism is characterised as a feature of Gemeinschaft-type societies, based on Weberian notions of traditional power, where individuals and groups are bound into relations of reciprocity, with social and material benefits being disbursed in exchange for commitment and support. Clientelism is thus seen as a form of politics which is the product of local culture.

> In Europe political clientelism and patronage are commonly considered as phenomena typical of only some countries, normally the Latin and Mediterranean. The ascription of clientelism and patronage to given political areas goes hand in hand with their attribution of cultural traits that supposedly uniquely characterize these countries such as familism, tribalism, clannism, 'Orientalism'. Political clientelism and patronage are thus generally understood as cultural phenomena, the reflection onto the political sphere of a generalised way of conceiving interpersonal relations, particularly those between the powerful and powerless.
>
> (Piattoni 2001: p. 2)

In parallel to the European phenomenon, in the Asian context, the traditional concept of 'guanxi', reciprocal relationships based on notions of trust, face and hierarchy (Gold *et al.* 2002), has characterised business and political relationships, particularly in situations such as that of Taiwan's (until recently) authoritarian system where mistrust of strangers and reliance on personal relationships and networks were fostered by political exclusion of ethnic Taiwanese (Solinger 2006).

The second type of explanation of clientelism is 'developmentalist' in that it is explained as a function of the distorted or incomplete development of particular political systems. Those who have articulated a modernisation thesis, whether of Marxist or liberal orientation, have implied that clientelism and similar kinship, friendship or community-based relations represent a transitory stage in the development of class-based or interest-based politics (Roniger and Gunes-Ayata 1994). Such explanations have assumed that patronage based on familial patterns would be replaced by rational allocation of resources on the basis of universal (rather than personal) rights and that these rights would be administered through the organisational form of state bureaucracy and the political form of the liberal, democratic, welfare state (Kurer 1993; Papatheodorou and Machin 2003; Sotiropoulos 1994, 2004). In modernising societies, parties are taken to provide a form of social anchoring previously provided by the traditional community:

> political parties serve two-fold functions. They become the means through which bargaining over resource allocation can occur, according to both clientelistic intercessions and universalistic principles. Moreover they serve as the basis for the establishing of a new kind of identity, a sense of belonging to a community, as a potential means of access to power centers.
>
> (Gunes-Ayata 1994: p. 22)

However, the survival of clientelistic relations embedded in newly emerging forms of social relations reflects both the persistence of the phenomenon and the limitations of teleological modernisation perspectives (Gunes-Ayata 1994; Mingione 1994; Petmesidou 1996; Roniger 2004).

In this chapter, we are reviewing political party-directed clientelism, in Greece during the 1980s and early 1990s, and in Taiwan across the late 1990s and into the twenty-first century, in a policy arena (that of sports policy) which tends to be undeveloped in pre-modern social contexts. Southern European democracies, South East Asian republics as well as African and South American states and, more recently, the republics of the former Soviet Union have been seen as ripe for the development of political clientelism (Davaki and Mossialos 2005; Featherstone 2005; Hallin and Papathanassopoulos 2002; Ho 2003; Nazareno *et al.* 2006; Shefner 2001; Sotiropoulos 2004; Zimmer 2005). This is not to say that such 'selective material incentives in networks of direct exchange' (Kitschelt 2000) do not feature in the mature polities of Western Europe and North America (Piattoni 2001). Clientelism has proved to be more prevalent than earlier accounts of the phenomenon assumed (Roniger 2004). Nevertheless, the particular forms which clientelism takes will vary from one social and political culture to another, and it is therefore to the description of the political contexts of Greece and Taiwan that we now turn.

The Greek political context

The immediate post-war history of Greek politics was particularly turbulent. The Civil War of 1946–9 provided a victory for right-wing forces but left deep scars and lasting bitter divisions in Greek society. It was only after the fall of the military Junta (1967–74), with the restoration of democratic freedoms, that parties of the left were truly able to participate in political life and that a moderate party of the right was also able to emerge. This was reflected in the participation of the Communist Party in 1974 elections (for the first time since 1936), the formation of the Pan-Hellenic Socialist Movement (PASOK) and the revitalisation of the right in the form of the New Democracy Party under Konstantinos Karamanlis (Clogg 1987; Diamandouros 1983). Under Karamanlis, the New Democracy governments of 1974–81 sought to expand public expenditure, significantly increasing public sector employment, though not expenditure on social services. The expansion of the Greek economy and of the public sector was based on three principal sources of revenue, tourism, shipping and remittances from Greeks working overseas (Vergopoulos 1986). However, the global economic crisis of the early 1970s had intensified, and by the end of the decade, it had had severe consequences for the Greek economy. The gradual decline in overseas remittances, and in the shipping and tourism industries combined with a decline in domestic industrial investment, brought about by rising labour costs, undermined the alliance between the New Democracy government and the middle classes (Kurth 1993). PASOK came to power in 1981, on a platform designed to appeal to a wide constituency, promising financial solvency and progressive social legislation, while abandoning its previous opposition to membership of NATO and Greece's joining the European Community. This policy admixture successfully attracted broad electoral support, and PASOK gained 48 per cent of the vote.

Thus, the beginning of the 1980s marked two significant developments in Greece's post-war politics. In the early part of the decade, the country experienced the first socialist government of its modern history while its position in the global polity was also significantly altered, with its entry into the European Community. PASOK attempted in its first term in office (1981–5) to realise its 'catch all' pre-election programme, and to meet the aspirations of its supporters, drawn mainly from the lower and middle classes (Lyrintzis 1989; Petras *et al.* 1993). The incremental reduction of social inequalities was to be achieved by increasing the role of the state in the economy and introducing a form of welfare state provision (Karambelias 1989; Manesis 1986; Tzanatos 1986). In a period when the Greek and world economy were in recession, extensive government spending for the finance of PASOK's policies was sustained through foreign borrowing and the inflow of European Community funds (Kazakos 1990). However, this policy could not be sustained for an extended period, and thus, PASOK's economic policy in its second term in government (1985–9) was characterised by the introduction of a 'stabilisation programme' in the form of a series of tight economic measures (Petras *et al.* 1993).

However, the austerity programme undermined the government's electoral support, and in conjunction with the deepening crisis of the economy and the economic scandals of the party's leadership, the socialist party's position deteriorated, and voter support slumped in the 1989 election (Kazakos 1990). After three consecutive elections in ten months, with coalitions involving New Democracy and Communist Party partners, the right-wing party, New

Democracy, regained office in its own right in 1990. Its programme was inspired by a New Right doctrine which called for a minimal role for the state in social life and in the economy with an increasingly significant role in economic development to be played by market forces. In terms of policy, the reduction of government spending, the shrinking of the public sector and the denationalisation of a number of public companies were among the most significant initiatives which characterised the New Democracy approach in the early 1990s. The period of policy review which this research covers is that from the beginning of PASOK rule in 1981 to its return to power in 1993 and, specifically, focuses on what this period of rapid political change brought about for sports policy.

In order to contextualise this study, it is necessary to provide the reader with a brief introduction to the way sport is organised in Greece. The smallest unit of organised sport in Greece is the sports club, which, for its foundation and administration, depends on private initiatives (either voluntary or commercial). By the end of the 1980s, approximately 5,000 sports clubs were officially recognised, with approximately 500,000 athletes as members (Brademas 1988). Those clubs are represented by national sports federations and the NGBs, which have responsibility for specific sports and organisations. Above these bodies in the governmental sector stands the Ministry of Culture, which directs central government funds and implements the government's policies for sport through an appointed Junior Minister of Sport and a governmental agency, the General Secretariat for Sport (GSS) (Figure 5.1).

The majority of sports clubs in Greece are multi-sports organisations (though single-sport organisations also exist), and they receive money from government via the NGBs for each of the sports they serve. The GSS provides funding to a

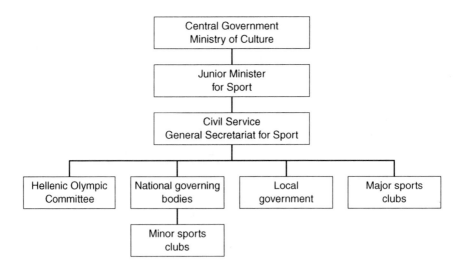

Figure 5.1 Sports funding structure in Greece.

small number of major sports clubs which provide high-performance coaching for elite competitors, in particular sports. For the most part, coaching is provided within the club structures and funded by the NGBs and clubs. Assemblies of clubs affiliated to the NGBs elect representatives to the board of each national governing body.

The GSS is funded both through the state ordinary budget, but also from revenues from football pools and lottery games, and, in some cases, through the programme of public investments. The NGBs depend very heavily, or virtually entirely, on state funds and are grant aided through four types of subsidies: (a) ordinary subsidy, allocated directly from GSS funds from the state budget; (b) additional subsidy for contingencies; (c) subsidy for specific projects (e.g. athletic equipment, participation in international events) and (d) subsidy to cover the cost of the organisation of international events in Greece. The last three types of subsidy are funded from GSS revenues from football pools and lotteries. Along with sports clubs and the NGBs, local authorities have emerged (since the mid-1980s) as a major provider of sporting opportunities at local level.

Although the Greek state had traditionally not exerted an overtly direct influence in sport, policy and funding of sport became an area of increasing government interest in the 1980s. As Figure 5.2 illustrates, direct state spending for sport (funds from the state budget and public investments programme) increased gradually from the restoration of democratic government up to the mid-1980s. In particular, the first term of office for PASOK (1981–5) was the period when government expenditure on sport peaked in percentage terms, an increase which reflected budgetary growth for sport in real terms. From this point, government spending for sport reduced both in relative and in real terms.

The emphasis in state funding up to the mid-1980s was on the development of physical infrastructure for sport but from the mid-1980s to the end of our

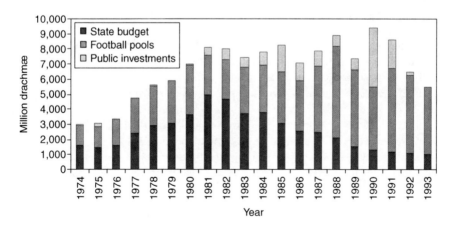

Figure 5.2 The General Secretariat of Sport (GSS) funds from the state budget, football pools and public investments 1974–93 in real terms (1981 prices).

period of investigation in 1993, this gave way to an emphasis on grant aid to NGBs, sports clubs and associations. In addition, the PASOK government sought to foster 'Sport for All' initiatives with local government providing grant aid for the employment of sporting animateurs. The direction of sports policy by the 1990s had, however, taken a different turn. The abandonment of the social objectives of the 'Sport for All' programmes, the reduction of government funds allocated to sport, the shift of resources to the promotion of elite sport and the introduction of commercialisation in some of the most popular sports were directions of change in sports policy, introduced by the New Democracy government when it returned to office in 1990–3.

The political context in Taiwan

The political context of Taiwan shares some features with that of Greece, in particular the forging of the political system post-Second World War, following a period of civil war. Following the arrival of Chiang Kai Shek in Taiwan, the Nationalist leader ousted from the mainland by the Communists in 1947, local opposition was suppressed with brutal force (Lia et al. 1991) and a single party government was established under the nationalist KMT party. Single party, authoritarian rule on the part of the KMT, was constructed on a quadripartite foundation – an elaborate and centralised party apparatus, a system of extra-constitutional legal arrangements and emergency decrees, a controlled electoral pluralism implemented at the local level and structural symbiosis between the party and the state in the post-1949 period (Chu and Lin 2001). In addition, the monopolistic government also enforced martial law in order to maintain social order and security and to promote stability. The imposition of martial law greatly expanded the scope and power of the Taiwan garrison command and suspended the protection of civil rights guaranteed in the 1947 Constitution (Fu 1987). During this period, despite the KMT government implementing tight political control from 1950 to 1954, the government introduced popular elections, such as those for the Provincial Assembly, in order to incorporate a diversified local elite into the process of party building and provide the authoritarian system with a modicum of democratic legitimation.

Enjoying a monopoly of economic and political privilege permitted the KMT regime to construct alliances with local factions by sharing political power and material benefits with them in exchange for their long-term allegiance (Brown et al. 1998; Hood 1996a; Kau 1996; Kuo 2000; Wang 1994; Wu 2001a, 2003). Factions arose to mediate between the 'mainlander' KMT state and local Taiwanese society, earning power and prestige by their ability to help individuals unable to appeal directly to the KMT-controlled government and courts (Bosco 1992). These approaches were generally successful, and the system of shared economic and political interests between the KMT and local factions provided the foundation for political stability and increased legitimacy for the regime. However, such kinds of patron–client relationship provided a space for criminal links to the political domain to develop, and this became widely evident with implications as we shall see for the governance of professional sport (Bosco 1992; Cai 1998; Hood 1996b; Kuo 2000; Liu 2001b). Indeed, looking at the dark side of Taiwan's history and culture, organised crime had been an accepted agent of power when the KMT had been in power in China. The KMT on the mainland had not only tolerated but often courted crime syndicates, and their ties with organised crime continued to develop in Taiwan (Brown *et al.* 1998; Reaves 2002). This phenomenon threatened to undermine Taiwan's political and economic system. With the creation of a corrupt political environment came a reduction of public confidence in judicial independence and an under-mining of the area for fair and competitive economic activity (Liu 2001a).

In the early 1980s, the détente between both sides of the Taiwan Straits began to mitigate the siege mentality among Taiwan's citizens and weakened the rationale for retaining martial law. The KMT government was aware of the need to reflect the context by enhancing its own democratic legitimacy in Taiwan through a gradual opening up of the electoral process. Limited open elections to national representative bodies were first instituted in 1972 and were expanded in 1980 and again in 1989 (Chu 1992). The lifting of martial law in 1987 with, for example, the granting of freedom of association, and the forma-tion of party competition, created opportunities for ordinary citizens to particip-ate in new modes of social organisation. With the upgrading of education among the population and increasing channels of communication, a plethora of associations and social movements began to develop in the 1980s. Over the period, the Vice President Lee Teng-Hui, of Taiwanese (rather than mainland Chinese) origin, succeeded to two significant positions (the Chairmanship of the KMT and the Presidency of Taiwan) following on from President Chiang Ching-Kuo (son of Chiang Kai-Shek) who died on 13 January 1988. Subse-quently, after surviving a competitive internal political power struggle within the KMT, in May 1991, President Lee regained the Taiwanese Presidency and secured full control of the operation of the KMT. In 1988, the main opposition party, the Democratic Progressive Party (DPP), was set up and subsequently achieved important political victories, most notably the 2000 Presidential elec-tion in Taiwan.

Although the DPP gained victory in the election with 39.3 per cent of the vote, the proportion of the vote was not enough to dominate national policy in Taiwan and the outcome thus limited the policy mandate of the winner (Liu 2003). After 20 months, the DPP defeated the other parties including KMT at the 2001 general election, gaining the biggest parliamentary majority of seats, which squeezed the position of KMT to a mere 68 seats from their previously held 123, representing a completely new political situation for Taiwan, and the end of the election also signalled the start of cross-party cooperation (Lin 2001). Lien, the Chairman of the KMT, reflecting on his party's failure, com-mitted the KMT to negotiate with other parties in the Legislature to reach con-sensus for the purposes of national development and national stabilisation (Yang 2001). These political changes were taken to imply that the liberal rights of citizens had been largely achieved, and political transformation such as free elections, and the establishment of various political parties, provided visible indicators to illustrate that Taiwan had acceded to a more democratic political situation (Chu and Lin 2001).

In 2004, President Chen Shui-Bian was re-elected, though by a small margin with 50.12 per cent of the votes against 49.88 per cent, in a controversial election. Though the DPP had had to fight hard to win, the party's absolute majority was widely seen as symbolising the formation of a majority consensus in favour of a 'Taiwanese national identity', since this was a core element of the DPP programme. Thus, even though the formal name employed by the government of Taiwan officially remains the 'Republic of China' (mainland China has the title of the People's Republic of China), the roots of legitimacy of the government have shifted from the 'virtual' identity of part of a 'Greater China' promoted during the KMT authoritarian era to the identity of Taiwan as an entirely independent, sovereign state though this brought heightened tensions with the People's Republic (*Taiwan News* 2004).

Thus, what we see in these two political systems is a strong series of parallels. Both are the product of deep-rooted and long-standing civil strife. Both have experienced totalitarian rule, and both are characterised by historically deep ideological divisions, between the left (PASOK and the Communist Party) and the right (New Democracy) in the case of Greece and between Chinese nationalists (KMT) who see Taiwan as part of greater China and Taiwan nationalists (DPP) who wish to regard Taiwan as independent. Both systems also have been dependent on their relations with external parties – the USA in the case of Taiwan and the European Union in the case of Greece. These strong cleavages, external dependencies and relatively young systems of democratic pluralism provide parallel contexts for the embedding of sports policy.

Exploring clientelistic relations: methodological considerations in the two case studies

Clearly, investigating clientelistic relations in operation presents potential difficulties, since client–patron relationships may imply activity which involves political patrons failing to invoke legal requirements or being more actively involved in illegal activity. Petmesidou (1996), for example, refers to phenomena such as illegal house building on a massive scale, informal economic activities, and large-scale tax evasion, or abuse of the system of invalidity benefits being tolerated by the state. In the case of Taiwan, patron–client links in illegal activities are also well documented (Bosco 1992). Thus, standard interviewing approaches, for example, may be much less likely to elicit frank and open responses.

In addressing the nature and operation of clientelistic networks in sports policy, in Greece, our focus was on NGBs. Initially, it was decided that a number of NGBs (12 in total) would be selected and that representatives (in key positions) in each of the 12 NGBs would be asked to cite the political affiliation of the remaining 11 NGBs. Representatives of the 12 NGBs would then be interviewed, focusing on the process of interaction with government departments, the outcomes of such interactions, perceptions of the significance of party political influence and the impact of changes of government across the period. The 12 NGBs were selected in part on the basis of whether they had a 'known' political affiliation (i.e. some NGBs were 'known' to the authors before the investigation as either PASOK or New Democracy affiliated and some were also selected because their affiliation was unknown or known to be regarded as 'neutral') and in part on the basis of responsiveness of officials to requests for interview. Eleven of the NGBs approached agreed to allow officers to be interviewed.

In fact, despite our perceived need for the type of 'reputational grid' approach outlined earlier, there was little difficulty in terms of frankness about political affiliation in the Greek context. Interviewed officials of the NGBs, without exception, declared the affiliation of their association (in terms of the party membership of their leading members) to be that which their colleagues in other NGBs had identified for us. Indeed, as the interviews progressed, what was remarkable was the openness with which NGB officials discussed not only their political affiliation but the implications of this for their relations with governments of different political persuasions in the period under review.

The analysis of the Greek case that follows provides an account of the explanations given by key figures in sport in central government, the GSS and NGBs' administrators, of the reasons for the existence of clientelistic relations in Greek sport and the ways these kinds of relations are sustained. Tables 5.1 and 5.2 indicate the nature and number of interviews conducted. Of the

Table 5.1 Political affiliation of Greek NGBs and interviewees

National Governing Body	Position of interviewee	Political affiliation of NGB
Hellenic Federation of Athletics and Gymnastics Clubs	Chairman	PASOK
Hellenic Volleyball Federation	Chairman	PASOK
Hellenic Federation of Wrestling	Chairman	PASOK
Hellenic Weight Lifting Federation	General Secretary and Technical Director	PASOK
Hellenic Fencing Federation	General Secretary	PASOK
Hellenic Boxing Federation	General Secretary	New Democracy
Hellenic Sailing Federation	Chairman	Neutral/no political majority on the Board
Hellenic Cycling Federation	Chairman	Neutral/no political majority on the Board
Hellenic Federation of Judo	Chairman	Neutral/no political majority on the Board
Hellenic Karate Federation	Chairman	Neutral/no political majority on the Board
Hellenic Tai Kwan Do Federation	Chairman	Neutral/no political majority on the Board

Table 5.2 Government ministers, party officials and party appointed bureaucrats interviewed

New Democracy	PASOK
Junior Minister of Sport: December 1992– October 1993	Junior Minister of Sport 1985–8
Junior Minister of Sport: August 1991– December 1992	General Secretary of Sport: 1981–5
General Secretary of Sport: September 1989–February 1991	Head of Department of Competitive Sport in the General Secretariat of Sport: 1985–8
Head of Department of Competitive Sport in the General Secretariat of Sport: 1989–93	Chairman of 'Sport for All' Committee: 1983–9 and 1993

Note
The following were unavailable or declined to take part: Junior Minister of Sport: 1989–1991 (New
Democracy; unavailable); Junior Minister of Sport: 1981–5 (PASOK; unavailable); General Secret-
ary of Sport: 1991–3 (New Democracy: unavailable); General Secretary of Sport: 1985–88
(PASOK; unavailable); Junior Minister of Sport: 1988–89 (PASOK; unavailable); General Secret-
ary of Sport: 1988–9 (PASOK; deceased).

12 interviews with key members of 11 NGBs, five were with representatives of
NGBs associated with PASOK, one with an NGB associated with New Democracy and five with representatives from neutral NGBs. All ministers of sport
and former heads of the GSS who held office in the period 1981–93 were
approached with a request for interview. Table 5.2 lists the responses to this
request. Of the politicians and political appointees interviewed from central
government, four were interviewed from New Democracy (two former ministers
of sport and two senior political appointees to the GSS) and four from PASOK,
including one former minister of sport and three senior political appointees to
the GSS. In terms of political balance, it was regarded as desirable to have a bal-
anced sample of NGBs; however, the majority of PASOK NGBs evident in the
sample was the product of refusal by one New Democracy-associated NGB to
participate, and the discovery that the NGBs of unknown affiliation in the
sample chosen were associated with either PASOK or neutral.

   In the case of Taiwan, the aspects of sports policy upon which the study
focused were threefold: first, that of the government's treatment of an illegal
betting scandal which emerged in 1997; second, the staging of the 2001 Baseball World Cup in Taiwan; and third, the merging in 2003 for Taiwan's two
professional baseball leagues. Less emphasis could be placed on interviews with
politicians and government administrators in the Taiwan study since the political sensitivity, and legal implications of the issue and the cultural reticence of
Taiwanese political culture rendered it difficult to gain access and/or frankness
in a number of instances. Nevertheless, in the Taiwan case study, 16 interviews
(ranging from 40 minutes to just over two hours in duration) were conducted
between March and July 2003 by one of the authors and subsequently transcribed and partially translated. Published, or publicly available, documents and

records were employed to assist in the appraisal of the wider context that the case inhabited. In this study, 158 government reports/proceedings of parliamentary debates, which derived mainly from administrative records held by the Executive Yuan (the Cabinet), the Legislative Yuan (Parliament), the National Council on Physical Fitness and Sport (NCPFS) and the Ministry of Education, were reviewed. Such documents provided useful data shedding light on issues such as the impact of political, economic and cultural transformations external to Taiwan on the development of professional baseball within Taiwan. Finally, media and press commentary and academic analysis were also reviewed, and particular items were selected from national newspapers reflecting a range of political perspectives and academic journal articles commenting on studies of baseball in Taiwan.

Table 5.3 provides a summary of the strategic actors identified and the approaches adopted to obtaining data relating to their own commentaries and that of other observers/commentators on their perspective.

In Greece, fieldwork took place in the early 1990s. Interviews were conducted by one of the authors, tape recorded, translated and transcribed. Interviews lasted between 30 minutes and two hours and were conducted across the period October 1992 to May 1994. Other information sources employed were GSS expenditure records for the NGBs for the period 1988–93 (complete records were available for the period for five of the 11 NGBs). In addition, party policy documents relating to sport were consulted, and records of Parliamentary debates relating to sport were evaluated across the period 1981–93.

In both case studies, interview transcripts were subjected to thematic analysis broadly in line with Altheide's (1996) approach of Ethnographic Content Analysis placing particular emphasis on understanding accounts from the perspective of the interviewees/stakeholders themselves.

Clientelistic relations between the NGBs and the PASOK and New Democracy governments

Exploration of the nature and functioning of clientelistic relations in the Greek system focused on four principal themes: the nature of the relations between the NGBs favoured by particular parties and the party itself; the conditions under which clientelism survived and flourished in sport; the process of exercising clientelistic relations; and the financial outcomes of the exercising of clientelistic relations, in particular, over the period 1988–93 when government control shifted from PASOK to New Democracy and back again. These are discussed in the following sections.

The nature of the relations between the sport, the NGBs and the political parties

Perhaps the first point to make in relation to the 'favouring' of certain sports governing bodies by the two major political parties is that the promotion of the

Table 5.3 The summary of commentaries of stakeholders and other observers/
commentators

Strategic actors/ Stakeholders	Interviews	Government reports/ proceedings of parliamentary debates	Media/press commentary
Politicians	2 (KMT, DPP)	42	15
The Executive Yuan	0	4	3
Ministry of Education	2	4	2
Ministry of Interior	0	2	3
Ministry of Justice	0	4	3
Managers	1	3	9
Coaches	1	5	10
Players	2	23	21
Fans	1	3	8
Media	1	6	16
Chinese Professional Baseball League	0	15	17
Chinese Taiwan Baseball Association	1	2	5
Sporting Universities	3	0	3
National Council for Physical Fitness & Sports	2	14	11
Criminal Groups*	0	31	21
Total	16	158	147

Note
* It should be noted that among the key stakeholders identified here are the criminal gangs themselves. Although it was clearly not possible to include members of such groups in interviews it
was deemed important to include consideration of their position and their interaction with
other stakeholders in the analysis. Such groups are often omitted from consideration in studies
of this kind, but despite lack of interview data such an omission would render the analysis less
complete.

NGBs' interests was not on the basis of political ideology (e.g. socialist parties
were not promoting 'socialist' sports or commercial sector-oriented parties supporting commercial activity in sport) or was support given on the basis of the
participation profile of the sports concerned (e.g. where working class sports
might be supported by socialist parties which anticipate the electoral support of
participants), rather the determining variable was the political affiliation of the
members of the boards of the particular NGB. Where key members of the board
identified themselves as affiliated to a particular party, the NGB was identified
as a potential beneficiary. The comments of the Chairman of the NGB for Athletics and Gymnastics are typical: 'every governing body is subsidised according
to its board, [that is] whether it [the board] is affiliated politically with the
government or not. ... The federation's programme and success are of minor
importance'.

The conditions under which grant aid to NGBs was awarded: reasons for the survival of clientelistic relations

The conditions under which political clientelism is expected to flourish are defined in the literature as: first, the existence of a strong state (in particular, one which controls a considerable proportion of the economy); second, a lack of consensus concerning the operationalisation of objective measures of social justice (such a consensus might be said to be inscribed within a welfare state system with 'objective' measures of need calculated by welfare bureaucracies); and third, a lack of public confidence in the objectivity of measures and processes employed in resource allocation, such that the legitimacy of political intervention on more partial grounds is accepted as legitimate and/or inevitable. These conditions are deemed to hold true for the Greek governmental context as a whole (Sotiropoulos 1994) but also might be said to apply more specifically in relation to the political economy of sport in Greece.

The first of these three conditions, the strength of the Greek state, is certainly apparent in sport. It is clear that NGBs (and local governments) are very heavily dependent (and in some cases virtually wholly dependent) on state funding. As a New Democracy General Secretary of the GSS (1989–91) argued:

> the governing bodies receive a subsidy allocated by the state. They have no other potential to bid for grant-in-aid. Neither can they exercise pressure on, nor threaten the GSS, because they are non-profit administrative federations of the sports clubs, rather than union groups. Apart from that, they do not have their own sources.

The strength of the party in power in central government is reinforced therefore by the perceived resource dependency of the client groups.

The second condition which under which clientelism is likely to flourish is also met in the case of Greek sport, the lack of objective criteria for resource allocation. This was clearly identified by one of the New Democracy Ministers for Sport: 'the lack of any criteria for the assessment of sports governing bodies, which leave room for political or any other sympathies to mediate this process' (New Democracy Minister for Sport, 1991–2). There was some recognition that objective criteria should be used in deciding the relative size of subsidies allocated to each NGB (e.g. number of athletes and sports clubs, the NGB's success in the international field, its administration expenses and the cost of running leagues), but these were deemed, at best, only to form part of the evaluation process by the GSS. In addition, decisions were taken by the *political* leadership within the GSS (i.e. individuals appointed by the party in power) and within the Ministry, concerning the development and support of certain sports, and these decisions, taken on political grounds, were considered to be at least as important as any objective criteria of the financial needs of the NGB. Thus, the process of decision-making in respect of grant aid to particular NGBs was permeated by a number of inputs, which might range from the sport's potential for success and its appeal to the public to personal and political factors. This view was reflected by the majority of interviewees at NGB level. There were also interviewees who adopted more extreme views:

> there are no [objective] criteria. What is missing is an evaluation by the GSS of all governing bodies. ... I have the impression that the political position of the members of the bodies' board is a very strong factor for the allocation of the bodies' subsidies.
>
> (Chairman of the Volleyball NGB)

Only in one exceptional case was the allocation of subsidies to NGBs described as being independent of any factors relating to the government's political persuasion (by the Chairman of Judo).

The third condition germane to the survival of clientelistic approaches, that is, the perceived legitimacy (or at least the tacit acceptance) of the intervention of political parties in the sports funding decision-making process, is also met in the Greek case. The fact that respondents were willing to talk openly about the party political nature of the process perhaps illustrates this point best. Clientelism was not seen by participants as a set of politically corrupt practices, though there was a recognition in some political and sporting circles that it was undesirable, and both political parties had argued that change should be sought in this respect. Two statements in public forums reflect this view. In the PASOK National Congress for Sport, the Chairman of the Wrestling NGB argued that NGBs 'had to realise that by confusing the political party with the wider field of sport we have made a great mistake' (Chamakos 1994: p. 2) while in Parliament also PASOK and New Democracy had been critical of clientelistic relations in sport: 'we have to eliminate the governing bodies' dependence on the state, which is used by governments as a means to secure their political support' (former PASOK Minister of Culture, Parliamentary Records 4 July 1991: p. 478).

The process of exercising clientelistic relations in funding negotiations

The key to the process of establishing annual funding levels for the NGBs was the annual negotiation which took place between each NGB and the GSS. Bargaining took the form of making a bid for funding the organisation's activities. The amount granted was in effect that which was accounted for as 'ordinary subsidy'. As we have noted, additional subsides were, however, made available under three other headings: 'international events', 'extra subsidy for contingencies' and 'subsidy for specific projects'. These additional subsidies were funded in the main from football pools and lottery revenues.

In order for the clientelistic relations between the government and a number of sports bodies to be sustained, key figures of the bodies' boards were granted access to the decision-making process at central (GSS) level, which could secure the means for the resourcing of the individuals' and the bodies' objectives:

> I was GSS consultant for heavy sports. There was a certain contact with the GSS and its departments. ... We were provided with athletic equipment, a number of indoor halls were constructed, a number of facilities belonging to sports clubs were maintained, all the training centres for the national team were enriched with sports equipment, and in general there was a close contact [with the GSS]. This contact was completely cut off after 1990.
>
> (Chairman, Wrestling NGB)

The importance of direct access, for sports development and capital expenditure, is underlined in the following comments by interviewees: 'the need to develop certain sports dictated the decision for the construction of new facilities, which was a point of discussion with those bodies considered as of high priority...' (PASOK appointee, Head of GSS Competitive Sports Department, 1985–8). The same kind of relation was evidenced between the governing body of weightlifting (also affiliated with PASOK) and the GSS:

> before 1990 there was a very close co-operation with the GSS. There was an exchange of opinions even with the General Secretary and the Minister on the development of weight lifting. ... After 1990 there was no co-operation at all. ... When the new government took over [PASOK in 1993], we asked for an appointment with the Minister and we were accepted the next day.
>
> (General Secretary, Weightlifting NGB)

Clientelistic relations might secure direct access to GSS resources, though the manner in which additional resources were channelled may be not through the mainstream budget ('ordinary subsidy') but rather through ancillary budgets funded through football pools and lottery money:

> extra subsidies granted to some governing bodies through vague procedures ... extra subsidies were granted in several ways, either through the executive committee for the organisation of major events, where the subsidies exceed the needs of the events, or under the label 'provision of sports equipment', granted to the same NGBs every year.
>
> (Chairman, Wrestling NGB)

This approach (of using additional funds rather than mainstream budgets) was common to governments of both political persuasions: 'extra subsidies, financed from football pools revenues, are directed to the governing bodies and are not included in the ordinary GSS budget ...' (New Democracy appointee, General

Secretary of GSS, 1989–91) and 'increasing football pools revenues gave us the potential to allocate extra money in agreement with governing bodies, sports clubs and local government …' (PASOK Minister for Sport, 1985–8).

Reviewing financial outcomes for five NGBs: the impact of the change of government in 1989–90

Thus, increasing GSS sources from football pools in the late 1980s seemed to be absorbed by certain of the governing bodies in the form of ordinary or extra subsidies. Clientelistic relations were thus most evident in the bargaining for these additional resources. 'Normal' bargaining processes, as described earlier, involved the NGB in making bids to the GSS which would be reduced or only partially met by the grant from the GSS. However, as far as the NGBs of wrestling, weightlifting and volleyball (all three affiliated with PASOK) were concerned, 'bargaining' with the GSS (while PASOK was in power) resulted in major benefits for the respective bodies;

> in 1989 we received 310 million drachmae … which was the amount we had asked for. And suddenly in 1990 the GSS and the political leadership, … reduced this amount to 120 million prompted by the government's vengeful policy.
>
> (General Secretary, Weightlifting NGB)

> in 1989 we had announced a five year development programme that was approved by the political leadership and as a result the state subsidy to our body reached a very high level. Following that year we suffered a major disaster.
>
> (Chairman, Volleyball NGB)

Indeed, for one NGB, it was not always even a case of bargaining for additional resources: 'we received whatever we claimed from 1985, the year we took over the body, to 1989 (the year of government change). On two occasions the government granted an amount which was higher than we had asked for' (Chairman, Wrestling NGB). Those arguments can be contrasted with the case of non-PASOK-affiliated NGBs (both those affiliated to New Democracy and those which were neutral): 'if you did not belong to PASOK, then you had a problem even if you did not belong to New Democracy either. You needed the PASOK label in order to have access' (General Secretary, Boxing NGB). The change of government in 1990 resulted in changes in the relations between the mentioned actors and groups and the governmental agency for sport. This change did not end clientelistic relationships but simply replaced the actors at both ends of the chain. A number of organisations emerged as the main beneficiaries of this change, and GSS financial support shifted to some of those bodies which, under PASOK, had been excluded from access to state resources: 'there was political intervention by the New Democracy government as well, but those who belonged to the New Democracy Party complained that they had not the opportunity to recover from the injustice suffered during PASOK' (General Secretary, Boxing NGB). Exclusion from the process of decision-making at central government level, and the associated shifting of resources, severely affected those bodies affiliated with the opposition (such as the NGBs of athletics, volleyball, wrestling and weightlifting):

> New Democracy government adopted an avenging policy which reached its peak with the policy of subsidies to those bodies regarded as belonging to PASOK. ... In that way the GSS started reducing financial resources to the bodies of athletics, weight lifting, and wrestling.
>
> (General Secretary, Weightlifting NGB)

> the previous government (ND) followed a selective policy in terms of subsidies, by making the distinction between 'ours' and 'theirs'. As a consequence, big bodies with major success, such as the bodies of basketball, athletics and gymnastics, volleyball, weight lifting, and wrestling suffered a financial disaster.
>
> (Chairman, Volleyball NGB)

> government change adversely affected our body. ... In 1989 our budget was 580 million drachmae and in 1993 it was only 425 million. Certainly this reduction had to do with the governmental change. Our board was not a favourite of the political leadership.
>
> (Chairman, Wrestling NGB)

Reduction of subsidies was not deemed to be merely the result of the government's hostility towards those bodies, since there was a general reduction, after 1989, of the total amount granted to governing bodies in real terms. However, interviewees regarded the cuts they faced as being disproportionately targeted to the PASOK-dominated NGBs. According to the Technical Director of Weightlifting NGB, 'there might be a direct relationship with the revenues of football pools and lottery games. [However] in addition, the reduction of our subsidy came as the result of the negative change in our relationship with the GSS in 1990', and according to the Chairman of Volleyball NGB, 'certainly there was a reduction of GSS resources, due to the reduction of football pools revenues, but our governing body along with four more bodies (affiliated with the opposition) suffered a major reduction'. During the period over which the interviews took place, PASOK regained power (in 1993), this change was seen by some as an opportunity to recover from the financial restrictions placed on their budget by the previous government:

> the GSS will show respect to our programme without a tendency of intervention.
>
> (General Secretary, Weightlifting NGB)

we now have a positive change in the sense that there is state interest towards the body of weight lifting.

> (Technical Director, Weightlifting NGB)

this year we are claiming 981 million dr. in order to recover from what we have suffered in the last four years.

> (Chairman, Wrestling NGB)

the new government has promised to support our programme, through which we will reverse the whole negative climate

> (Chairman, Athletics and Gymnastics NGB)

we expect the new leadership to pay close attention to our sport in order to recover from what we suffered in the last three years

> (Chairman, Volleyball NGB)

The given accounts draw on respondents' perceptions and descriptions of the grant-aiding processes and outcomes. Figure 5.3, however, draws on the data held by the GSS for grant aid for four of the PASOK-controlled NGBs and for the single New Democracy-controlled NGB (Boxing) in our sample for the period 1988–93. In relation to the four PASOK-affiliated NGBs, grant aid peaks in 1988 in one case (Olympic year for the Athletics and Gymnastics NGB) and for the remaining three in 1989 (the year PASOK was to lose power), and parity is never recovered. However, the evidence of the impact of political favour is not necessarily unequivocal. Each of these NGBs received various

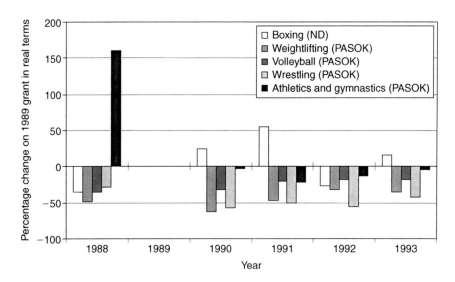

Figure 5.3 GSS grants to NGBs – percentage change on 1989 grant in real terms.

additional elements of funding in the post-1989 period, and for three of the four, annual grant aid 1990–3 generally exceeds that for 1988. Nevertheless, these figures contrast sharply with the picture for the New Democracy-affiliated Boxing Federation, for which a significant increase in grant over the 1989 figure is evident in each year of the New Democracy government except one. Figure 5.3 highlights this point. It does not show absolute amounts of grant aid, but rather the percentage change over the 1989 grant is mapped, demonstrating the contrasting fortunes of PASOK- and New Democracy-affiliated organisations in the period of New Democracy Government. Thus, the data held by the GSS in terms of the sources of income of the NGBs across the period 1988–93 support the accounts of interviewees of clientelism in operation.

Political clientelism and professional baseball in Taiwan

The study on which this commentary on clientelism in Taiwan draws was part of a wider analysis of the changing governance of professional baseball in Taiwan (Lee 2005). However, following a brief outline of the development of professional baseball in Taiwan in the 1990s, we will focus on political involvement in three sets of events to illustrate the nature of client–patron relations in Taiwanese baseball. These are the unfolding of a major bribery scandal in baseball from 1997; the staging of the Baseball World Cup in 2001; and the merging of the two Taiwanese professional leagues, the Chinese Professional Baseball League (CPBL) and the Taiwan Major League (TML), in 2003. These three sets of incidents provide us with the opportunity to evaluate the interconnection of professional sporting interests with those of political parties in Taiwan.

Professional baseball in Taiwan is still a recent phenomenon. With Taiwan's rapid political and economic development during the 1980s (Wu 2003), and following the national baseball team's regularly impressive performances in international tournaments, such as the bronze medal in the Olympic Games of Los Angeles in 1984, governmental, sporting and business interests became convinced that Taiwan could sustain professional baseball (Wilson 1999). After the Olympic Games in Seoul in 1988, several prominent domestic corporations embarked on a plan to set up a professional baseball league. In 1989, the CPBL, which owned four clubs – Brother Elephants, Weichuan Dragons, Uni-President Lions and Mercury Tigers – was established and had its debut in Taipei in 1990. Because the Chinese Taipei Baseball team had won the silver medal at the Olympic Games in Barcelona in 1992, more spectators came to see the games and all the players of the national baseball team subsequently joined the league. In 1993, two new clubs, the China Times Eagles and Jingo Bears, which were composed of players from the national team in Barcelona, were added to the CPBL.

This led the China Trust Whales to joining the CPBL, but fierce competition developed with the emergence of a new rival organisation, the TML. Since the inauguration of the CPBL, the Sampo Corporation and TVBS Corporation had supplied a significant amount of the finance required for the League through media contracts and had sought membership of the CPBL. The president of the Sampo Corporation, Chen, had lobbied vigorously but without success for his Sampo Giants club to join the CPBL from 1992 (Lin 2003; Tsai 2003). As a consequence of its failure in bidding for broadcasting rights to the CPBL, the Sampo Corporation and the TVBS Corporation jointly established the Naluwan Corporation in 1996 which was set up to operate a new league (the TML) in 1997, incorporating ten popular former players of the CPBL who transferred to the TML just at the time the bribery scandal was about to break (Lee 2003).

Immediately prior to the challenge posed by the formation of the TML in 1997, the CPBL suffered a crisis of public confidence when it was rumoured that some players had fixed matches. These rumours quickly led to accusations of connections between bribed or threatened players and criminal groups (Lee 1996; Pan 1996). On 16 June 1996, Hsu, the coach of the Weichuan Dragons, received a letter from a criminal group, attempting to blackmail him to fix games, and this revelation exposed the influence of gambling and the involvement of violent criminal groups in the CPBL (Lin 2001). On 3 August 1996, criminals kidnapped five players of the Brother Elephants team to influence the outcome of matches making manifest what had previously been suspected, that attempts at match fixing were rife. It was gradually revealed that criminal groups had pressured players to throw games, and this provided evidence of a long-suspected problem. On 7 August 1996, after the arrest of two of the criminals involved in the city of Taichung, Kuo, Chairman of the Player's Union, and Chen, the CPBL Commissioner, jointly issued a statement promising fans that no games had been rigged (Chen 1999). Ironically, on 28 January 1997, Kuo was one of the first three players to be placed on charges for brokering deals between players and gamblers (Huang 1997). It transpired that Kuo was a ringleader of the game-fixing network, and he admitted accepting US$1.5 million from criminals. He received the heaviest sentence among the 22 players convicted, and he was sentenced to 30 months in jail with an NT$3 million[1] fine (Wilson 2002). The continuing emergence of cases where players were associated with gambling compelled the CPBL Commissioner, on 14 February 1997, to apologise to the general public and to outline the action to be taken to deal with this crisis: 'Players, taken into custody, have to be suspended from duties and payment of salary; players, released on bail, withdraw from games but still receive 50% salary; players, convicted by the court, will be dropped from this league forever' (Su 1998, translated by one of the authors). Despite this declaration, the formal powers for intervention in this scandal on the part of the CPBL were still limited, and a steady flow of information concerning bribery continued to emerge. On 13 March 1997, Chen, the coach of the China Times Eagles, was the first coach to be charged though he was released on bail of NT$100,000. Then, on 20 June 1997, nine players of the China Times Eagles and one player from the Uni-President Lions team were interrogated by the public prosecutor and subsequently released on bail. During that period, there were only two domestic players of the China Times team available for selection since players who were under suspicion were suspended and could not play games in the CPBL. The China Times Eagles finished the rest of the season's games by using the other clubs' bench players, and in 1998, it was decided to disband the club. On 2 August 1997, criminals kidnapped seven players of the Mercury Tigers team and four other foreign players in Kaohsiung to get them to throw games, deepening the crisis of the CPBL. Thus, the China Times Eagles bribery scandal and the subsequent uncovering of this series of criminal links undermined the operation of the CPBL and threatened the whole baseball market, reflecting a crisis of confidence in professional matches as fair contests.

Political involvement in the 1997 baseball bribery scandal

A central aspect of the context of professional baseball in Taiwan, which goes some way to explain the emergence of the bribery problem, relates to the political development of Taiwan and, in particular, the existence of strong clientelistic relations. While political clientelism was both visible and acknowledged by the majority of actors in the Greek case, this was much less evident in the case of political interviewees in Taiwan. This is in part because of a more reserved political and social culture (Chang *et al.* 2005: p. 178; Chun 2000: p. 179; Hsieh 2000: p. 55); however, it also reflects illicit nature of much of this clientelistic activity. The existence of clientelism in the Taiwanese case is related to traditional 'guanxi' sets of relations. Guanxi is a central concept in Chinese culture. It relates to the network of social relations and obligations in which an individual or group of individuals is implicated. Such networks form the basis of much business activity where individuals and companies tend to work with known parties whom they can trust (Weidenbaum and Hughes 1996). Thus, being introduced into a network by an already known and respected party is critical, and as Solinger (2006) comments, 'The personal relationships so nurtured are based implicitly on mutual interest and benefit, and on an expectation that a favor entails a debt to be repaid; they have a binding power and primacy'. Clearly then, guanxi structures and practices can form the basis for political clientelism, but guanxi networks can also violate bureaucratic, legal or commercial principles spilling over into illegal activity (Gold *et al.* 2002; Yang 2002).

Political and social analysts have regularly commented both on the existence of patron–client relations between the KMT party (especially in its long period of political rule) and local groups and more specifically on the existence of such links with criminal groups (Reaves 2002). As we have noted, for decades, a monopoly of economic and political privilege permitted the KMT regime to construct alliances with local factions (with little concern shown for their backgrounds), sharing political power and material benefits with them in exchange for their allegiance to the party (Brown *et al.* 1998; Hood 1996a; Wu 2001b, 2003). Thus, it was hardly surprising that organised crime with political support should involve itself in gambling in professional baseball, with huge potential profits. Despite the traditional reticence of the politicians and others interviewed, one interviewee who was a DPP legislator (member of the Legislative Yuan or Parliament) was particularly forthright:

> What happened in the development of baseball was mainly the extension of long-standing 'patron-client' relationship between crime triads and Taiwan's ruling political party [KMT]. Gangs' attempts to control professional baseball are a manifestation of the problems of Taiwan's politics, not just the sport of baseball itself.
> (Interview with DPP MP, 15 May 2003, translated by one of the authors)

In the case of the gambling scandal, media commentators noted that members of the criminal underworld were able to act with the support of some political actors, which governmental organisations (such as the Ministry of Justice) seemed afraid to challenge (Kuo 2000; Reaves 2002). As the press subsequently argued, this culture of 'dirty money' in politics is such an entrenched part of the political system that the KMT government's anti-corruption campaign barely scratched the surface of the problem (*Taipei Times* 2003).

The revelations about the widespread abuse of the sport for gambling profits emerged in 1997 when the KMT was still in power in government. There had been rumours for some time that illegal gambling profits were being made, and there were those in the media who were surprised when the government decided to act. As the *China News* (1997) reported during the height of the scandal in 1997, even though gambling itself was illegal,

> Gambling in [Taiwanese] baseball has long been a known, even tacitly accepted, fact. Claims of match rigging have been rife for years, with huge sums involved as players throw games in return for kickbacks from gamblers. But not many followers of the sport expected the justice ministry's (sic) investigators to be quite so ruthless in their crackdown and some seriously heavyweight business interests must have been caught off-guard.

Two specific examples serve to illustrate the nature and diversity of patron–client relations between different regimes, groups of politicians and organised crime in this sphere. Hsiao, a former KMT supporter and one of the alleged 'gangsters-turned-politicians' in Taiwan, came from a noted political family in the Chiayi County (*The China Post* 2001b). In 1997, he was arrested in an organised nationwide anti-crime campaign, implemented jointly by the Ministry of Justice and the Ministry of the Interior, for his alleged role in a series of professional game fixes and several other scandals (*The China Post* 2001a). He was later released on bail and decided to distance himself from the KMT party after one of his brothers came under judicial investigation for alleged involvement in illegal activities (*The China Post* 2001a). Subsequently, by 21 August 2003, the Taiwan High Court had further considered Hsiao's case confirming the charge that he had approached and bribed China Times Eagles players, including the captain Kuo (the most crucial intermediary between players and gangsters), to throw games making a huge (illegal) gambling profit in 1997. The court approved a two-and-half-year sentence for Hsiao (*Taiwan Daily News* 2003).

This judgment both demonstrated the DPP government's determination to clean up professional sport and rid it of criminal influences while it also attacked the former KMT patron–client networks. The change of government in 2000 from KMT (which had enjoyed 50 years of unbroken political rule) to DPP undoubtedly helped to give momentum to the anti-corruption campaign.

The second member of the Legislative Yuan[2] (a former KMT member), who was subsequently unaffiliated with any political party, is another example of a politician with reported links to criminal elements in Taiwan. The importance of political patronage is evident in that, despite disputed claims about this individual's criminal background, his support was surprisingly sought by three main candidates from KMT, DPP and the People First Party (PFP) in the Presidential elections in 2000 and in 2004 (Lin 2003; Prelypchan 2000; *Taipei Times* 2000). This prominent politician, with alleged criminal links, was described by political commentators as 'involved in connections between organised crime, political influence and local and central government' (Liu 2001a). This individual had also been accused of running an illegal lottery and masterminding baseball gambling activities, though investigators had found no evidence to support these claims (*Taipei Times* 2000). Relevant investigations were still proceeding at the time of writing despite the fact that this politician was shielded by his political position with privilege against court summons and arrest while the legislature was 'in session' (Kennedy 2000).

Thus, at the level of political legitimacy and party politics, it is clear that the crisis had a significant impact on the reputation of the KMT government and on individual politicians. Direct criticism is difficult to identify in the cultural context of an interview in Taiwan with its traditional adherence to Confucian respect for authority. While KMT politicians in referring to the crisis tended to locate blame among the players and the criminals involved in match fixing, the DPP politicians were much more ready to require government to shoulder the blame and by implication to criticise KMT's involvement. The only arrests of political figures in relation to the scandal were of those former KMT politicians referred to earlier, and the DPP legislator (member of parliament) interviewed was keen to distinguish his own party's response to the crisis from that of the KMT: 'The DPP always takes concern with events of professional baseball in Taiwan. The MPs automatically asked the Ministry of the Justice to take real actions to prevent a gambling scandal from happening again' (interview with DPP MP, 15 May 2003, translated by one of the authors). However, the DPP itself, even though in the past it had strongly denounced local factions and economic favours, was subject to claims of similar behaviour, once it had come to power: 'the DPP now pursues a faction-based electoral strategy of the increased political and economic privileges associated with patronage' (Wu 2003: p. 106).

The politics of the staging of the Baseball World Cup

In May 1999, the Chinese Taipei Baseball Association (CTBA) and the Taipei City government successfully bid to stage the 2001 Baseball World Cup. The city of Taipei was KMT controlled, and KMT still held office in central government until 2000. The government supported the bid and established a plan through the NCPFS, the *Programme for Development of Baseball in the ROC 2001–4*, which would be funded to the sum of NT$115.6 million. Through this plan, the government clearly announced its intention to use the event as a vehicle to revitalise the sport of baseball.

However, after the DPP gained power in central government in 2000, the hosting issue became problematic, with the Executive Yuan's (the Cabinet) proposal that the NCPFS should negotiate with the Taipei City government and the International Baseball Federation (IBAF) to see whether it was possible to move the opening and closing ceremonies to Kaohsiung County (a DPP-controlled local authority). Liu emphasises this point and indicates that, 'The political intervention by the DPP and ensuing power struggles amongst the international governing body, central government, and two local governments with different political affiliations were evident' (Liu 2003: p. 226). Thus, arguments among political actors, such as the Executive Yuan, the Legislative Yuan (the Parliament), Taipei City (KMT) and Kaohsiung County (DPP), and sport governing bodies, such as the IBAF and the CTBA, gained momentum.

With the successful experience of having staged the World Senior Youth Baseball Tournament in 1999 behind it, the Kaohsiung County government sought to be involved in the 2001 Baseball World Cup. The Kaohsiung County DPP Magistrate, Yu, suggested it would be 'logical' for his county to jointly host the event with Taipei City and accused Taipei City of trying to monopolise the tournament. However, the reality was that Taipei City would only host 21 of the tournament's 68 matches and 14 would be held at the Kaohsiung County baseball stadium, Chengching Lake.

> Indeed, when the IBAF chief executive Ortin visited Taiwan in March 2001 to inspect baseball facilities, the National Sport Council [NCPFS] asked that the final game be held at the Chengching Lake [in Kaohsiung]. But the association chose Tienmu stadium in Taipei instead and approved the tournament schedule.
>
> (*Taipei Times* 2001a)

Despite the fact that the IBAF had made its decision, the Kaohsiung County government still clamoured for the final game and the closing ceremony. This matter was then raised with the Executive Yuan (the Cabinet), which '... supported the Kaohsiung County government's proposal to negotiate this issue with the Taipei City government. The head of the DPP supports the request of the Chief Magistrate of Kaohsiung County to discuss this issue with Taipei City government' (*China Times* 2001, as quoted in Liu 2003: p. 228). A DPP legislator (member of parliament) Yen had previously (at the beginning of 2000) proposed that the 2001 Baseball World Cup should be placed in the Kaohsiung Greater area, and he had tried to place pressure on the KMT Minister.

> Hosting international sport events could promote cities' diplomacy and let foreigners further understand what the cities are. I suggest that the 2001 Baseball World Cup should be held in the Kaohsiung area, but not Taipei City where many international activities have taken place for many years. … I am looking forward to your Minister's promise to hold this event in Kaohsiung, which has many strengths that Taipei is unable to offer.
>
> (Yen 2000: pp. 33–91, translated by one of the authors)

At that time, the KMT Minister Chao, who was responsible for the NCPFS, responded indicating that:

> As far as I am concerned, the NCPFS is still evaluating in which city to hold this specific tournament. We are negotiating with Taipei City and Kaohsiung County and decision-making is yet to come. Importantly, the NCPFS will finish the evaluation in one month and make a final decision.
>
> (Chao 2000: pp. 33–91, translated by one of the authors)

However, the NCPFS made no proposals at this time since the KMT government lost power later in 2000. Such arguments concerning the hosting arrangements were re-addressed in 2001. Following its victory, the new DPP central government decided to support Kaohsiung's proposal, and the new Minister responsible for the NCPFS, as a member of the Cabinet, was urged to liaise not only with the local governments but also with the IBAF and the CTBA to renegotiate the location of the opening ceremony, the closing ceremony and the schedule of play-offs. Press reports suggested that, 'The NCPFS is under pressure both from the local governments and from the International Baseball Association [IBAF]. It claims to serve as the "negotiator to work out everything relating to the World Cup" ' (*China Times* 2001, as quoted in Liu 2003: p. 228).

The 'political interference' by the NCPFS immediately led to criticism from both the Taipei City government and the CTBA. The KMT Mayor of Taipei City, Ma, complaining about the DPP political intervention, responded that it was inappropriate to reschedule the tournament under international sport regulations. He remarked that 'I have no idea how the Executive Yuan could change the schedule of the World Cup without going against international rules' (*China Times* 2001a). Subsequently, he further reported in the weekly Cabinet meeting of the Executive Yuan that:

> The International Baseball Federation, on June 26, notified all sixteen participating countries of its schedule, finalised June 2, which it said couldn't

be changed. I therefore don't see either the possibility or the reason for a change of venues ... if the Cabinet insists on making changes, damage will be done to the nation's image. Only in the event of a national disaster can a change be made.

(*Taipei Times* 2001b)

However, Premier Chang, supporting his DPP Magistrate from Kaohsiung County, tried to instigate a renegotiation between the two local authorities. Chang argued that this would be a matter decided by a special task force set up by the Executive Yuan to deal with the organisation of the World Cup, thus in theory distancing the decision from direct political influence, though he left little to the imagination in terms of the outcome he anticipated.

I would leave the decision to be reviewed by the Cabinet's ad hoc task force, which is in charge of coordinating the tournament. I hope the Taipei City government would not be offended by the likely change and 'turn it into a clash' between the central and local government.

(*Taipei Times* 2001d)

The debate over who should host the ceremonies thus became a string of political spats between Taiwan's two major local government bodies (and the two political parties which controlled them). Although Premier Chang made the above comment in response to criticism that political intervention and party interests lay behind the Cabinet's proposal, rather than objective and neutral concerns, cynicism was expressed in the media. 'One of the reasons for this, according to the Cabinet, is to help create a better balance between the country's north and south by benefiting the southern counties. Interestingly, most southern cities and counties are controlled by the DPP' (*Taipei Times* 2001d). Also countering the accounts of political intervention from the Taipei City Mayor, the central government spokesman Su re-emphasised the state's attitude towards this matter as he indicated that:

The Cabinet's proposal was simply intended to provide the tournament with a better stadium than Taipei could offer. The tournament, which aims to promote the sport and increase the country's supporters, is not a regional one ... the Chengching Lake Baseball Stadium in Kaohsiung County can accommodate 20,000 spectators, three times as many as Taipei's Tienmu Stadium.

(*Taipei Times* 2001d)

In the end, with the start of the tournament approaching, the IBAF was able to rule that the original plans for opening and closing the World Cup in Taipei would remain, and the DPP was forced to accept this outcome.

The merger of the TML and CPBL

The success of staging the baseball World Cup and Taiwan's positive performance (placed third) did much to rehabilitate the reputation and standing of the sport, and attendances at professional league games began to recover. However, notwithstanding this improvement in spectator numbers, it was clear that the two professional leagues could not both survive. Both had effectively lost money since their inception, but the TML was significantly weaker. The negotiations between the two leagues proved sensitive and turbulent, but the DPP government decided to intervene to facilitate the process of a merger, with the President of the Republic himself making a number of personal interventions. Baseball, it was argued, was too important in terms of national identity and pride to leave to the market. As one commentator put it:

> For Taiwan, baseball is politics …. The game has been utilised as a means to exercise the governments' political hegemony …. No matter how much people may want the game [to be] free from politics, whilst power networks exist, baseball is never going to be free from politics.
>
> (Lin 2003: p. 232)

Reflecting on this point, we should consider the political circumstances surrounding the CPBL, which was established and sponsored by some corporations with strong connections to political interests, in particular to the KMT (Liang 1993). For example, Ku, the president of the China Trust Corporation, and Lin, the president of Uni-President Corporation, were both members of the Central Committee of the KMT, which was so powerful and influential when the KMT was in office, that it was said to exert influence in all significant policy areas in Taiwan. The professional baseball clubs (China Trust Whales and Uni-President Lions) sponsored by the China Trust Corporation or the Uni-President Corporation remain as important stakeholders in the CPBL. Interestingly, in the former TML, key leaders were either parliamentarians or government officials from the DPP with the exception of the Commissioner Wang (who was Vice Chairman of the KMT). Thus, it is clear that there has been a complicated relation between political parties and professional baseball leagues, as a comment by Krich illustrates: 'Only in Taiwan, where connections to political parties are crucial in operating franchises and constructing ballparks, would a baseball official, TML Executive Director Robin Tseng, explain "our league is more DPP while the other league (CPBL) is more KMT"' (Krich 2002). Despite these very evident party affiliations, the DPP government and its President succeeded in persuading its supporters who owned the TML to swallow the bitter pill of a one-sided merger in which only two of the TML's four clubs survived. The only overtly partial move made by the government in favour of the TML position was to promote a proposal for the CPBL to compensate the TML to the tune of NT$80 million for each of the two teams to go out of existence. This move was, however, rejected by the CPBL.

Although the merger took place on CPBL terms, from the TML perspective, this was a better outcome than simply allowing the weaker of the two leagues to wither and die.

> When we look at this successful merger from a different angle, the merger reflected the fact that the owners wanted to maintain their good political and economic relationships with the government, especially after understanding the President's attitude towards this issue. Here, we cannot over emphasise how powerful the political force is.
>
> (Interview with the Media commentator, 6 May 2003, translated by one of the authors)

> Because the owners of the TML have good political relationships with the central government, the league was successful in communicating its views to the government. We can see the DPP MPs, the President, the NCPFS were greatly involved in this issue and the CPBL accepted such an arrangement without many dissenting voices (there are always different opinions in the CPBL). Therefore, I think party political power really worked this time.
>
> (Interview with the Principal of a Higher Education Institution and researcher, 13 May 2003, translated by one of the authors)

Indeed, it is clear that leaders of the CPBL, despite their KMT affiliation, sought to establish good political relationships with the DPP ruling government in terms of access to relevant resources. In other words, what the leaders of the CPBL considered important was the long-term development of the baseball industry, and they clearly felt that the government's attitude would play a vital role in the future.

Conclusions

Clientelism is a persistent feature of social and political relations in both Greece and Taiwan, affecting a wide range of policy fields in both cases, including sport. The question this invites is why such arrangements, associated as they are with traditional forms of social organisation, should persist in the contemporary context, since both politico-economic systems have been subject to the impact of pressures in relation to modernisation of their polities and economies.

Greece developed rapidly in political terms after the fall of the Junta in 1974, and its politics were no longer simply a parochial matter. It became a member of the European Union and of NATO. It has developed economically, though not without problems, with initial industrialisation (industrial employment peaking in 1981 at 28 per cent) giving way to a structure dominated by small business and a growing tertiary sector.

In Taiwan, political liberalisation has been in train for a relatively shorter period since the lifting of martial law in 1987, the development of multi-party politics and the introduction of popular elections for the Presidency in 1996. Taiwan has developed into a dynamic capitalist economy with decreasing state intervention. When the Nationalists took control of the island, the economy was significantly reliant on agricultural production (32 per cent of GDP in 1950). Over the 1960s and 1970s, Taiwan enjoyed rapid growth and industrialisation as one of the Asia's Tiger Economies, and this has been followed by rapid growth in the service sector which by 2005 accounted for 69 per cent of GDP. The country enjoys a major trade surplus, and its foreign reserves are the world's third largest.

However, global forces are mediated in local contexts, and invariably local responses to global contexts will vary in political, social, cultural and economic terms. The forms of clientelism in these two cases are clearly characterised by local differences. In the Greek case, it is the use of state support for national federations, contrasts with the support of individual business and other interests evident in Taiwan. However, there are a number of key commonalities which we would suggest characterise both systems. We would suggest survival of clientelism in these two contexts can be explained by reference to three sets of factors[3]: at the level of the individual, an explanation can be given in terms of personal histories; at the level of political parties, an explanation can be generated in terms of the tactical difficulties in moving away from this system; and at the societal level, an explanation can be generated in terms of the forms of social regulation fostered and/or constrained by the social and economic structures of the two societies.

Perhaps the simplest of these forms of explanation is that of the individual response to clientelism. As we have noted earlier in this chapter, it is claimed that political parties form an alternative basis for individual identity, particularly when traditional forms of solidarity are undermined by 'modernising' phenomena such as urbanisation and industrialisation. However, an additional feature of both political systems, which goes some way to explaining the strength of personal affiliation to a party (or the distrust of the 'other' parties), is the relatively recent role which party affiliation played in internal civil strife, the Civil War in the Greek case and the (initially brutal) imposition of the KMT in 1949, reinforced a form of distrust, or at least an unwillingness to trust, which helps to perpetuate reliance on the political patronage of one's own party, or reliance on guanxi networks which helped to shape relationships with political entities. As the memory of civil struggle recedes, and there is an opening out of business and political relations beyond the local, different attitudes may be developed, but as we argue further, it is difficult to wholly disengage from political, business and social cultures which have been so deeply rooted.

The second type of explanation to which we refer is that of the difficulties faced by the political parties, which, though they agree that clientelism is something which should not be promoted, they continue to perpetuate. The political party's problem is akin to the classic prisoner's dilemma, in that while both the major parties recognise that there would be benefits to all in terms of the reduced inefficiencies of a non-clientelistic, 'rational' system of resource allocation, if one party chooses to stop disbursing benefits to its supporters while in power, it cannot be absolutely sure that the other major party will do likewise. Thus, while a party might maximise its interests by doing away with clientelism, it risks undermining its own interests if the opposition does not follow suit, and maintaining the status quo may therefore be seen as the safest option. The DPP's action in promoting a solution to the baseball merger of the leagues provides an example of one-side conceding ground and persuading its supporters (TML owners) to accept a deal which principally benefited sports entrepreneurs associated with the KMT. However, this example is one in which DPP-affiliated owners would have inevitably lost out more heavily if a merger had not been agreed.

The third type of explanation for the survival of clientelism is perhaps the most complex, drawing as it does on regulation theory approaches to understanding social and political structures. Clientelism is strongly associated with the political systems of Southern Europe, Latin America, the former Soviet republics and the Gulf States, as well as those of South East Asia. These are political systems which have not been subject to smooth or gradual modernisation processes. Petmesidou argues in relation to Greece that its rapid shift from a pre-industrial (and pre-Fordist) society to a post-industrial and post-Fordist society is a major factor in explaining the prevalence of clientelistic relations, since Greece, in a sense, missed out on the rationalism of modernisation inherent in the social and political arrangements which accompany industrial development. She points out that Greece experienced a rapid rise in industrial activity from the 1960s, with industrial employment peaking in 1981, but subsequently declining:

> ever since the early 1970s Greece has been experiencing a shift to post-Fordist social and economic structures (tertiarisation of the economy, flexible work relations, informality etc.), well before industrialization had deepened and Fordist production structures with their accompanying patterns of collective solidarity and universalist social citizenship had been fully developed.
>
> (Petmesidou 1996: p. 328)

Fordist patterns of social regulation have also been historically less evident in Taiwanese society in which the development of a liberal welfare ideology was to some extent undermined by traditional family-based systems of welfare provision and guanxi structures of social obligation and mutual interdependence. We need to be cautious here to avoid slipping into a cultural determinism. Nevertheless, it is important to note that guanxi structures provided a resource for achieving some of the things which were provided by the 'open but regulated' markets and welfare systems associated with Fordism in the West.

We do not necessarily accept Petmesidou's description of the Greek economy as post-Fordist, though there are certainly some features of such an economic structure, and here, there are strong parallels with the Taiwanese history of rapid development thorough industrialisation to a service sector-dominated economy. The forms of social regulation and political compromise evident in late-twentieth-century Greek and Taiwanese politics are certainly not Fordist, in the sense of being a negotiated compromise between labour and capital as in the case of the social democratic political arrangement evident in, say, post-war Britain, France or the Netherlands (Bramham *et al.* 1993). If the welfare state and social democratic politics represent the rational politics of modernity, clientelistic politics may represent the 'arational' politics of (if not post-modernity) high modernity (Giddens 1990). The locus of control in modernist/Fordist political arrangements was conceived as being much more a matter of internal politics (bargaining between national capital and labour), whereas the locus of control in the high modern or neo-Fordist context is deemed to be at least partially displaced to the transnational level (transnational corporations, the European Union, etc.), reducing the opportunity for meaningful bargaining between capital and labour on the macro scale. Party loyalty may thus be important in order to maintain political parties in office (hence the survival of clientelism), while the compliance and commitment of the labour force is sustained by the level of unemployment and a concern to attract inward investment into national and local economies.

In this chapter, we have sought to demonstrate ways in which clientelism exists in two very different social contexts, to illustrate how it operates and to explain why it persists. While there are global structures which are emerging rendering decisions much less local and providing resources for local actors, the continued availability of local structures such as guanxi and the adaptability of those employing such structures, whether in business or politics, are evident phenomena. As Yang (2002) argues, in relation to guanxi, one should avoid the determinist teleology of modernisation theories.

> *guanxi* must be treated historically as a repertoire of cultural patterns and resources which are continuously transformed in their adaptation to, as well as shaping of, new social institutions and structures, and by the particular Chinese experience with globalization. ... [we should] ... take issue with approaches which treat *guanxi* as a fixed essentialised phenomenon which can only wither away with the onslaught of new legal and commercial regimes. Rather, as the examples of Taiwan and post-socialist Russia's encounter with capitalism suggest, guanxi practice may decline in some social domains, but find new areas to flourish, such as business transactions, and display new social forms and expressions.

The same argument can be made by extension to other clientelistic forms or structures, as in the Greek case which should also be regarded as a contingent outcome, and thus amenable to change given appropriate action in the right circumstances. Whether in relation to sport, such clientelistic interactions decline is thus a matter for empirical investigation rather than functionalist teleology.

6 Multiculturalism, interculturalism, assimilation and sports policy in Europe

Ian Henry, Mahfoud Amara and Dawn Aquilina

Introduction

Claims about the use of sport as a vehicle for promoting social integration of socially excluded groups in general, and specifically ethnic minority groups, are not new, though they have been increasingly evident in recent years. Initiatives such as the United Nations' (UN) appointment of Adolf Ogi as Special Adviser to Kofi Annan on the use of Sport for Development and Peace, the announcement of the year 2005 as the UN Year of Sport and Physical Education, the funding of projects as part of the European Union's (EU) Year of Education through Sport (Amara *et al.* 2005) and by the Council of Europe (Niessen 2000) reflect a growing concern to explore the uses of sport for such purposes. The concern, particularly in a European context, with the use of sport as a cultural 'bridge' is unsurprising given the growing level of international migration and subsequent cultural heterogeneity. Figure 6.1 illustrates the rapid growth of

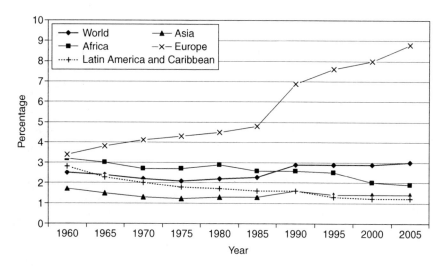

Figure 6.1 International migrants as a percentage of the population.

migrant populations (those persons born in a country other than that in which they live), which is estimated as 8.8 per cent in the case of Europe (United Nations 2006).

However, claims about the 'integrating' potential of sport have tended to be made without reference to detailed evidence of the effectiveness of such measures or indeed without explicit statements of what integration might mean in such policy contexts and therefore of the precise goals of these policy initiatives, prompting both the Council of Europe (Niessen 2000) and the European Commission (Amara *et al.* 2005) to foster research in this field. This chapter draws on the latter study (a project led by the research team from the Institute of Sport and Leisure Policy at Loughborough, directed by the first-named author of this chapter, but which incorporated research teams from each of the 25 Member States of the EU[1]).

The approach adopted here is to begin with a clarification of key terms. Conceptual clarity is essential since different understandings of such terms imply very different philosophies with significant implications in relation to the use of sport for forms of cultural 'integration' (or multiculturalism, interculturalism, assimilation, cultural cohesion etc.). This chapter, thus, subsequently outlines in ideal typical terms a range of policy orientations which stem from the differential understanding of social integration through sport. Finally, we go on to provide a conceptual framework for characterising the different approaches evident in the 25 EU Member States.

Key terms and approaches to national identity and citizenship

In the literature on multiculturalism and policy, perhaps the commonest distinction made is between policies of 'integration' on the one hand and 'assimilation' on the other. Integration is seen as the process whereby a minority group adapts itself to a majority society and is accorded equality of rights and treatment, whereas the term 'assimilation' is used in relation to the 'absorption' of ethnic minority and immigrant population cultures into the cultures and practices of the host society. Assimilation thus implies *acculturation* both in the adoption of mainstream cultural norms and in the gradual loss of indigenous cultural distinctiveness.

Different concepts of integration/assimilation are bound up with the way that different states understand national identity, and these concepts are a product of the processes of nation-building, democratisation and their experience of international relations, particularly colonial and post-colonial relations. In our study of EU Member States, we chose to look in particular detail at four national policy systems, those of France, Germany, Poland and the UK[2]. Three of these nation states have historically distinctive concepts of national identity and citizenship and the fourth (Poland) finds itself establishing new forms of citizenship as it entered the EU in May 2004.

The origins of modern French thought in relation to national identity derive from the French Revolution with the replacement of allegiance to a monarchy by the voluntary adoption of republican values of freedom and equality. Nationalism was an expression of the willingness of groups with differing cultural, linguistic, religious or ethnic backgrounds to accept a common political project guaranteeing universal rights for all (Kastoryano 2002). Acceptance of the political project, however, also required acceptance of norms of citizenship, organised around a secular and unified notion of French identity. Thus just as languages spoken regionally, such as Breton, were suppressed in the nineteenth and early twentieth century, the cultural symbols of ethnic or religious difference are banished from public life by the French state in the contemporary context (as in the recent case of discussions about the wearing of the veil in schools or in other public institutions such as sports centres).

Whereas the French notion of a national culture depends upon shared political will, the German tradition of nationalism stemming from Herder and Fichte emphasises nationhood as shared culture, language and ethnos. For the French, shared culture was a product of political nationalism, whereas in the German tradition, political nationalism was seen as the natural consequence of a shared national culture (Boswell 2003). Until relatively recently, the naturalisation of non-Germans (such as the Turkish minority) was the exception, though social rights (such as access to welfare services) were widely available to immigrant groups (Miller 2000). Thus, social citizenship rather than political rights of being a German national was what was available to such groups.

The implication of both of these views of national identity is that 'foreign' cultures should not be 'accommodated' within the national culture but rather should be assimilated.

In contrast to these two models, the concept of multiculturalism is most clearly associated with the liberal pluralist state which promotes the individual freedoms of its members, fostering the potential for cultural diversity. The existence of national minorities within the borders of the UK state may well have fostered cultural pluralism, but the colonial experience and the associated notion of British subjecthood also fuelled such pluralism with Commonwealth immigrants (at least until the late 1960s) having the right to British citizenship. Political rights in such a context were the product not of hereditary membership of a particular group (as in the case of Germany) or of the voluntary political adherence to the nation (as in the case of France) but rather by reference to territorial residence.

While the political circumstances of contemporary Britain, France and Germany may well have shifted from these traditional positions, with the liberalisation of naturalisation rights particularly for second- and third-generation 'foreign' inhabitants in Germany and the tightening of access to citizenship in Britain, one might nevertheless expect to see a greater propensity to adopt multicultural or integrationist policy stances in Britain with a parallel assimilationist tendency on the part of the German and French states.

The Polish context is somewhat different. Social organisation and thus questions of nationality and citizenship were constructed under very different circumstances, and within the communist system, the importance of immigration, ethnicity and of national minorities was minimised. Poland like other new Member States was still in process of working through its approach to citizenship at the time of this study. However, in drawing up its new internal administrative boundaries, the significance of national minorities has been recognised.

Policy approaches to sport, cultural identity and citizenship

This schematic representation of the different approaches to national identity and citizenship is significant for the discussion of multiculturalism and sport; therefore, in this section of the chapter we will seek to map the development of sports policy for minorities onto the competing concepts of integration and assimilation and the traditions of national identity and citizenship discussed earlier.

Figure 6.2 seeks to spell out five ideal typical policy approaches, three of which are most closely associated with pluralism and multiculturalism and two with assimilationist concerns with social cohesion and a unitary national culture. In each of these policy approaches, we seek to identify the values that underpin them, their relationship to mainstream political values and programmes and their implications for sports policy.

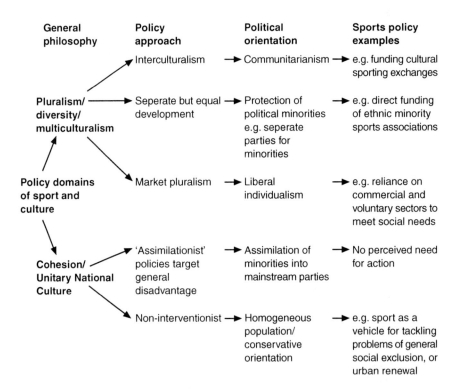

Figure 6.2 Ideal typical representation of sport/cultural policy orientations.

The first of the pluralist approaches is that of *interculturalism*, a situation that describes the equal valuation placed on cultures, the best elements of which are brought together to produce a new cultural mix. Such a cultural approach is consistent with the politics of communitarianism (Etzioni 1993; Tam 1998) or at least what Miller (2000) terms 'left communitarianism'. Such a political position values, amongst other things, diversity as a cultural and political resource. A typical sports policy associated with such thinking would be the promotion of cultural interchange between sporting groups.

The second of the pluralist approaches characterises what French commentators refer to in a pejorative manner as *communautarisme*, meaning separate but equal development. Such a philosophy is evident in political terms in the protection of political minorities, for example, in providing reserved parliamentary seats as quotas. In sports policy terms, this approach would be manifest in a policy of funding ethnic minority sports associations.

The final multicultural policy approach might be termed *market pluralism*, associated with the classical liberal individualism of the Anglo-Saxon model of the state. Sports policy in such a context would involve the fostering of commercial and voluntary sectors as being the optimal deliverers of diversity in sporting opportunity.

The first of the two 'unitary' policy approaches is thus described as *assimilationist* in that policies are targeted at general conditions (such as social exclusion) and not at serving the needs of particular specific minorities. The political orientation associated with this philosophy sees the absorption of minorities into mainstream parties and of minority interests into mainstream policy programmes. Sports policy approaches consistent with this approach address generalist problems, such as the use of sport in combating social exclusion, rather than focusing on the sporting and social needs of specific target ethnic groups.

The final policy approach, *non-intervention*, stems from the perception by politicians of a homogenous population. Politics (in particular, cultural politics) in such contexts may tend to be conservative as is also the case with sports policies, since with a homogeneous population there will be little perceived need for targeted policy programmes.

Categorising the policy positions of Member States

The outlining of these five ideal types illustrates a range of policy responses in relation to multicultural and unitary cultural thinking, and it invites a further key question – where do particular nation states find themselves within this framework in respect of sports policy? In order to be able to evaluate the policy positions of the EU states, data were sought in two stages from the 25 research teams.

The first stage of data collection aimed to establish the nature of the system for delivery and the types of projects that were promoted and to generate sporting opportunities targeted at ethnic (and national) minorities, immigrant groups, refugees and asylum seekers. Thus, four forms of information were sought for each of the 25 Member States at this stage.

1   The level of cultural homogeneity or heterogeneity of the population;
2   The nature of the bodies which had responsibility for sports provision and policy in each country;

  • Whether these bodies (public, voluntary, commercial) had policies explicitly targeted at ethnically diverse groups;
  • If so, what were those policies programmes?
  • What level of resource was expended on such policies or schemes?
  • Whether such schemes were targeted at particular ethnic minority groups or simply targeted at disadvantaged groups more generally?

3   The nature of governmental organisations responsible for providing general services/generating policy in relation to ethnic minorities within the national population and for immigrants, refugees, asylum seekers and displaced persons; and specifically, whether these bodies (public, voluntary, commercial) had policies which employ sport as a vehicle for working with ethnically diverse groups.
4   Examples of schemes in which sport was being used for the purposes of working with culturally diverse populations and in particular, where such schemes were being used to foster dialogue between different cultural communities.

Following receipt of information from stage one, for those states which had examples of policies targeting ethnic minorities and employing sport, stage two of the research sought to identify secondary data on these schemes in relation to the following questions.

  • How common or widespread was the existence of such projects? Who resources them, and how long had they been in operation?
  • What were the goals of the projects?
  • Who were the actors involved in this type of provision?
  • Were projects monitored and evaluated? If so, what data existed and how successful had the projects been?
  • What difficulties had been reported in implementation and the attainment of goals?

A further stage of data collection took place for the four core nations studies. While stages 1 and 2 relied on secondary data in the 25 Member States, stage 3 involved some primary research in developing case study materials of specific policies and projects in four states, France, Germany, the UK and Poland.

Figure 6.3 seeks to illustrate the ways in which the policy positions of Member States were categorised on the basis of responses to stages 1 and 2 of the data collection. The figure is organised around two dimensions. On the horizontal axis is the level of homogeneity of the population. This is assessed qualitatively rather than operationalised quantitatively because of the difficulties of finding common bases for conceptualisation and measurement. For example,

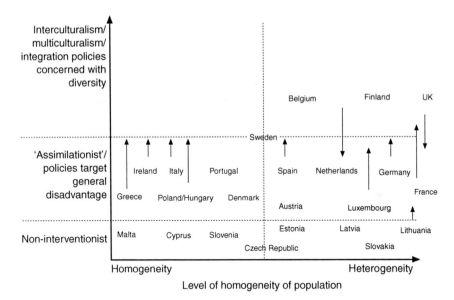

Figure 6.3 Ideal typical location of national sports policies for minorities.

Britain and France have considerable proportions of their populations from ethnic origins derived from their colonial past, from North Africa and from the Indian subcontinent and the Caribbean respectively. However, in the French case, census data do not record ethnic origin but describe all citizens as simply French by definition. Thus, records of immigrant population cannot be compared across nation states.

The vertical axis assigns countries to the categories of multicultural/ intercultural or assimilationist policy. Here again, some caution in interpretation has to be exercised because, as some commentators point out, positions on multiculturalism and assimilation

> should not be seen as unified or fixed. One can discern multiple traditions of thought on citizenship and identity within most states, and it is not always a foregone conclusion which concept will come to dominate policy when states are confronted with new immigration challenges.
>
> (Boswell 2003: p. 76)

With such caveats in mind, however, it is helpful to categorise policy approaches, albeit in ideal typical terms. Figure 6.3 presents a 'snapshot' of the policy positions of each of the Member States with regard to national sports policies for minorities. The commentary which follows provides a rationale for the location of the individual nation states. Where there is evidence of a shifting position on the part of a particular nation state, this is indicated by directional arrows.

Taking the **United Kingdom** as our first case, the United Kingdom's population can be described as heterogeneous by European standards. Not only does it have a strong tradition of receiving labour migrants from the Commonwealth in the twentieth century, and before this from Ireland and Eastern Europe in the nineteenth century, but also it has its own national minorities in Scotland, Wales and Northern Ireland. In policy terms, the participation of ethnic minorities has been a very visible issue, with policies under the general theme of race equality being developed from the 1960s onwards. There is also a history of periodic social disorder and 'race riots', which go alongside this, from Nottingham and London in 1958 through to the beginning of the new century.

A plethora of governmental and non-governmental agencies provide general services targeted at ethnic minorities, together with sporting initiatives such as *Sporting Equals* (Commission for Racial Equality and Sport England 2001) and the *Equality and Diversity Strategy* of UK Sport (2004). The focus on ethnic minority sports participation is evident in the commissioned research by Sport England (2000) and sportscotland (Scott Porter Research and Marketing Ltd 2000) and by the development of a system of good practice guidelines for national sports governing bodies by Sporting Equals (2000). In addition, the need for action to achieve equity is acknowledged in the Government's Plans for Sport (Department of Culture, Media and Sport 2000).

In recent years, however, the British Labour government has sought to be seen as taking a strong line on limiting immigration and the numbers of asylum seekers, to the criticism of its own supporters. In similar vein, Trevor Phillips, Chairman for the Commission on Racial Equality, in April 2004, argued that Britain's policy of multiculturalism had gone too far and that there was a need to ensure that a core of British values remained intact (Modood 2005). More recently, the Home Secretary Jack Straw publicly opposed the wearing of the veil by Muslim constituents in particular contexts (Sturcke 2006). Thus, there is evidence, in some areas of government and the quasi-government sector, of a shift from dominantly multicultural or intercultural positions to the monocultural and assimilationist position with an emphasis on protecting cohesion rather than diversity.

The case of **France** is something of a contrast. Heterogeneous by virtue of immigration but also with its own national minorities (Corsican, Basque, Catalan, Breton, Roma), the country's dominant philosophy has been, as we have argued, assimilationist, so policy measures in all domains will be seen as 'general' in their target, rather than specifically focusing on given minorities. However, the spatial or social concentration of ethnic minorities in particular contexts (parts of the city or among groups such as *les jeunes en difficulté*) means that services may be de facto, delivered largely to ethnic minority elements by virtue of their spatial or social concentration. The *Direction Central des Renseignements Généraux* (DCRG) presented to the Ministry of Interior in June 2004 a report (described by *Le Monde* newspaper as 'alarming') about the tendency of urban ghettoisation or *repli communautaire* among families from immigrant backgrounds. The DCRG report, which covered 630 zones (*quartiers sensibles*) incorporating a population of 1.8

million, indicates that half of those areas are 'ghettoised or in the process of ghet-toisation'. The DCRG notes also that within those areas, there is a high concentration of families from immigrant backgrounds suffering cumulative 'social and cultural handicaps' (*Le Monde* 6 July 2004).

In relation to sports services, Lionel Arnaud (1999b) illustrates this point convincingly in his book *Politiques Sportives et Minorités Ethniques*.

In general, if not in sporting terms, however, we can see some movement in the direction of multiculturalism (or at least equality and anti-discrimination policies) in French society. Examples include the establishment of the first elected National Islamic Congress, representative of different Muslim communities in France, and the opening of the first Islamic high school Ibn Ruchd in the region of Lille. Further examples include appointments at the political level such as the nomination (in the first Raffarin government) of Tokia Saïfi, a French of Algerian origin, to the post of Secrétaire d'Etat au Développement Durable; Hamlaoui Mekachera as Secrétaire d'Etat aux Anciens Combatants; Aïssa Dermouche, the ex-Director de l'Ecole Supérieure de Commerce de Nantes, as a préfet of the region of Jura; and the Algerian-born sociologist Azouz Beggag as Minister of Equal Opportunities in the government of Dominique de Villepin.

Germany has experienced considerable immigration with the growth of its economy from the 1960s onwards. Following the German tradition of ethno-nationalism and citizenship, referred to earlier in this chapter, the distinction which has traditionally been made in policy commentary has been that between 'German' and 'foreigner'. There is no official definition of the expression 'ethnic minority' in the governmental context. In principle, the Federal Ministry of the Interior refers to minorities only in connection with those national minorities that have traditionally been resident in Germany, such as the Serb, Danish, Friesian, Sinti and Roma minorities. All other groups living in Germany and differing from the majority of the society by nationality or other characteristics are not referred to as minorities.

There has, however, been a recent change of language used within the Ministries. Until relatively recently, the term 'migrant' was not used. Questions of status were focused upon the distinction between 'Germans' and 'foreigners' or 'immigrants'. However, the term 'foreigner' tends no longer to be employed in official discourse. Nevertheless, children born to foreigners in Germany (second and third generation) are still non-German. However, as of 2000, these individuals have the option of taking German nationality in addition to their foreign nationality after reaching the age of majority.

There are some German citizens, national minorities living in the Federal Republic of Germany whose home country is traditionally Germany but who have a different mother tongue and a 'different culture'. These national minorities live under the protection of the European Convention for Human Rights and of international agreements concerning civil and political rights. The Federal Government provides a regulatory framework to protect the cultural freedom of such groups.

Although legal rights for national minorities are provided for and the rights of 'foreigners' to take on German citizenship have been liberalised to some degree, provision for ethnic minorities in German sports policy is fragmented and limited. Much of such policy relates to activity at Länder level. Some schemes are targeted not simply at the minorities themselves but at xenophobic youth, such as the *Street Soccer for Tolerance* project promoted by the German Football Association and Länder organisations in Brandenburg, which aims to resocialise young people prone to violence by playing in mixed teams with negotiated rules. This fragmented picture is one that reflects the principle of subsidiarity in the German federal system. Nevertheless, commentators continue to refer the dominant focus on assimilation into German culture.

With a heterogeneous population by virtue of its colonial past, **the Netherlands**, until the late 1990s, pursued a relatively multiculturalist strategy in line with its traditional pluralist, 'pillarised', political system. However, by the late 1990s, sympathy for such an approach was on the wane. The right made political gains (for example, under Pym Fortuyn, a high profile opponent of immigration and critic of Islam) and local authorities began to reduce activities and resources spent on multicultural sports initiatives. Indeed, following the murders of Fortuyn in 2002 (by an animal rights extremist, Volkert van der Graaf, of ethnic Dutch origin) and of Theo van Gogh, the Dutch film maker and supporter of Fortuyn in 2004, opposition to multiculturalism has continued to grow. What had been the twin objectives of the integration of ethnic minorities into mainstream Dutch sports provision on the one hand and the promotion of ethnic sporting groups on the other gave way to a simple emphasis on the former approach.

Schemes such as *Als racisme wint, verliest de sport* (If racism wins, sport loses), a multimedia campaign and development of a special commission for complaints on racism in sport, and the provision of advisors by provincial and municipal governments in the 1990s have all been subject to financial cutbacks in the first decade of the twenty-first century. Also in the 1990s, the National Olympic Committee and national sports federations, in close cooperation with NPS, a Dutch national broadcasting service, broadcast a series of programmes entitled *Nieuwe sporters; Nieuw kader* (New sportsmen; new volunteers). These were television documentaries about the ways in which sport clubs operate (their practices, rules, costs, subscription fees, volunteering, decision-making, etc.) that were broadcast during hours reserved for minorities. They were also made available on video cassette. The soundtrack was provided in different languages (Turkish, Berber, Arabic, French, English, German) with subtitles in Dutch.

Finland is ascribed the status of being relatively heterogeneous by virtue particularly of its important Swedish- and Russian-speaking minorities and of the Sami population as an indigenous group. Multiculturalism or interculturalism has been in a sense built into the Finnish system with Finnish and Swedish as the country's two official languages. In the sports domain, the founding of the Finnish Multicultural Sports Federation (FIMU) in 1999 (affiliated to the

Finnish Sports Federation in 2000) signals the intent to deal with multicultural-ism in sport. The aim of the organisation is to promote sports opportunities for immigrants and to safeguard the interests of all immigrant associations. In 2004, the Finnish Sports Federation supported 42 projects promoting tolerance and multicultural activities in sports with 50,000 euros provided by the Ministry of Education. The 2004 application procedure for this programme favoured pro-jects in which sports opportunities for immigrant families and women were pro-vided; education on tolerance, multiculturalism and attitudes were promoted; and sports activities, education, events and/or dissemination of information were jointly planned and realised by immigrants and the majority population

The position of **Luxembourg** is quite unique. From an outsider's perspective one might expect that Luxembourg because of its size would be closer to the Maltese or Slovenian contexts, but the reality is quite different. Luxembourg has one of the most diverse populations in the EU and is one of its most poly-ethnic societies. However, in policy terms, it tends to follow the French 'univer-salist' model, Luxembourg's policies and services are geared towards voluntary integration on the part of foreigners. Refugees and asylum seekers are, therefore, integrated into the existing judicial, economic and social structures. Thus, sports activities put in place specifically for this group of people were rare, and such examples as did exist were driven by the voluntary sector. Thus, for example, Caritas, a non-governmental organisation (NGO) organised the *Sports Passe-Partout* scheme targeted at refugees and asylum seekers, which incorpor-ates such events as football tournaments to bring the Caritas team into closer contact with these groups, breaking down formal barriers. Caritas has arranged with sporting clubs to allow asylum seekers and refugees to participate in train-ing sessions, including, for example, young Africans who want to take up boxing again. Thus, in general terms, Caritas has sought to integrate asylum seekers and refugees into existing sports organisations; so, for instance, it will encourage them to join the sports events organised by the municipalities.

Asylum seekers, refugees and immigrants in general, are not accounted for as ethnic groups. The government body in charge of national statistics, Statec, carries out its population census employing the categories of 'Luxembourgers' and 'Aliens'. Among those incorporated in the category 'Alien' are the main immigrant groups whose countries of origin tend to be EU Member States. In fact, non-EU Aliens come under the simplified denomination of 'Other' and represent 24,600 people (out of a national population of 448,300) for the 2003 census.

Belgium has a relatively heterogeneous population. In 2002, 8.2 per cent of its population were immigrants, and, given its own federal structure and linguis-tic and cultural cleavages, cultural diversity is considered the norm. The country's policy of integration seeks to balance between general and specific measures of integration, with a more decentralised consideration or application at federal and regional levels. The Royal Commissariat for Immigration Policy, *Le Commissariat Royal a la politique des immigrés* (CRPI), is the consultative insti-tution responsible for defining the orientation of a new federal policy in terms of immigration. It was established in 1989 as a response, according to Bousetta and Marechal (2003), to the increase in popularity of the far right after the municipal elections of 1988, particularly in the Flanders region. The CRPI has proposed a number of measures in order to facilitate linguistic and economic integration as well as prevention of the social exclusion of migrants and minorities. The work of the CRPI was followed by the Centre for Equality and by other communities and regions, which have adopted elements of integration policy that are proper to their roles in the decentralised Belgian system.

Public community sports services often work together with local youth and integration institutes on multicultural programmes or initiatives. The Institute for Sport Management (ISB), for example, took over the co-ordination of the annual Neighbourhood Ball campaigns (after the withdrawal of the King Boudewijn Foundation) in cities and communities with a high concentration of ethnically diverse groups.

Similarly, the *Koninklijke Belgische Voetbalbond* (KBVB), Belgium's national soccer federation, started a campaign 'Fighting Racism in Football' in the 1990s. Initiatives were developed through the co-operation of the clubs – the KBVB and FIFA to work on two themes, racism among football fans and discrimination in the clubs; with programmes such as 'The United Colours of Football', 'Show Racism the Red Card' and 'Go for Girls', they have tried to eliminate racism from football stadiums.

In 1978, the new constitution of **Spain** established a federal parliamentary structure in the public sector. The federal structure comprises 17 regional autonomous communities, which have their own statutes and elected parliaments. The level of responsibilities assumed by the communities varies, some having greater powers vis-à-vis central government than others. Central government has responsibility for the political economy and international affairs, whereas the communities deal with social policies and provision including health care, social services, education and culture. The Communities are divided into smaller territories governed by elected *Diputaciones* (Provincial County Councils), which form a link between the town halls and the central government. The town halls (*ayuntamientos*) are governed by the Law Governing Bases of Local Government and have the most direct contact with citizens. Town halls are governed by elected mayors and are key actors in the provision of sport.

Immigration is a relatively recent social, political and economic issue in Spain, and the policy and provision responses to immigration are thus new in comparison to other EU countries such as the United Kingdom or Germany. Before entering the European Community (EC) in 1986, Spain conformed to European legislation that restricted immigration by people from outside the EC by establishing its first immigration law, or *Ley de Extranjería*. The focus of this legislation was on the short-term control of existing immigrant residents particularly in relation to access to the labour market. In 1996, the law was amended with the aim of shifting the focus to immigrant rights (civil, social, legal and political) in acceptance of immigration as a structural fact in Spanish society. The emphasis of immigration policy, therefore, changed from control to integration. This prioritising of integration was established as part of Spanish law in January 2000 with the Law on the Rights and Freedoms of Foreigners in Spain and their Integration (Law 4/2000).

The Plan Greco was an initiative of the Immigration Department within the Interior Ministry, rather than under the Labour Ministry where immigration policy had previously been formulated. It was implemented during the period 2001–4 and involved cross-ministry action including the Ministries of Foreign Affairs; Justice; Internal Affairs; Education, Culture and Sports; Employment and Social Affairs; Public Administration; and Health and Consumption. A key role was thus acknowledged for the regional governments in the integration of immigrants.

The notion of national minorities is built into the Spanish constitution with the establishment of the regional governmental units, the Autonomous Communities. Those with the strongest claims on the part of national minorities for independent political and cultural expression are Catalonia, Euskadi (the Basque Country), Galicia and Navarra and these Autonomous Communities have the strongest regional powers.

Despite the existence of groups such as the 'Vaqueiros de alzada' in Asturias and the 'Agotes' in Navarra that could be described as ethnically distinct – the only major ethnic minority is the Gitano (a subgrouping of the European Roma population). This nomadic group arrived in Spain towards the end of the Middle Ages and is located around the country, with concentrations found in Madrid, Barcelona and the larger cities in Andalusia. The first programme targeted at the Gitano population began in 1988 under the Ministry of Social Affairs in collaboration with the Communities, town halls and Gitano organisations. The main areas of action focused on employment, training, adult literacy, health care, housing and preservation of cultural identity.

Immigration in Spain is concentrated in certain geographic areas: Barcelona, Madrid, Andalusia, Valencia, Canary Islands and the Balearic Islands. The control and integration of immigrant populations is largely the responsibility of the regional and local governments in collaboration with the regional and local branches of NGOs and thus varies according to locality. The NGOs have considerable responsibility in policy implementation, as an active role for civil society is promoted but at the same time controlled through the allocation of resources by regional and local government. In order to gain a full picture of policy and provision, it would be necessary to undertake a separate analysis of the Communities, Provisional County Councils and the Town Halls.

There appears to be little or no published literature on policy and provision of sporting services for ethnic minorities in Spain at the national level. At the regional level, each Community decides its own policy regarding sport provision for immigrants, refugees and asylum seekers. The Communities with highest levels of immigration have been among the first to include immigrants in sport policy formulation. It must be stressed that these are the first examples of including immigrants in sport policy, and policy development is still in its infancy.

There are no clear examples of sport and immigration programmes as such. Rather, ad hoc collaborations existed between voluntary and regional/local level public sector organisations. In Catalonia for example, the Generalitat (regional autonomous government for Catalonia) has included immigration in its sports policy, stating that

> sport is probably one of the most effective means of integration. When we take part in sport we are all equal, and so cultural, ethnic and racial differences disappear. Thanks to sport, we are able to create links with immigrants that can be maintained in day to day life.

In Catalonia, immigration is included as a main area of sport policy along with education, health, work, the environment, urbanism and tourism.

In the Community of Madrid, the commitment is less explicit, with a broad commitment being made to 'the diffusion of physical and sports activities among all sectors of the population, in particular those that are most disadvantaged'. While women and people with disabilities are identified as disadvantaged groups, there is no specific mention of immigrants, refugees or asylum seekers.

The example of Barcelona's municipal sports plan highlights similarities to the Generalitat and the Community of Madrid. One of the three main policy commitments stated was to make Barcelona, 'a city that enabled and promoted the practice of sport – sport that socially constructs the city'. As part of the expert panel discussions that contributed to the formulation of the municipal plan, immigration was identified as a key issue, having a role to play in the redistribution of economic resources to young immigrants.

These examples from the national and more particularly the regional and local levels highlight how sport has been identified as a key means to integrating immigrants into the local community, but that this has still not moved much beyond a policy commitment, with few examples of concrete activities or programmes.

It was difficult to identify action in the voluntary sports sector by NGOs. This is perhaps a result of the lack of research in this area. At a seminar on sport and immigration held in November 2001 at the National Institute of Physical Education of Catalonia (INEFC), research findings were presented from Spanish studies on immigration in general, but little was presented specifically on sport and immigration. Some examples were, however, highlighted of localised action involving local immigrant associations and local authorities.

One such example from Barcelona was the Ramadan indoor football tournament, organised by the Socio-cultural Association Ibn Batula from the Raval neighbourhood, which has a large immigration population, particularly from North Africa. This competition was organised annually during the period of Ramadan after 8 p.m. Most of the participants are immigrants or members of ethnic minorities, but the tournament is open to everyone. Another example from the province of Barcelona comes from the area of Sant Adrià de Besos, where the Hispano-Pakistani Cultural Association organises cricket courses in collaboration with the town hall. These examples highlight the existence of collaborations between the voluntary (particularly associations representing immigrant populations) and public sector in the provision of sports activities for immigrants.

As König and Perchinig (2003) point out, despite a long history of immigration and emigration and despite its historical role as a bridge between Eastern and Western Europe, **Austria** does not officially see itself as a country of immigration. Pressure following the demise of the communist bloc and the rise of the right-wing Freedom Party under Jörg Haider resulted in the introduction of significant restrictions for immigrants in the early 1990s.

> Whereas in many European countries the legal differences between citizens and non-citizens have gradually been reduced, the legal restrictions governing non-EU-immigrants with regard to employment, housing, social and political rights are the most important obstacles to social and political integration in Austria.
>
> (König and Perchinig 2003: p. 7)

Nevertheless, in the 2001 census, the Austrian population stood at 8,032,926 inhabitants, with 709,926 foreign inhabitants of whom 116,016 were born in Austria. One-third of these 'foreign' inhabitants came from the former Yugoslavia, one-fifth from Turkey and the rest from the EU and other nationalities.

The recent introduction of language tests for immigrants reflected a strong emphasis on assimilationist policy, reflecting something of German ethno-nationalist philosophy:

> The term 'integration' is mostly used in debates on immigration control, where it serves as an argument to stop further legal immigration: 'Integration (shall come) before new immigration' ('Integration vor Neuzuwanderung') is a key concept of the government since 1997, when it was introduced by the Social democratic–Conservative coalition, with a strong emphasis on understanding 'integration' as German language acquisition and adapting to an 'Austrian way of life'. It was used to legitimate further restrictions on legal immigration and asylum.
>
> (König and Perchinig 2003: p. 7)

Despite the somewhat tougher stance on new immigrants, sporting initiatives aimed at integrating minorities and at combating discrimination have been launched and sustained. The Fair Play-vidc campaign, for example, has been operating in various schemes since 1997, with partnership from the European Commission and Union of European Football Associations (UEFA). It promotes football as a vehicle for tackling discrimination and has been used, for example, to promote European-African sporting relations in particular.

Sweden straddles the homogeneous/heterogeneous divide. On the one hand, it has a population that records an 85 per cent membership of the Lutheran Church of Sweden. On the other hand, it has a national minority in the form of the Sami, and, since 1940, immigration has accounted for 40 per cent of population growth. Sports policy also straddles the divide between multiculturalism and assimilation. On the one hand, the Swedish Sports Federation (SISU) provides support for training ethnic minority sports leaders and for sports projects targeting such groups, while on the other, much policy effort goes into assimilating immigrant groups into 'mainstream' Swedish civic society.

Since the publishing of the government Bill paper *Sweden, The Future and Diversity: from Immigration to Integration Policy* (Nr 1997/98:16), greater emphasis has been placed on dealing with individuals from ethnic groups rather than the groups themselves. For new arrivals, for example, there is a special induction programme lasting approximately two years, which is offered to each individual on arrival in a municipality. A state grant of 154,000 SEK is paid for each adult refugee resettled in a municipality; for children, the equivalent figure is 94,500 SEK (2001 figures). This sum is expected to cover the extra costs arising in conjunction with the reception of the refugee in the municipality, including any financial assistance paid out under the Social Assistance Act, accommodation, Swedish tuition, childcare, education and training, interpreters' fees, administrative costs, and so on. The grant is expected to suffice for all costs paid by the municipality during the entire introductory period. An additional grant is payable for elderly or disabled refugees and for unaccompanied minor children.

There has been a discernable shift in Swedish society since the 1950s from integration, in the sense of accepting and promoting cultural difference and cultural distinctiveness, towards integration, in the sense of 'togetherness' (assimilation into existing Swedish institutions) which is reflected in the mixed composition of sports clubs.

A range of local initiatives has been developed within this general policy philosophy. An example is a Health Improvement Project organised by SISU in the community of Tensta, a multicultural area of Stockholm. This was a two-year programme focusing on the unemployed or early-retired (through ill health) and women from immigrant communities. The aims of the project included prevention of social isolation; physical, psychological, social and cultural development of the participants; improvement of knowledge about sport; development of positive attitudes and improvement in general health. The project involved 200 members of immigrant groups, and cooperation was established with health consultants, sport clubs, sport facilities and arenas, SISU representatives and the Women's Centre in Stockholm. The activities were organised emphasising training in leadership, elementary gymnastics, discussion groups in preventive drug abuse work, training in social interaction, aqua-gymnastics, nutrition and public health, swimming and lectures in specific themes like massage, dance or self-defence. SISU organised leaders and guest speakers for all groups.

Denmark has a tradition of assimilationist policy. Immigration became a politically significant topic and was associated with political gains by the Far Right in Danish politics in the 1990s. In fact, since 1973, the official position has been that immigration is only possible on two grounds, asylum and family reunification.

There have been relatively few policies at national level that have specifically targeted ethnic minorities in relation to sport and culture. Ethnic minorities are seen as benefiting from the same measures as those aimed at meeting the general needs of the Danish population, and there has traditionally been resistance in government to providing funding for ethnic minorities even up to the same level as for Danish citizens. For instance, legislation on integration of refugees reduces their social benefits by up to 50 per cent compared with Danish citizens for a period of seven years. Thus, funding for special schemes has tended to be viewed negatively by many who see it as rendering such groups as clients of social services rather than self-sustaining citizens. As the Minister for Refugees, Immigration and Integration Affairs expressed it, 'the crucial mechanism of integration is the sound of cash boxes being snapped shut' (*Jyllandsposten* 17 November 2002: quoted in Stenum 2003).

At central government level, there has been a recent reorganisation. The Ministry for Refugee, Immigration and Integration Affairs was created in November 2001, following the establishment of a think tank on integration in 2000. When the Ministry was created, several fields were transferred from already existing ministries, in particular that of integration. There are a number of projects (for example, in the field of urban regeneration) that have subsequently been launched and which benefit ethnic minorities. The most recent project, announced in March 2004 by the Minister for Integration, Bertel Haarder, represented an initiative of the two major Danish Sport Federations – *Danmarks Idrætsfor-bund* (DIF), *Danske Gymnastik- og Idrætsforeninger* (DGI) with the Danish Youth Association *Dansk Ungdoms Fællesråd* (DUF). The project is called 'Participation of Children Coming From Difficult Family Backgrounds in Sport and Club Life' and provides finance to allow membership of sports clubs. It is recognised that this will disproportionately assist members of ethnic minorities, helping them to establish networks and social capital useful for fostering employment possibilities.

However, it is at the local authority level that much policy activity takes place seeking to integrate ethnic minorities into mainstream culture. The situation in each local authority can be very different, for example, with regard to the social and ethnic background of the population and the political priorities of the administration. Some local authorities not only support the local clubs financially, among other things by giving money for sports instructors, but also initiate projects that motivate the public engagement of immigrants (among others) in joining a club. Furthermore, some authorities offer counselling and funding of specific projects with the aim of promoting sporting activities including some projects that target ethnic minorities. However, funds are normally given to the clubs that conduct the projects, and thus assistance from the state is 'at arm's length'.

Those policies that do exist, in formal terms at least, emphasise assimilation rather than multiculturalism. For example, the counselling project 'Diversity, Culture, Leisure', with five workers funded by the municipality of Copenhagen, despite its use of the term 'diversity' in the title, has the principal goal of integrating ethnic minorities into existing sporting and cultural organisations.

In **Portugal**, in 1995, the government appointed a High Commissioner for Immigration and Ethnic Minorities (HCIEM), whose office forms part of the Presidency of the Council of Ministers. The creation of this organisation was due to the recognition of the new challenges faced by Portugal as a country of immigration, which required social integration measures for migrant families and ethnic minorities in general, in order to avoid situations of social exclusion that generate racism and xenophobia. The High Commissioner's mandate is to accompany and support the integration of immigrants at inter-ministerial level.

A new law on entry and regulation of foreign citizens was introduced in February 2003. Despite referring to the respect for the immigrants' social and cultural identity, the law is clear when defining the responsibilities of the High Commissariat as: 'the promotion of the knowledge and acceptance of the Portuguese language, laws, and also of the cultural and moral values of the Portuguese Nation as conditions for a complete integration' (Article no. 2b, DL no. 251/2002, 22 November). Noteworthy here is the explicit requirement of acceptance by immigrants of the moral and cultural values of the nation.

As Esteves *et al.* (2003: p. 3) point out: 'Considering that immigrants will be part of the Portuguese society, one might wonder if their moral and cultural values can also be incorporated into the Portuguese Nation in order to enrich it.' In order to develop closer work with immigrant communities living in the municipalities, some local authorities have established immigrant consultative councils or special offices to attend to immigrants' needs. Lisbon and Amadora were the pioneers in founding consultative councils where associations representing immigrants and local authorities discuss issues pertinent to both parties. However, budgetary constraints due to an environment of economic recession have led to a substantial reduction of expenditures, and the activities developed in the scope of the consultative councils have had to be included in general activities of the municipalities.

No budget provision, therefore, is now made for the activities developed with immigrants' associations. This is a prejudicial situation to them, as through consultative councils, associations had a privileged contact with local authorities. Their requests and needs were 'more efficiently' attended to, and they voiced their opinions about local policies directly to the mayor and deputy mayors. Now, they must fill their requests for financing and support to the respective municipal department (sports, health, culture) just like other associations, which makes it more difficult for them to obtain the help needed (Esteves *et al.* 2003).

Nevertheless, a number of governmental and NGOs aim to meet the general and sporting needs of national ethnic minorities and immigrant populations. These include the State Secretariat for Sport, the Ministry of Defence, Higher

Sports Council, Portuguese Council for Refugees, High Commission for Immigrants and Ethnic minorities, the Cape Verdean United Association, Guinea Association, Casa do Brasil, SOS Racisme and Olho Vivo. The Cape Verdean United Association incorporates associations from, for example, Sines, Oeiras and Lisbon and organise formal and non-formal sports competitions and, in some cases, also have teams competing at a national level (for example, a female handball team) from the ethnic population.

In **Poland** in the post-communist period, there is evidence of some attention being paid to issues of multiculturalism, though Poland is still relatively homogeneous (ethnic populations make up around 3 per cent of the total population). Poland introduced new legislation to reflect the requirements of EU membership in 2001 in the form of the Amended Act on Aliens. However, this regulation was preoccupied with dealing with the control of immigration flows rather than with social provision for the ethnic minorities themselves.

> Immigration has not been discussed in terms of social or economic policy, nor was it perceived as an option within these policies. This is understandable in light of high unemployment among the Poles, whose reduction formed the main objective of both policies. The presence of foreigners in Poland is, at the same time, a relatively new social phenomenon, and constituting just a fraction of the population, the foreigners are not perceived as a burning social issue.
>
> (Iglicka *et al.* 2003: p. 8)

Policies dealing with national minorities do exist. The construction of county level Voivodships, in the new political system in 1989 took account of the distribution of national minorities, and thus policy at Voivod level may de facto incorporate provision for ethnic groups by virtue of their regional concentration. Education programmes in 620 institutions are provided in languages other than Polish, and many of these institutions are responsible for delivery of the physical education curriculum.

A major initiative currently being introduced is the Programme for the Roma Community 2004–13. This follows a pilot programme in the Malopolski Province (2001–03) and focuses on employment, health, hygiene, living conditions and Roma participation in civic society. Although sport is not explicitly mentioned in the programme outline, it could be incorporated into certain aspects of the programme such as 'Roma involvement in civic society' and 'educational integration of children and youth'.

However, beyond state initiatives, in respect of religious-affiliated groups, there are a number of voluntary sector organisations that provide sporting opportunities for ethnic (national) minorities by virtue of their religious affiliation. Such groups include: the Lutheran Sports Organisations in Poland, Greek Orthodox Sports Organisation in Poland, the YMCA, the 'MACABI' Sports Club, Salezian Sports Organisation, Jozef Kalasancjusz Associations *Parafiada*, and the *Katolickie Stowarzyszenie Sportowe RP*.

The Parafiada is particularly significant since it has used sport in bringing together Catholic young people from Poland and other European countries, most significantly Ukraine, Latvia, Lithuania, Estonia, Russia, Belarus and Moldova, to promote common understanding in a festival each year since 1988. In 2004, 1,800 participants took part in a week's activity, which involved religious and cultural activity as well as sport. The Parafiada Organisation was successful in obtaining funding from the European Year of Education through Sport (EYES) programme for its activities, and its explicit goals included (amongst others) the following:

- the integration of children and youth groups from various communities, including disabled;
- the acquisition of skills of solidarity and mutual tolerance and understanding in a multicultural environment;
- the integration of children and youth from countries of Central and Eastern Europe.

The use of sport for social integration purposes is thus only indirectly supported by government, where, for example, the resources of the Academy of Physical Education and of the armed forces are provided to support initiatives such as that of Parafiada.

Hungary, like Poland, has a relatively homogeneous population (approximately 3 per cent are members of ethnic minorities). It has traditionally been more concerned with policing immigration than with enhancing their integration.

> The OIN [Office of Immigration and Nationality] decided to launch, in March 2003, a project targeting the formulation of a policy for the integration of refugees and other migrants, funded by the Dutch Government and implemented by a Dutch consulting agency in co-operation with the Welfare and Logistics Department of the OIN's Asylum Division (the fact that the OIN designated its asylum branch to deal with immigrant integration reflects the continuing lack of recognition of immigration as a social issue, but possibly also points toward increasing awareness of that issue within the agency).
>
> (Kováts *et al.* 2003: p. 3)

Notwithstanding this, the Hungarian government has promoted support for initiatives with the Roma population, which constitutes 1.95 per cent of the population, in sport and in education. The second National Anti-Racism Day organised in 2004 by the Ministry of Sport, the Hungarian Football Association and the Ministry of the Interior incorporated matches involving the national Roma and Slovene minorities' teams at senior and junior levels.

Based on the 2000 census data for **Italy**, there are about one million immigrant residents (including economic migrants, refugees and asylum seekers) of foreign origin, which corresponds to 2.6 per cent in a total population of 56.8 million. The majority of the immigrant population are from Albania, Morocco, Tunisia, Romania and the Philippines. In addition, a number of foreigners without legal status ('clandestini' or 'irregolari'), generally estimated at between 200,000 and 300,000 persons, are also present in Italy. However, most of the 'clandestini' who have entered Italy since the mid-1990s have obtained legal status.

There are few specific policies that target ethnic communities in Italy. Italian society is perceived as homogeneous, where the presence of foreign migrants, seeking asylum and/or better socio-economic conditions, is quite a new phenomenon. Providing specific policies that target a particular ethnic community is generally conceived as reflecting separatism and discrimination. Thus, integration in the Italian context is assimilationist, aiming more at applying general measures for social cohesion, rather than integration in the sense of diversity.

The rare examples of government and non-government agencies providing sporting services to ethnic minorities and immigrant communities include: the Ministry of Social Solidarity, Ministry of Internal Affairs, Ministry of Education, Centre for Development Information and Education – Solidarity in Motion and Caritas.

The *Unione Italiana Sport Per tutti* (UISP) has developed a series of programmes that concentrate on communication and dialogue between migrants and Italians, while promoting initiatives to build contacts. The aim of these programmes is to assist immigrant communities to organise sports activities.

UISP works also with provinces in organising sporting projects which aim at intercultural dialogue and mutual acceptance. The organisation has five sets of aims:

1   to promote recreational, cultural and sport activities that aim at maintaining specific cultures and identities of immigrant communities in Italy;
2   to generate inter cultural dialogue, in particular the project of Centro Olympic Maghreb in Genoa aiming at immigrants from North Africa, South America, Eastern Europe;
3   promotion of events such as the Anti-racist World Cup which involves mixed teams (men and women) from different ethnic minorities;
4   development of initiatives to combat ethnic and social prejudices such as the 'Ultra Project' targeting football fans at national and international level; and
5   projects at the international level: for example, the Peace Games which aims to promote peace through sport and other recreational activities in areas of crisis in Africa, Middle East and the Balkans; and the campaign *Una speranza per il futuro* (A hope for the future) which provides funds for the reconstruction of a sport camp in Mostar.

Ireland is incorporated within the homogeneous group and has traditionally been a country of emigration, though this tendency has reversed with the long-term growth of the Irish economy. It has little by way of sport policy targeting the immigrant communities, an exception being Sport Against Racism in Ireland. This programme stages a festival each year with the aim of integrating ethnic minorities using sport as a tool. In addition, special measures have begun to be addressed at Ireland's national minority of Travellers, which were recognised as a distinct ethnic group in the 2002 census.

According to the January 2004 Monthly Statistics Report of the Reception and Integration Agency, there were 7,249 asylum seekers in the system of direct provision of accommodation – 0.19 per cent of the total population. Sixty-eight per cent had been in direct provision for six months or more, while 7 per cent have been in that situation for more than two years. Since 1992, over 59,000 people have applied for asylum in Ireland. Just under 9,000 have got either refugee status or temporary leave to remain. In 2003, over 1,100 asylum seekers were recognised as refugees in Ireland

According to the Irish Sports Council, the notion that sport can be a cohesive force in Irish society is accepted and initiatives are in place at local level to achieve this. There is a lack of a clearly formulated and articulated national policy on this issue on the part of government and the agencies involved in sport. The view has been expressed that it is more appropriate to use a 'bottom up' approach with respect to sport acting as a cohesive force, which may explain the absence of a documented policy.

Integration of the Irish Travellers ethnic minority is a new concern for the Irish government. They have been recognised officially as an ethnic minority category or ethnically distinct community in the 2002 population census. Travellers are an indigenous minority who have been part of Irish society for centuries. They have a long shared history, cultural values, language, customs and traditions that make them a self-defined group, both recognisable and distinct. Their culture and way of life, of which nomadism is an important factor, distinguishes them from the sedentary population and clarifies their ethnic status. The median age for the traveller community is 18 years compared with the national figure of 32. Traveller infant mortality is three times greater than the national average. Although the number of traveller children attending school has increased in recent years, the numbers decrease substantially as children get older and in 2004, there were only 16 young Travellers in any form of higher education.

The sport with which male members of the Traveller community have been most closely associated is boxing. One of their members, Francie Barrett has represented Ireland in the Olympic Games, and many are members of clubs and participate in national and international competitions. In the case of the club located in Crumlin (Dublin), as of June 2004, one-third of its members (approximately 80) are from the Traveller Community. One club member (a Traveller) holds two Irish titles and has been invited to join the Irish Amateur Boxing Association (IABA) High Performance Programme. In discussing the popularity of boxing among Travellers, tradition was frequently mentioned as being a facilitating factor. There is a culture of toughness among this ethnic group and being able to defend oneself is considered important.

The sport of handball operates under the auspices of the Gaelic Athletic Association and used to be very popular among members of the Traveller Community. Currently, its popularity is concentrated in certain parts of the country and County Clare is one such area. While St. Joseph's Training Centre in Ennis does not have sports facilities, since 1989 it has had handball teams participating in local league competitions with considerable success. This initiative was a product of voluntary effort and received a small amount of funding from the public sector through Clare Local Sports Partnership and a more significant sum from the St. Joseph's Training Centre itself.

In **Greece**, nationality is defined by descent or ethnic affiliation. Thus, all Greek minorities living all over the world can retain full citizenship rights as long as they wish. The ethnic make-up of the population of Greece has been significantly affected by the situation in the Balkans, with substantial movement from Albania, Bulgaria and other Balkan states (an inflow of 300,000 in the early 1990s). It is estimated that Greece now has some one million immigrants, many illegal, and this has placed considerable strain on internal relations with ethnic groups.

> It must be noted that Greece, which is a country with a high level of cultural and ethnic homogeneity related mostly to language and religion, has increasingly come under scrutiny and partial challenge, a factor which plays a significant role in the policy and public debates concerning immigration. On the one hand, Greek policies seem to disapprove of the cultural diversity within the country and adopt a forced tolerance towards minority rights. On the other hand, public opinion, a considerable portion of the political leadership, and the Church believe that the recent history of the Balkans and Greece's fragile contemporary geopolitical position in the region, are legitimate reasons to impose restrictions on minority behaviours and foreign nationals.
>
> In addition, the sudden demographic transformation caused by the flow of immigrants from Eastern European countries during the 1990s has connected the presence of about one million of immigrants with the economic recession, the rise of unemployment and the rise of criminality in recent years.
>
> (Lykovardi and Petroula 2003: p. 5)

Given these difficulties, it is perhaps unsurprising that social and cultural integration policy has not been a priority and that where it has existed it has tended to be assimilationist in orientation. Traditionally, Greece has seen itself as having a strong, historical core culture, with a homogeneous population, the exception to this being the Turkish, Muslim population of Western Thrace. Recent policy attention has also been focused on the situation of the Roma minority. These groups are served by general programmes, which are targeted locally (such as 'Sport for All'). These programmes are, in some cases, located in areas of spatial concentration of minority groups rather than specifically initiated for them. The programme Immigrants in Greece 2003–06 is intended to focus comprehensively on the needs of immigrant populations, and as this initiative is further developed, it will be interesting to see whether sport is employed within the programme.

The three small states of **Malta, Cyprus** and **Slovenia** declare themselves as relatively homogeneous, though membership of the EU may add to immigration pressures. The description of policy given by our Slovene respondents expresses succinctly the approach adopted here: 'since culturally diverse populations are not treated differently in Slovenia. .. there are no sport related programmes that would attempt to establish a dialogue between different cultural communities (Tusak and Kajtna, 2004: private correspondence) Cyprus is something of a special case. The response to our questions in the research template returned for Cyprus related to the situation in the Greek community, but the possibility of an eventual reuniting of the Greek and Turkish populations seems likely to provide the need for a new response, since effectively a large national minority will be evident and the relations between the two communities in cultural terms (as well as political and economic terms) will become critical. One relevant example of a sport-based initiative is the Trust Games, established by informal groups (because of the difficulty of relations between Greek and Turkish Cypriot formal bodies) which brought together young people from both sides of the border through sport to engage in dialogue and to promote understanding.

The **Czech Republic** became much more homogenous at a stroke, as far as the ethnic structure is concerned, with its separation from Slovakia. Although national/ethnic minorities represent 5.2 per cent of the demographic structure of the population, the most numerous is the newly recognised Slovak national minority which is strongly culturally and linguistically integrated. Conversely, assimilation, especially linguistic, has affected the Roma, Slovak, German, Polish and other minorities. With the exception of numerous, but dispersed, groups of Slovaks and Roma, no national minority occupies a prominent position in the current ethnic make-up of the Czech population. Public sector sports providers do not make specific provision for national or ethnic minorities though voluntary sector organisations such as the Centre for Refugees and the Society of Citizens Assisting Emigrants use occasional sporting projects.

There has, however, been significant concern expressed in relation to the treatment of the Roma minority:

> De facto discrimination against ethnic Roma in the country remained the most disturbing human rights problem in 2001, affecting access to justice, education, housing, employment, and public services. Little progress was made in implementing the Czech government's long-term strategy to improve the situation of the Romany minority, adopted in June 2000.
>
> (Human Rights Watch 2002)

Provision for the Roma community in terms of sport is neglected, as are more basic forms of social provision.

The position of ethnic minorities in **Slovakia** has traditionally been very difficult. Of the population of 5.4 million in the 2001 census, 85.7 per cent described themselves as Slovak, 9.7 per cent as Hungarians, 1.7 per cent as Roma, with Czechs, Russians, Ukrainians, Germans and others representing less than 1 per cent each. The Roma population is, however, regarded as significantly underestimated in these figures, and its size was estimated as 500,000 at the time of the 1992 census.

While both the major ethnic minority groups suffer from major disadvantages in social and economic terms, political representation for the Hungarian population has been reasonably developed. The Party of the Hungarian Coalition (SMK) gained 11.2 per cent of the vote and 20 seats in the unicameral National Council (Slovak Parliament) in the 2002 elections. The Roma community was not represented in either the National Council (Slovak parliament) or in regional parliaments. The marginalisation of the community as well as its internal fragmentation has resulted in a lack of political unity and thus in inadequate representation even in most self-governing communities.

The Hungarian Slovak population has been involved in protracted and often bitter dispute with the Slovakian state about its rights in various cultural and political spheres. The Hungarian Government has also been drawn into the development of Treaty provisions with Slovakia in relation to protection of Hungarian population's rights. A succession of right wing governmental initiatives aimed at a strong version of assimilation provided a backdrop to this concern on the part of the Hungarian Government.

The Roma population has, however, been subject to political as well as social and economic exclusion. It has no political representation at either national or local levels, and its socio-economic circumstances are significantly worse than those of its disadvantaged Hungarian compatriots. A recent report describes their situation in the following terms:

> The Roma minority in Slovakia is linguistically and culturally a non-homogenous group comprising some 10 percent of the total population of the country. Slovak Roma generally live in very poor social conditions. Their rate of unemployment exceeds the national average by far, reaching close to 100 percent in settlements located in Central and Eastern Slovakia. Lack of education, segregation, and poverty lead to create extremely poor health conditions and low life expectancy among the Roma. Empirical evidence on this has been provided by a recent study [which] ... found that in poor Roma settlements the average age is 25.7 years and average life expectancy is 35 years. An environment without safe potable water and proper sewage contributes to dramatically high mortality.

> (European Commission 2003: pp. 1–2)

The Slovak Government prepared in 2003 a *Concept Strategy for Roma Integration*, but although this deals with a range of forms of integration including cultural action, it makes no specific reference to the use of sport.

Each of the Baltic States has its own political and cultural trajectories, though in terms of the important issues relating to inter-ethnic relations, the situations in **Latvia** and **Estonia** have been quite different from that in **Lithuania**. While Estonia's population consists of 61.5 per cent Estonians and 30.3 per cent Russians, Latvia's consists of 52 per cent Latvians and 34 per cent Russians and Lithuania's population consists of 79.6 per cent Lithuanian and 9.4 per cent Russian together with 7 per cent Poles. In addition, upon restoration of independence, the Lithuanian Government offered free choice of citizenship to all permanent residents except Soviet military personnel and their families, and the vast majority opted for Lithuanian citizenship.

In Estonia and Latvia the situation is very different.

> In Estonia and Latvia, a large part of the population was – and still is – ethnically non-Estonian (40% in 1993, 35% today) or non-Latvian (almost half then, 44% today). The great majority of these peoples were not accepted as Estonian or Latvian citizens when these states regained their independence in 1991. Instead of offering citizenship to all residents on the basis of a 'zero-option' formula, like all other states on the territory of the former Soviet Union did, the Estonian and Latvian Governments restricted automatic citizenship to those who had held it before the Soviet occupation and their direct descendants.
>
> (Zaagman 1999: p. 23)

Zaagman goes on to describe the reasons for adopting this initial post-independence strategy in relation to citizenship.

> The non-citizens were for the most part not integrated in Estonian or Latvian society and often did not speak the national language. Most ethnic Estonians and Latvians considered them as illegal immigrants, their presence a product of the policy of enforced Russification .... Many Estonians and Latvians still fear that they will one day find themselves a minority in their own country, unable to preserve their language and national identity.
>
> (Zaagman 1999: p. 23)

Although citizenship laws have subsequently been liberalised to some degree in both countries, largely as a product of external pressures, this has not been without difficulties (in Latvia, for example, a national referendum on the liberalising legislation was forced on the government by opposition), and as late as July 2004, a Russian-sponsored resolution to the meeting of the Organisation for Security and Cooperation in Europe was debated, which criticised both countries for failing to implement legislation. In these circumstances, it is perhaps unsurprising that in both of these states, there is little evidence that the use of sport for integration has been developed. In both cases, and in particular in Latvia, the fear of eventual domination of a Russian-speaking population (emotively referred to as 'statistical genocide') has led to an emphasis on linguistic and cultural assimilation.

Some rare examples of generic efforts in the field of cultural integration are evident. For example, in 2001, the Latvian government launched the national program 'The Integration of Society in Latvia'. However, according to the researcher Svetlana Diatchkova:

> The Integration Program and governmental policy in general do not pay sufficient attention to the concerns of civil society and minorities in the field of minority rights, such as the need for greater access to education and electronic media in the mother tongue, greater promotion of minority languages, the need for dialogue between minorities and the state, and the effective participation of minorities in public life.
>
> (Terskinas 2002)

There are also some efforts on the part of the voluntary sector to promote sporting opportunities for national minorities such as the Latvian Lithuanian Communities whose team of athletes:

> participated in the V World Lithuanian Games, winning 30 medals (14 gold and 16 silver), and in the VI Games, 9 gold medals. Other sports events [organised by the LLC included]: the Latvian National Minorities Sports Festival of children and youth, health and sports festivals, and the best-sporting-family competitions.
>
> (Lithuanian Community in Latvia 2004)

Although the situation of the minorities in terms of citizenship and political participation is much more settled than in the neighbouring Baltic states, the public sector in Lithuania, particularly in relation to sport, is not specifically orientated towards the particular problems and needs of ethnic minorities. The prevailing orientation is for competitive/achievement sport and this reduces the impetus to discover and use the social, educational and cultural potential of sports activities.

Focusing on representative sport, national sport organisations are generally unprepared for participation in ethnic integration processes. Government policy, however, is oriented to providing equal sporting possibilities, that is, the ability to join existing sport organisations or create one's own club (for which small amounts of financial support is available). Thus, the Lithuanian public authorities and sporting associations adopt a strategy of social cohesion (assimilation) in relation to the Russian, Tatar, Ukrainian and Byelorussian minorities with some evidence of more of an emphasis on diversity (integration) in relation to the Polish and Jewish community.

There is some provision of sporting opportunities for ethnic minorities in

Lithuania on the part of central governmental and national public bodies (e.g. Centres of Ethnic Culture, Department of National Minorities and Lithuanians Living Abroad and the Police) that are not directly related to the sport domain. Some sport-related activities for younger members of ethnic groups, refugees and asylum seekers are provided through educational, cultural and socialisation or entertainment programmes without the direct involvement of sport organisations.

The initiatives to promote national identity or intercultural dialogue through sport come predominantly from the ethnic communities themselves or from external agencies (such as UEFA and the Council of Europe) and may meet with little approval in the local environment. Our research respondent in Lithuania argued that, for historical and social reasons, the level of association and communal activity of Lithuanian ethnic minorities was not high; consequently, the ethnic integration policy of local and national authorities has had a status which has been more symbolic than real.

Examples of support for Jewish and Polish communities are provided by the Lithuanian State Department of Physical Education and Sport's support for ethnic sports organisations, such as SC *Makabi* and SU *Polonija*. However, these organisations are supported as part of the 'Sport for All' initiative which targets all groups rather than ethnic minorities specifically.

Other examples include provision of basic facilities at Refugee Reception Centres, the use of sport by the Lithuanian Red Cross working with asylum seekers to combat apathy and depression and campaigns by the Lithuanian Football Federation, UEFA and sponsors to combat racism in sport through the project 'Our Nationality is Football'.

Conclusions

The pattern which we see emerging in this review of policy is one of diversity between and occasionally within states in terms of attitudes to social integration and in policy action employing sport. One of the dominant themes reported by the research teams was a lack of understanding on the part of some professionals working in sport of the policy aims of social integration, but equally a lack of understanding on the part of those working in the broader field of social and cultural integration of the potential which sport might have for engaging groups which are otherwise excluded and for bringing groups together in ways which can have positive consequences for social interaction if managed appropriately. As a consequence, there is a need for incorporation of the understanding gained from detailed local studies of good practice into the training both sports development workers and policy makers and of those working in the social and community work domain (Amara *et al.* 2005).

The empirical work for this review took place at an important juncture for the EU, with the biggest ever expansion of the EU from 15 to 25 Member States. This expansion presented further opportunities for celebration of the richness and diversity of Europe's culture, but also posed problems of ensuring social integration and cohesion. Recognition of the role which sport could play in positive terms was reflected in part in the inclusion of a competence in sport in the Draft Treaty establishing a Constitution for Europe agreed at the Intergovernmental Conference on 18 June 2004. The inclusion of sport as a competence for the first time reflected the growing pressure that had resulted first in the Declaration on Sport annexed to the Treaty of Amsterdam which came into force in 1999 and which was more fully articulated in the Declaration of Nice in 2000. With the addition of the article on sport, the responsibilities of the EU in this area of policy were to be further underlined.

At the time of writing, the introduction of the Treaty in the form proposed by the Council of Ministers in 2004 seems unlikely to be accepted having been rejected in referenda by two major members. However, even without a competence in sport per se, the EU has a strong set of rationales for intervention in sport deriving from its longer established competences. Thus, in the areas of social policy and combating social exclusion, regional policy and regional development, cultural policy and the protection of cultural identity, tourism, education and youth policy, and external relations, sport activity on the part of the EU can still have a role to play in ways which are related to aspects of multiculturalism and social cohesion of different ethnic and religious groups.

Indeed, the pursuit of non-sporting policy goals themselves has impacted on the multicultural nature of the everyday sporting experience of European citizens. One aspect of the Bosman judgement, for example, which defined certain restrictions on the nationality of players in professional football teams in Member States as contrary to the principle of freedom of movement, has rendered the professional football teams watched weekly by sports fans into multicultural playing units. For fans, sporting heroes to be drawn from a wide set of cultural backgrounds provides strong, positive images, particularly for young people.

With the expansion of the EU to 27 Member States with accession of Bulgaria and Romania in January 2007, international migration within Europe seems set to be further promoted.

7 Sport and social regulation in the city

The cases of Grenoble and Sheffield

Ian Henry and Christine Dulac

Alongside the (contested) claims about the relative decline in significance of the nation state in the face of increasing globalisation are claims about the increasing significance of the roles of transnational bodies (Chapter 6) and of cities in the development of both social and economic policy. In this context, urban sports policy and associated urban sports politics have also become increasingly significant (Cochrane *et al.* 1996; Henry 1997, 2001b). Nevertheless, with some exceptions, the comparative politics of urban sport has to date been a largely neglected phenomenon (Arnaud 1999a; Gratton and Henry 2001; Henry and Paramio Salcines 1999a). This chapter follows on from the discussion of national and transnational policy contexts in Chapter 6 to address comparative policy at the urban level, undertaking an historical analysis of the development of sports policy in a French and a British city (Grenoble and Sheffield, respectively), from the late 1960s to the end of the century. Both the cities, though very different, had given considerable prominence to sport as a policy area, and in both cases, the nature of sports policy has undergone radical change across the period in question. In undertaking this analysis, this chapter draws on the frame of social regulation theory, seeking to evaluate the theorisation of transnational phenomena within the context of this framework.

The issue of whether local politics matter has been a question of significance to political analysts for some considerable time (John and Cole 2000). The changing significance of the nation state and the city (and of transnational government) in a variety of policy domains is, as we have already noted, bound up with the phenomenon of globalisation, and social analysis has been preoccupied with attempts to conceptualise the relationship between local and global forces and actions. The rapidly increasing scope, pace and depth of economic, social and political change mean that policy actors find themselves enmeshed in a globally changing policy context. In order to explain local policy outcomes, one must make reference to global context, but the global is both context and outcome of local actions. Thus, most commentaries in characterising the local policy context seek to avoid the excesses of, on the one hand, crude determinism, where local actors are powerless to effect change when faced with global forces, and on the other hand, naïve voluntarism, with explanations of policy options adopted at local level being based on the unconstrained choices of local actors (Harding and Le Galès 1997). In the analysis presented in this chapter, we seek to articulate, within the context of regulation theory, the enabling and constraining factors which have impacted upon the urban sports policy context in these two contrasting cities which have become identified with distinctive approaches to sports policy. This represents the rationale for characterising the study reported here as a Type III study, 'theorising the transnational'.

The theoretical context: local government, sports policy and regulation theory

In developing an analysis of urban policy change in sport, this chapter seeks to consider the extent to which such change can be said to reflect changing forms of social regulation. The regulation approach, derived initially from studies of the labour process in capital accumulation (Aglietta 1998; Boyer 1986), argues that particular modes of capital accumulation are accompanied by complement-ary regimes of social regulation if they are to be sustained. This is not to suggest that specific forms of capital accumulation *require* specific forms of social regula-tion in a functionalist sense. Such forms will vary from one context to the next, but social regulation will invariably be, in some measure, compatible with eco-nomic processes (Mayer 1994).

The use of regulation theory in non-western contexts has been the subject of considerable debate, and certainly, in any teleological sense, it would be diffi-cult to make a sensible argument for societies proceeding through a shared process of development. In this sense, if we extend the use of alliteration, we are involved in 'theorising the transnational' rather than 'generalising the global'. Nevertheless, for many of the developed economies of the capitalist system of the West, three periods of capital accumulation are generally acknowledged: competitive regulation (from the mid-nineteenth century to the 1920s), Fordist regulation (1920s until early 1970s) and the transition from Fordism (some-times referred to as post-Fordism or neo-Fordism – from the early 1970s to the present day). Our focus in this chapter is on the latter two periods. In practical terms, the welfare state is said to reflect a set of social arrangements which was complementary to the conditions that held, particularly under post-Second World War Fordism, of relatively full employment and continued economic growth. Welfare provision was seen as an element of the social wage which, together with rising incomes, secured worker commitment to production in a Fordist society dominated by mass production (with work forms characterised by worker alienation). Welfare rights implied access to health, housing, education and other basic forms of social provision as well as, ultimately, the more luxury services of sport, culture and leisure. As production changed in western economies to a post-Fordist or neo-Fordist scenario (Allen 1992) in which full employment for mass production was to be replaced by automated production processes and high skill niche production, requiring lower levels of employment, so the social arrangements which accompanied this changed set of circum-stances were themselves to change. Welfare provision for all was to be replaced by the development of a two-tier policy to reflect the needs of two-tier society. One tier (those in employment and benefiting from economic growth) requires consumer rights, freedom to buy on the open market, while the second tier (those unemployed or underemployed) was likely to be provided with lower level welfare rights (to reduce national taxation levels and ensure the global competitiveness of industry), which together with increased policing and security investment would serve to guard against social instability (Christopherson 1994). 'Sport for all' in such a scenario is thus replaced by 'sport for some', residual welfare policies targeted at disadvantaged groups. The other shift implied in post-Fordist sports policy is the use of sport for city marketing. As traditional industry is replaced by service sector provision, the use of cultural provision (including sport) to capture global publicity and to attract service sector professionals is evident, as cities become more entrepreneurial in selling themselves on the global market (Boyle and Hughes 1994; Heeg *et al.* 2003; Quilley 2000; Wood 1998).

There has been a range of work which has sought to address the question of whether local government in general terms has reflected a shift in the nature of social regulation of the British (Jones 1998; Peck and Tickell 1992, 1995; Tickell and Peck 1995) and other (Boyer 2005; Fujita 2003; Kipfer and Keil 2002) contexts, but with few exceptions, little attempt has been made to address the issue of whether sports or leisure policy might form an element in a new set of approaches to local social regulation (Henry 2001a; Ravenscroft 1993). Thus, this study sets out to evaluate whether the developments in sports policy in these two contrasting cities can be accommodated within the context of a regulation theory-based account of change in the city.

Grenoble and Sheffield – leading lights in the French and British local government context

The two cities presented in this account have contrasting political, economic and cultural histories. The very particular political culture of the city of Sheffield is rooted in the nature of the local economy and social structure. The city was, until recently, renowned for its steel industry, and the concentration of employment in steel-related activity meant that the major decline in the demand for steel in the 1970s hits the local economy particularly hard (Benington 1987). From the beginning of the 1980s, the decline accelerated with local unemployment exceeding the national average from 1981 and unemployment growing threefold from 5.1 per cent in January 1980 to 15.5 per cent in September 1984. In 1971, almost half of the workforce was engaged in manufacturing industry, but this had fallen to 24 per cent by 1984, with job loss in the metal-based manufacturing sector between 1981 and 1984 being double the rate for the UK generally (Sheffield City Council 1983).

The decline of steel-related industry was compounded by the relatively poorly developed service sector, with growth in the business, financial and high-technology sectors being well below the national average (Strange 1995). The growth of 25,000 in service jobs between 1971 and 1984 in the city failed to compensate for the loss of jobs from the shrinkage in manufacturing employment.

The political control of the city had since the Second World War rested almost entirely with the Labour Party. The nature of Labour politics at the local level was nevertheless subject to local variations as well as to change over time (Gyford 1985), and after an extended period of resisting central government's attempts to reduce the size and significance of local government service provision, Sheffield adopted a series of partnership projects with local capital from the late 1980s. One such partnership project was the bid to stage the World Student Games of 1991, which was to have a profound effect, not only on local sports policy but also on urban policy more generally for the city (Lawless 1990; Seyd 1993; Strange 1993).

While Sheffield had been predominantly associated with a single traditional industry, with deindustrialisation and a relatively drab urban environment, Grenoble enjoyed a reputation for research-led economic development with, in the late 1960s and early 1970s, high-technology companies such as Hewlett-Packard (computers), Péchiny (electro-chemical research) and Becton Dickinson (paramedical development) establishing production, research and administrative headquarters in the city. With a population of 400,000 (including the suburbs) in 1975, Grenoble was seen as a good centre for attracting high-level international staff, in part because of its strong educational base but also because of the quality of the local environment, in particular the physical proximity of the city to winter sports opportunities. Unlike Sheffield, Grenoble had had a relatively indistinct political history at municipal level. As Ardagh (1990: p. 181) points out, 'Through the boom years of 1950–65 the mairie had remained in the hands of the old guard Grenoble-born notables, in turn Socialist or Gaullist by label, conservative by temperament'. With the arrival of the Dubedout administration in the city in 1965, however, the city gained a high-profile socialist mayor (though he had initially been elected as an independent) with an innovative set of policy approaches.

If the nature and reputation of the cities were very different, they also existed within very different contexts in terms of their relationship with the state in the period under review. In the French case, the state was seen to give way to growing pressures for decentralisation, with de facto powers being to some extent assumed by leading cities such as Grenoble prior to legislation, and subsequently, the legal basis of decentralisation being established in the early 1980s (Schmidt 1990). This contrasts with the UK case in which, during the 1980s, increasingly centralised power was imposed by a Conservative central government on local government in Britain, in order to curb local government expenditure (Farnham and Horton 1993; Goodwin *et al.* 1993; Leach *et al.* 1994). While Grenoble was to the fore in developing local autonomy for French cities, Sheffield was equally prominent in its (ultimately unsuccessful) attempts to oppose the dilution of local government powers by Margaret Thatcher's governments in England (Seyd 1993).

Methodology: dimensions for comparison

In order to undertake an analysis of sports policy change across the period, key stages of generic policy significance were identified in the political development of the two cities. Subsequently, following an approach derived from strategic analysis (Bernoux 1985; Friedberg 1993), policy and change were evaluated across four dimensions: ideologies or rationales for policy, objectives, strategies employed and policy outcomes (Table 7.1).

In the case of Grenoble, identifying the stages of significant political development in the city and their dates is fairly straightforward. The period divides neatly into two, covering the political control of the city by two charismatic mayors, Henri Dubedout (1965–83) and Alain Carignon (1983–95). Dubedout came to power and inherited a city which had successfully captured the Winter Olympic Games for 1968 but which had had little in the way of strategic policy goals in respect of social or physical planning. Dubedout, in addition to changes in the physical infrastructure of the city, successfully developed policies to enhance community development such that the city became known as a 'social laboratory' for urban policy, and he successfully forged a stronger role for Grenoble *vis-à-vis* the central state in the French urban policy system (Bruneteau 1998; Frappat 1979). When Alain Carignon came to power, though initially maintaining some of the Dubedout approach in respect of social development, he subsequently promoted a business agenda for the city which favoured economic development over social goals (Avrillier and Descamps 1995).

The periodisation of Sheffield's political development is slightly more

Table 7.1 Indicators employed in the analysis of the politics of sport in Grenoble and Sheffield

Dimensions	The politicians responsible for sports policy
Ideology	Distinguishing political tendencies (e.g. decentralisation/participation/community development; neo-liberal individualism/centralised control/market development)
Objectives	Dimensions of sports policy • Élite/mass participation • Image promotion/needs • Prioritising groups in need/undifferentiated provision for all
Strategies	Decisions voted upon Origins of proposals (who initiates the decision; what process is adopted in the progressing of particular proposals) Nature of the proposal – what types of intervention are proposed (e.g. provision of facilities, staff, subsidies etc).
Outcomes	The implementation of decisions How are resources spent across the sectors of facility provision, staffing and subsidy of sporting associations.

complex. Comparison with Grenoble is complicated by the different history of institutional structures and periods of political control. Local government was reorganised in England in 1974, and prior to this, political constituency boundaries were rather different. In addition, Labour had held power in the city for all but two years from 1926 to 1999. Finally, in the absence of directly elected mayors, the key political figures in the city have been leaders of the Labour Group who were the Leaders of the Council (mayors being, up to the current decade, merely symbolic heads of municipal government in the English context). Notwithstanding these qualifications, three phases of political development in the period 1974–99 can be identified. In the first period, 1974–80, the City Council was dominated by Labour members from traditional backgrounds (trades unions, local working-class communities, etc.) (Seyd 1993), with traditional goals of maintaining levels of public expenditure, service provision, public sector employment and support for local industry. Such a strategy brought the city into direct conflict with central government, particularly after 1979 when Margaret Thatcher's administration took power.

A second and transitional period, 1980–7, was one in which this stance was increasingly recognised as futile. A new group of young left-wing politicians, led by David Blunkett, gained control of the City Labour Party in 1980. Similar groups emerged in a number of British cities and were termed the New Urban Left by political commentators – new because they represented a break from traditional Labour, with many members being from the new service sector, and urban because this new group first began to appear in city, rather than national, politics (Gyford 1985). The New Urban Left group acknowledged that since economic restructuring was inevitable, a strategy of 'shaping', or 'influencing for the better', rather than resisting that restructuring was necessary. Unequivocal protection of existing local services was also called into question since it was recognised that some public sector services were not effective in serving the needs of the most disadvantaged in the city. However, the local Labour Party did remain committed to opposing central government cuts to local budgets, and in 1985, the Labour Group teetered on the brink of failing to set a legal (non-deficit) budget, which would have left individual councillors personally and financially liable for the financial shortfall and would thus have rendered them bankrupt. At the eleventh hour, sufficient numbers of Labour councillors drew back from the risk of bankruptcy, Sheffield set a legal budget and effective resistance to central government was over. Sheffield, which had been characterised in the press as the 'capital of the Socialist Republic of South Yorkshire', fell into line with other Labour local authorities which had accepted the futility of struggling against a Conservative central government that had the legislative means to ensure compliance (Stoker 1991).

In the later 1980s, it became apparent that the New Urban Left's policy initiatives were having only marginal effects in urban contexts, and in Sheffield, with the election of Blunkett to Parliament in 1987 and his resignation from the City Council (cumulative mandates are very rare in Britain), a new group of Labour Modernisers took control of the Council with Clive Betts as leader. This group sought direct involvement and partnership, with business as a central plank to their policy programme. Thus, in the Sheffield context, we can refer to the three distinct stages which are evident in the political developments affecting the city as control by traditional Labour, by the New Urban Left and by the Labour Modernisers. The first two of these periods are characterised by a relative antipathy to working through local business interests, while the last reflects a new approach by Labour, fostering partnership with capital.

As indicated earlier, for each of the stages of development of the two local political systems, analysis was undertaken along four dimensions. Three types of sources were employed to evaluate these dimensions, written documents (minutes of the meetings of the *Conseil municipal* and the City Council, books relating to local political and sporting history, articles in the local press, information materials and official reports from the local authorities), semi-structured interviews conducted in Grenoble with the politicians who fulfilled the role of *adjoint au sport* across the period (unfortunately, it was not possible to interview the mayors for the period, Dubedout having died in a climbing accident in 1986 and Carignon having been imprisoned for corruption in 1995). In Sheffield, interviews were conducted with local politicians of all three major local parties, local government officers and other stakeholders in the sports policy community locally.[1] Interviews took place in Grenoble over the period 1991–4 and in Sheffield over the period 1995–9. Official studies of local expenditure (comptes administratifs communaux and CIPFA 1976, 1982, 1984, 1988, 1990, 1992, 1993a,b, 1994a,b, 1995a,b, 1996a,b, 1997a–c, 1998a,b, 1999) and 'factual' items reported by the local press (e.g. opening, closure of facilities, changes in management arrangements) were employed particularly to document policy outcomes.

Sports policy in Grenoble – the city as a 'social laboratory' 1965–83

The ideologies and objectives of sports policy under the socialist administration of Dubedout

Between 1965 and 1983, a group of socialist politicians led by Hubert Dubedout (an engineer at the Centre of Nuclear Studies in Grenoble) controlled the local authority. Successful in three successive local elections, Dubedout was also elected to the *Assemblée nationale* and the *Conseil régional*.

The ideas and practical orientation of the Socialists were directed towards the development of social (public) housing, and of cultural facilities, as part of a wider project of reorganising urban space. The local authority proposed in its programme prevention of uncontrolled urban development and countering of the domination of urban development by private interests. In doing so, it opposed autocratic and unplanned urban management which had left some neighbourhoods under-provided and lacking facilities, while leaving others well provided for but too expensive for many local inhabitants. This policy approach also emphasised the importance of giving a voice in politics to local citizens and thus also gave prominence to various local organisations (Joly 1985). As a consequence, these local organisations were recognised by the municipality as privileged partners, and they thus became closely involved in the management of socio-cultural facilities. Indeed, Grenoble gained a reputation for the strength of its local voluntary sector.

> It has to be remembered that one is more likely to live in a community on the banks of the Isère, than elsewhere: it is a real indication, in effect that nearly 6 out of 10 grenoblois were members of some sort of association in 1975, while only 3 out of 10 French people were in the same situation. ... At the beginning of the 1960s, neighbourhood associations, organisations which already had some history, gained a new importance in the town, until in 1965 they were able to participate in municipal decision-making.
>
> (Parent 1982: p. 96, authors' translation)

Some of the community organisations served more particularly to support the implementation of this political experiment in socio-cultural development. Some examples include the *Maison du Cinéma et de l'Audiovisuel* in relation to the exhibiting and documenting of films and *l'Association Grenoble Animation Information*, which managed the development and publicising of information about the town, in relation to written material.

Thus, the affirmation of the strength of local power vis-à-vis the central state was the dominant policy theme in the post-1965 period. The concern of the city to assume a powerful role appeared to be a novelty in the mid-1960s when French cities were dominated by the state, negotiations concerning the built environment were directed towards the private sector and small concessions in decentralisation were directed towards the regions rather than to *communes*. Grenoble was thus one of the first examples of a city emerging out of the shadow of the power of the central state (Bonzy *et al.* 1988). It is in this sense that Grenoble can be described as a test bed for local democracy which was to be given formal expression in the decentralisation legislation of the early 1980s in France.

As far as sports policy was concerned, the priority until the end of the 1960s was with the staging of the Winter Olympic Games programme inherited from the previous municipal administration. The Games were held in 1968, three years after Dubedout came to power, and most of the construction plan was thus committed prior to his election. It was necessary to wait for the beginning of the 1970s, that is to say after Dubedout had been re-elected for a second term as mayor (1971–7), to see the emergence of more specific political objectives in the field of sports policy. Policy goals in the sports domain related to provision for the greatest number of local inhabitants, an objective which was evident in speeches and statements by the mayor reflecting a 'sport for all' approach: 'Sport is for everyone, and as such it should not lead to decisions which reinforce divisions' (Dubedout 1971) and in the proposals of the *adjoint au sport*:

> The activities of the masses are not incompatible with the practice of high
> level competition. The diverse nature of the former is not in opposition to
> the specialised nature of the latter. Both are implicated in the larger plan
> for sport.
>
> (Espagnac 1971)

One of the priorities was not to discriminate between clubs, in particular ensuring equity in subsidies, as Espagnac argued in an interview published in the
Dauphiné Libéré (Ribeaud 1973). This political discourse was expressed in the
refusal to engage in a bidding process relating to the funding of high-level sport
which would have been to the detriment of the policy of sport for all.

> The policy of funding the development of champions which we are reject-
> ing, by which I mean the entering into the scandalous game of bidding to
> pay to retain stars paying more and more, which renders it impossible for
> the municipality to promote and fund other sports.... An élite takes on the
> role of the rich and the town promotes its image through the players it has
> bought and which only represent it artificially. For ten years our objective
> has been to provide adequate sporting facilities for the town, with the goal
> of providing for our children the opportunity to obtain a satisfactory train-
> ing in sport, for our clubs to have access to the appropriate facilities, and
> finally for all inhabitants of Grenoble to participate in the sport of their
> choice.
>
> (Dubedout 1975a)

> The ideas which we have about sport corresponded well with socialist ideas
> about the sports movement. For many towns sport is reduced to élite teams,
> but we, for example have transformed gymnastics in schools into a policy of
> sports animation, because [for young people] to move into the sports clubs,
> it is necessary to go beyond the formal school context. And 'sport for all' it
> was necessary to strive to do that, and even at times it was necessary to
> intervene at the level of the élite clubs in the town.
>
> (Espagnac 1971, interview with C. Dulac, 5 January 1995)

This political discourse was expressed in the refusal to engage in a bidding
process relating to the funding of high-level sport which would have been to
the detriment of the policy of sport for all.

The strategies and outcomes of sports policy under the socialist administration of Dubedout

One element of the strategy of the politicians is manifest in the development of
facilities. The Socialist administration was not satisfied simply with existing
provision, and in particular with the infrastructure linked to the Olympic
Games financed in 1966 and 1967. A new programme of provision was

developed at the end of the 1960s, with construction oriented towards community recreation facilities in neighbourhoods. This policy orientation is one illustration of how Grenoble earned the title of 'social laboratory'. The policy of developing this type of facility, for which the town was a 'trail blazer', was effectively followed by central government in developing its programmes *Mille Piscines*, *Mille Tennis* and similar schemes for the whole of France. The growth of facilities in the Dubedout period had financial implications, because the capital costs were much more significant in comparison with revenue costs in the budget for sports facilities in the periods 1968–70 and 1972–4. The growth in capital costs was more significant during the second period: 11.4 per cent (1972–4) as compared with 2.35 per cent (1968–70).

In 1975, the orientation of the local authority was to open its facilities to the greatest number of people possible:

> We should be aware of the need to provide financial aid to allow large numbers of young people who do not even have sufficient resources to pay the symbolic amounts necessary to gain entry to swimming pools or sports halls.
> (*Nouvelle Revue d'Information et de Documentation* March 1971: p. 9)

In terms of facilities, the municipality had a two pronged strategy: to create neighbourhood facilities in Grenoble and to manage the large-scale sports provision in the city. This was in order to provide a diverse range of participants with access to the large-scale facilities, while giving sports participants free use of neighbourhood provision (Dubedout 1971). This strategy implied full usage of existing facilities, including those inherited from the period of Olympic investment (*Délibération du Conseil Municipal* 5 December 1968). Thus, 'indoor swimming pools, sports halls, indoor tennis courts, floodlit sports facilities, all were implicated in the strategy of full usage' (*Nouvelle Revue d'Information et de Documentation* March 1971: p. 8). As press statements indicated, this strategy incorporated school sport as well as provision through sports associations: 'It is absolutely essential that the sporting and cultural provision constructed for schools should be integrated into the life of the town, that is to say that it is useful not only for pupils but also for local people' (*Dauphiné Libéré* 22 September 1968: p. 8). As far as the distribution of subsidies was concerned, socialist policy was evident in the priority accorded to non-élite sport. In effect, during the period 1965–82, the share of subsidies provided for non-élite sport represented 50.15 per cent of the total sum allocated, while in comparison, high-level sport and the *Office Municipal des Sports*[2] obtained 39.42 and 10.43 per cent, respectively.

This orientation of the socialist policy in favour of mass sport rested on a particular strategic axis which consisted of controlling the financial management of high-level sports clubs and, in particular, that of the city's professional football team which played in the Second Division. This particular club had in effect adopted an unsustainable financial policy having overstretched itself, after twice gaining promotion to the national First Division (in 1960 and 1962), and subsequently recruiting the former coach of the French national team and of Stade de Reims, Albert Batteux, in 1963. As a consequence of this, the *adjoint au sport* was charged with overseeing the use of subsidies given to the club, in order to ensure that the club did not commit the same mistakes (*Délibération du Conseil Municipal* 7 July 1969). As a result of this intervention, there was a reduction in the amount of subsidy granted to high-level sport in the city during the period 1968–75, from 46 per cent of total subsidies for sports associations to 21 per cent. From 1976 onwards, the proportion of subsidy provided to high-level sport grew again until the end of the period of socialist control, standing at 44 per cent in 1982. In effect, when the municipality wished to pursue a policy of sport for all, it had to take account of the élite sports clubs but sought to do so without detriment of the other sports clubs.

> We are not going to get involved in bidding [by élite sports clubs for subsidy increases], but we will allow clubs which are doing very well [in national leagues] to be able to defend their interests, giving them a hand when necessary without burdening the municipal budget.
>
> (Dubedout 1975b)

This explains why the growth of the subsidies provided to high-level sport was always below that accorded to mass sport.

The second strategic approach used by the municipality was to encourage each of the élite sports clubs to take responsibility for its own affairs. The *adjoint au sport* suggested that they should find alternatives to municipal subsidy: 'The clubs must not rely solely on municipal aid to resolve their problems, it will be necessary to look for support elsewhere and to rely on spectator income' (Bergeaud 1980). He alluded to the paying public as a revenue source to be explored but also indirectly to appeals for sponsorship. The mayor also noted that certain sectors of sport with a high-spectator appeal managed without assistance from the local authority:

> the refusal to engage in an auction does not mean a rejection of high level competitive sport and its value as an example or inspiration. The large crowds at the *Palais des sports* during the *'Six jours'* [indoor cycling competition] or international events are a good example of this.
>
> (Dubedout 1975b: p. 16)

Thus, in the Dubedout period, widening access to facilities, involving local associations in decision-making in sports policy, maximising use of facilities and weaning local élite sports clubs off high levels of municipal subsidy characterised sports policy in Grenoble.

Grenoble under new managerialism 1983–95

In 1983, the socialist group led by Dubedout lost the municipal elections to a coalition of the right led by Alain Carignon. The new mayor sought to appropriate the benefits and publicity from projects developed by the preceding administration, while constructing his politics around a new neo-liberal pro-gramme: 'fewer taxes, less government intervention', 'a leaner municipality' and 'less involvement of the central state' at the local level (Avrillier and Descamps 1995). Thus, the new municipal administration of the right looked to promote a politics based on a liberal ideology, which manifested itself principally in the media projection of the city (Dulac 1998).

The ideologies and objectives of sports policy under the neo-liberal administration of Alain Carignon

Between 1983 and 1995, Alain Carignon won two successive elections. In addi-tion, he became a member of the *Conseil général*, of the *Département*, of the *Assemblée nationale* and of the European Parliament, and he was a minister in the *cohabitation* governments of Jacques Chirac (Environment, 1986–8) and Edouard Balladur (Communication, 1993–4).

During his first period in office, the mayor developed his policy programme around the central theme of city promotion and marketing. The 1980s saw the emergence of 'the entrepreneur' as an emblematic figure, with personalities emerging such as Messrs Bouygues, Lagardère and Tapie. In this context, Carignon declared directly to the local press that he wanted 'to manage the town like a business enterprise' (*Le Dauphiné Libéré* 10 May 1984). He developed this policy approach drawing on direct and privileged links with the business world, having himself come from a background within the local Chamber of Commerce and Industry (Avrillier and Descamps 1995).

In terms of sports policy, the Carignon administration inherited a consider-able investment in sports infrastructure, which is why it retained in part the dual orientation of its predecessor, of using the Olympic facilities and construct-ing neighbourhood facilities. As the 1980s progressed, the priority of the admin-istration in sports policy became more clearly oriented towards high-publicity sporting spectacle with media impact (rather than towards the promotion of high-level performance per se or of community recreation). This search for civic prestige was directly reflected in Carignon's local election manifesto in 1986. Of the 89 proposals contained within the manifesto, 5 were dedicated to sports policy and the majority of these were concerned with élite sport. Proposals 47–49, for example, advocated the promotion of the city through a major sports team, the development of a major sports complex and a system for developing élite young local sporting talent. Once elected, the Carignon administration confirmed the adoption of this approach in a press communiqué on 18 May 1983, concerned specifically with high-level sport and high-profile sporting events.

The strategies and outcomes of sports policy under the neo-liberal administration of Carignon

The dominant strategy of the Carignon team was to exploit the media potential represented in sport, emphasising the high-profile events (such as *Six jours cycliste* and the *Masters Pole Vault* event) and also high-profile sports teams in the city. The Masters Pole Vault competition in particular was the subject of a contract with Canal+ until 1989, then it was taken up by France 3 from 1990. By this time, the budget for this event had reached 1.6 MF, with the level of subsidy on the part of the town of Grenoble standing at approximately 20 per cent of the total budget for the event. The other competitive events on the evening of the Masters competition were simply included to legitimate the event as a general athletics competition recognised by the national governing body so that any records established would attract official recognition.

A second theme in the policy strategy related to support for high-prestige sporting teams. From 1983, the municipality allocated more than half of the total sum provided for sports club subsidy (excluding school sport) to the five major high-profile sports teams. These teams were competing at the highest level regionally or nationally in the sports of football, rugby, ice hockey, basketball and volleyball. The proportion of subsidies dedicated to this élite group oscillated between 60 and 65 per cent of the total sum allocated between 1983 and 1988, illustrating the precedence given to high-level sport over sport for all. The remainder of the monies had to be shared among 60 or so clubs.

When the Carignon team won its second term at the municipal elections of 1989, this signified a shift in the orientation of sports policy. In effect, the municipality decided to put a brake on the promotion of high-profile sport, because of a legal case in September 1989 against the *Football-Club Grenoble Dauphiné* (for a debt of 2.24 MF and a budgetary deficit of 8 MF at 30 June 1989: *France Football* 13 February 1990). However, the sporting and financial difficulties of the football club were not the only such difficulties the administration had to face. Table 7.2 illustrates the implication of the *Commune* and the *Département* in the financing of the five major sporting clubs in the town at the end of the 1980s.

Thus, the investment of the municipality in high-profile sport was in terms of not only subsidies but also the provision of access for the clubs to municipal facilities (for which the running costs could, in any given year, exceed the total subsidy to the club; for example, the renovation of the municipal stadium cost 2.85 MF in 1985, while the subsidy to the football club which used it was 1.91 MF). Furthermore, the town provided financial guarantees for the clubs. As Table 7.2 indicates, four of the five clubs were in this situation. These guarantees were to be renewed during the period of office of the Carignon administration, as was the case, for example, for the football club (*Délibération du Conseil Municipal* 13 December 1985) or for the basketball club (*Délibération du Conseil Municipal* 2 July 1990). In May 1988, the town of Grenoble and the *Département* guaranteed a loan of 12 MF for the football club.

Table 7.2 Financial relationships between the elite sport clubs, the city of Grenoble and the Département in 1989

Clubs	Budgets	Subsidy by the City	Subsidy by the Département*	Loans guaranteed by the city
ASG-Volley	1,800,000	935,000	–	No
FCGI (football)	Under judicial administration	2,250,000	364,080	Yes
FCG-Rugby	3,465,000	1,275,000	240,000	Yes
GBI (basket)	1,600,000	825,000	60,000	Yes
CSGH (hockey)	4,800,000	875,000	200,000	Yes

Source: *Grenoble Mensuel*, no. 3, 4–12 December 1990, pp. 8–9.

Note:
* Alain Carignon presided over the Le Conseil Général (i.e. Council of the Département/County Council) from 1985 to 1994.

The brake placed by the municipality on this policy of favouring the high-profile clubs was evident in a number of policy initiatives taken in 1989. The first of these concerned two prestigious facilities in Grenoble: the *Palais des Sports* and the 'Speed Rink'. After a period under municipal management, the *Palais des Sports* was handed over to a commercial company Alpexpo which also managed the city's exhibition centre and the 'Summum' (a location for major events). The Speed Rink, originally constructed for speed skating in the Olympic Games of 1968, was managed initially by central government, the municipality and the French Ice Sport Federation, then subsequently managed solely by the municipality. After 20 years of use, the facility had to have its refrigeration system renewed, and this renewal was beyond the budget of the municipality since it would cost 15.8 MF, on top of its operating costs, estimated at 1.6 MF for 1988–9. After an appeal to the Minister for Youth and Sport for financial aid had been turned down, this facility was abandoned and used only for informal activity and as a roller skating rink (Caubet 1993).

The second initiative concerned the organisation of the new *conseil municipal* elected in March 1989, in which the mayor wished to provide a specific role for well-known local sports persons (e.g. Longo, an international cycling champion, and Liénard, coach of the Grenoble rugby club). This policy was seen as part of an opening up of policy machinery to the influence of civil society, but also as a reflection of the fact that by the 1980s sport was seen as a point of 'social reference' to excellence (Ehrenberg 1988: p. 266) and therefore valuable as an element of political identity.

During this second term of office, Machefaux, *adjoint au sport*, shared his responsibilities with local élite sports personalities, Longo (who was given the brief of sports promotion and liaison with high-level sport) and Liénard (who was given responsibility for team sports). This strategy reflects the political will to control better the high-profile sport through a partitioning of tasks and responsibilities, while conserving a dynamic image for the town.

The third strategy was reflected in the creation of a commission to control high-level sport, in which a specified individual was to be responsible for the financial control of any given club. This initiative was the result of the catastrophic situation in which some clubs had found themselves, but the anticipated improvements were not forthcoming. Thus, the Administrative Tribunal announced in quick succession the liquidation of the ice hockey club in 1991 and the football club on two occasions (1989 and 1993). As a consequence, the town took on the responsibility for the debts of these two clubs (*Délibération du Conseil Municipal* 9 December 1991 and 4 May 1992).

These various initiatives of the local authority resulted in the necessity of modifying its financial policy of support for high-profile sport. At the same time, the municipality had to take account of sport for all, and in particular sport targeted at combating social exclusion for young people in local neighbourhoods (Arnaud 1999a), while effectively dealing with reduced resources in real terms for such social aspects of policy (Dulac 1999).

Sheffield – the city of steel: from traditional Labour to the New Urban Left

The development of Labour politics in the city is closely tied up with the fortunes of the steel industry. The traditional strength of the Labour Party in the city, up until the beginning of the 1980s, had lain with the strength of the working-class workforce in the metal-related industries and the Trades Union movement, from which many of its members and political representatives were drawn. The decline of the steel industry locally coincided with the decline of traditional Labour in Britain's cities generally, and Sheffield was no exception. Just as Dubedout's arrival in Grenoble signalled the electoral power of a new service class, the new figures in Labour politics in Sheffield in the 1980s were drawn from professional, often public service, backgrounds (Darke 1992). The New Urban Left, as they came to be referred to in collective terms (Gyford 1985), emerged in a number of British cities and sought a departure from traditional Labour politics. In Sheffield, the New Urban Left promoted a change in generic policy terms, and in cultural policy more specifically, though in terms of sports policy per se, there were few radical departures. (For this reason, and for pragmatic grounds of space, the two periods are considered together in the following commentary.) Radical departure in sports policy terms was, however, to follow in the period of the Labour Modernisers, from 1987 onwards.

The ideologies and objectives of sports policy under the control of traditional Labour (1974–80) and the New Urban Left (1980–7)

The reorganisation of local government in England in 1974 heralded a rapid expansion of public sector investment in sport. The first local government-funded sports centre in England had opened in Harlow in 1964, but by the end of the 1980s, there were well over 1,000 such facilities. The traditionalist Labour Group which controlled the local authority in Sheffield, however, chose not to expand its stock of sports facilities, many of which, particularly the swimming pools, were dated. As one of the local authority leisure services officers expressed it: 'While many local authorities were investing in new or improved sports facilities, Sheffield's priorities lay elsewhere and as a consequence it retained a number of outdated facilities, particularly swimming pools which were in need of upgrading or replacement' (Taylor 1990). The generic concerns of the local authority were with maintaining social service provision, sustaining low charges for municipal services, including public transport, and protecting public service employment, in the face of attacks from central government on local government spending levels. In addition, the mode of delivery of those services was through local government departmental bureaucracies with little wider involvement of voluntary organisations in the city. This was a common feature of service provision not simply in Sheffield but in most of the large-scale local government units established in the 1974 reorganisation of local government (Hambleton 1988). The end result of this approach to service provision was seen as inefficiency (because of bureaucratic waste) and ineffectiveness (the most disadvantaged groups in society were not well targeted by such provision). This was as true in sports provision as it was in other service areas (Audit Commission 1989). This promoted policy moves nationally in relation to the delivery of local government services: from the political left, the push was for decentralisation of services to be closer to communities, and from the right, the push was for greater commercialisation of such services (Hambleton et al. 1989; Henry and Bramham 1986).

Traditional Labour had opposed central government's attempts to squeeze local government expenditure, and the Sheffield Labour Group in the early 1980s pursued this policy aggressively. As central government introduced more and more legislation to curb local government spending, Sheffield City Council sought ways to circumvent this legislation and to continue to resource local services and public sector employment. This eventually brought the City Council into direct confrontation with central government as it refused to set a budget in line with the legal limits introduced by the Conservative Government. Faced with the threat of personal bankruptcy for local councillors, the Council eventually backed down in 1986, and resistance to central government's reduction of local government financial resources and policy powers was effectively ended in Sheffield (Stoker 1991).

The New Urban Left group subsequently began to drive policy in a different direction. Instead of opposing economic restructuring in the city, the local authority sought to maximise the opportunities for disadvantaged groups within the restructuring process. The city established an Economic Development Unit which looked at ways of promoting new investment and new jobs within the city to compensate for the loss of steel industry-related employment (Benington 1987; Sheffield City Council 1983). However, though cultural provision received a boost through new initiatives described in the following section, sports provision remained relatively low in terms of priorities.

The strategies and outcomes of sports policy under the control of traditional Labour (1974–80) and the New Urban Left (1980–7)

Thus, in general, the strategies and outcomes of this period were negative in relation to investment in sport. In the period of control by traditional Labour, provision was very much 'community oriented', with facilities concentrated in many traditional working-class housing areas but heavily reliant on an ageing stock of sports facilities (Sheffield City Council Recreation Department 1984). The implicit strategy was avoidance of the opportunity costs of investing in sporting or other infrastructure, focusing instead on investment in core social services. In 1976, the first year for which comparative data are available for the reorganised local government system, Sheffield, with 14 swimming pools and three sports halls, spent a total of £1.85 per head of population on indoor sport and recreation, ranking 27 out of 36 metropolitan districts in England (CIPFA 1976). By contrast, in the same year, it spent £1.61 per capita on cultural ser-vices, ranking second equal. This level of cultural expenditure reflects the city's traditional commitment to improving civic intellectual capital, which had left it with a heritage of traditional museums, theatres and art galleries, many of which also dated from the previous century. As the figures for 1980–1 provided in Table 7.3 indicate, the situation had changed little by the end of the period of traditional Labour control.

With the arrival of the New Urban Left on the local political scene from the early 1980s, the traditional Labour focus on core social services, the protection of public sector employment and support for traditional industries was to be called into question (Sheffield City Council 1983). The New Urban Left group sought new ways of promoting the interests of the local community. If eco-nomic restructuring could not be effectively resisted by governments, local or national, then how could that restructuring process be used positively to promote the needs of local people? The answer to this question favoured by the New Urban Left had few implications for sport but did signal important devel-opments in respect of culture, when the Council, following the lead of the Greater London Council (Garnham 1983; Greater London Enterprise Board nd), developed a cultural industries strategy, involving in particular the devel-opment of an Audio-visual Enterprise Centre incorporating a municipal record-ing studio and video and film production capacity (Betterton and Blanchard 1992).

The Council promoted cultural production within the local community with three principal rationales. First, the value thus implicitly placed on local culture (the culture of local communities and of disadvantaged groups) was intended as a boost to the morale of those groups, particularly those hard hit by the impact of the decline of the steel industry. Second, the cultural industries were part of the new service sector in which jobs were seen to be growing and thus were a

Table 7.3 Comparison of Sheffield expenditure on sport and culture with all metropolitan districts for selected years 1980/1–1991/2

	Net expenditure on indoor pools		Net expenditure on Indoor Sports Halls/ Leisure Centres with & without Pools	
	Sheffield	All metropolitan districts	Sheffield	All metropolitan districts
1980/1				
Total expendure	1,046	24,895	562	14,418
per capita expendure	1.92	2.14	1.03	1.24
1982/3				
Total expendure	1,246	29,709	665	22,251
per capita expendure	2.29	2.55	1.23	1.91
1987/8				
Total expendure	1,740	37,899	1,851	50,720
per capita expendure	3.2	3.25	3.41	4.36
1991/2				
Total expendure	1,267	38,779	6,695	104,497
per capita expendure	2.33	3.33	12.32	8.11

	Outdoor Sports Facilities		Cultural Facilities (e.g. theatres, museums)	
	Sheffield	All metropolitan districts	Sheffield	All metropolitan districts
1980/1				
Total expendure	29	3,187	1,242	11,380
per capita expendure	0.05	0.27	2.29	0.8
1982/3				
Total expendure	38	3,123	1,706	16,310
per capita expendure	0.07	0.27	3.14	1.4
1987/8				
Total expendure	380	6,947	2,579	29,298
per capita expendure	0.7	0.6	4.75	2.51
1991/2				
Total expendure	1,318	11,501	3,034	50,047
per capita expendure	2.43	0.99	5.58	4.30

potential source of employment. And finally, by improving the cultural infra-structure of the city, it was intended that it should become more attractive to inward investors. Thus, within the leisure sphere, investment in the city con-tinued with an emphasis on culture rather than sport. As Table 7.3 indicates, sports expenditure remained stubbornly low and little policy change was evident (Taylor 1990).

New realism in Sheffield Labour politics: Labour modernisers and partnership with business

After the debacle of the Council's climb down in its confrontation with central government, and with a deepening of the crisis of the steel industry, and the continuing squeeze on local government finance, Sheffield's Labour politicians acknowledged that finance and other resources had to come from sources other than local taxation (which had been effectively capped by central government legislation) or financial transfers from central government. Partnership with local capital provided one of the few ways forward. As the Labour Chair of the Finance Committee expressed it, most were initially reluctant to co-operate with business. There had been:

> a continuing and underlying suspicion within Labour Group against devel-oping too close a relationship with the private sector …. For many, if not all, Labour councilors, partnership was a marriage of convenience, even a shotgun bond, rather than the union of natural soul mates.
>
> (Darke 1992)

The partnership process was facilitated by a change in leadership within the Sheffield Labour Group. David Blunkett had departed to the national political scene, and leadership of the Council was taken up by Clive Betts, who was asso-ciated with a much more pragmatic and less ideological approach to politics. Formalisation of partnership arrangements came in December 1986 with the establishment of the Sheffield Economic Regeneration Committee in the City Council's Department of Employment and Economic Development (Seyd 1990; Strange 1993). This committee brought together representatives of the City Council, the business community, trades unions, higher education institutions, central government agencies and local organisations. The aim of the group, as stated in the principal planning document it produced, *Sheffield 2000* (Sheffield Economic Regeneration Committee nd), was to develop a long-term economic regeneration strategy for the city, with a particular focus on the Lower Don Valley in which most of the old steel plants had existed and which was now largely derelict.

As part of the regeneration process and following the recommendation of commercial consultants that a flagship project was required to spearhead the drive for regeneration, the city developed a successful bid over the period 1986–8 to stage the 1991 World Student Games. This project, as described next, stemmed from the partnership process (business and civic leaders together put forward the bid to the governing body of the World Student Games), and both further contributed to partnership activity. However, the Games were also the source of divisions which began to appear in the established partnerships as the Games approached.

The ideologies and objectives of sports policy under the 'new realism' of the Labour modernisers in Sheffield (1987–99)

If partnerships were to be the way forward and one of the new vehicles for partnership was to be the city's bid for the World Student Games to be held in 1991, how was sports policy affected in this context? The staging of the Games had several objectives. First, it was intended to reorient the image of Sheffield from 'City of Steel' to 'City of Sport'. Second, the bid was to promote tourism in the city. Third, the use of partnership with business was thought likely to erode central government's antagonism to the city and thus to improve the city's financial standing with central government. Fourth, the Games were intended to generate a range of new and exciting facilities for local people to use after the Games and would allow, in the post-Games era, the staging of international sporting events. Fifth, the building of new facilities in the Don Valley would enhance the environment, given that the Valley had been decimated by the closure of steel-related plants and factories and was an eyesore, a large swathe of highly visible derelict land.

The strategies and outcomes of sports policy under the control of the new realism of the Labour Group (1987–99)

The final period of new realism introduced by the Labour Modernisers under Clive Betts had a profound effect on sports policy in a number of ways. It determined the strategy to be adopted which was in effect an event-led planning approach, focused on the requirements for staging the World Student Games (Foley 1991; Roche 1992), rather than one which began with an analysis of local needs. In tandem with this was a strategy in terms of management of sports facilities which involved the 'debureaucratisation' of sports services, with the formation of private companies and trusts to operate some of the facilities opened for the World Student Games in particular. The medium for achieving this strategy was partnership. The outcomes can be summarised under four main headings: financial, sports development, environmental and political.

In financial terms, there were significant hidden costs in running the Games. In November 1986, the City Council had approved a bid, believing that the cost of running the Games would be met by generated income, and the capital costs of the facilities would be met by government grants, charities and private sources (Foley 1991; Roche 1992). However, by 1988, new central government legislation constrained the City Council's capital borrowing and spending. The city faced a critical dilemma and at the time estimated that at least

£110 million was needed to develop the facilities for the World Student Games. A private trust was created to run the facilities and to access private funding. This private trust, the Sheffield Leisure and Recreation Trust (SLRT), was established in March 1988 to provide the facilities and manage their future use. The capital was raised through foreign bank loans with a 20-year repayment period (Seyd 1993).

Subsequently, two subsidiaries of SLRT were established with different roles: first, Universiade (GB) Ltd to administer and raise finance for the Games, and second, a joint public–private board, Sheffield for Health Ltd to manage the World Student Games and three of the major facilities (Ponds Forge Swimming Pool and Sports Centre, the Don Valley Athletics Stadium and Hillsborough Sports Centre); the fourth major new facility, the Sheffield Arena, was put in the hands of an American company, SMGI, subcontracted to Sheffield for Health.

The World Student Games involved the largest sports facilities construction programme then seen in Britain with a total cost of the Games estimated at around £180 million. Construction of the new facilities accounted for nearly £150 million, with £27 million required for the running of the event itself (Middleton 1991; Seyd 1993). Except for the Arena which attracted some private funding, the rest of the construction was underwritten by the Council. By mid-1990, only £500,000 had been raised and the company Universiade (GB) Ltd was forced to cease trading and wind up with debts of nearly £3 million. Thus, in June 1990, the city was compelled to take direct responsibility for the running of the Games.

As a result, the city's commitment to the World Student Games was criticised as a high-risk strategy, being financially questionable (Roche 1992). It was also criticised as a being the product of a lack of consideration of alternatives (Critcher 1991). Due to the escalation of the facilities costs from £110 million in 1988 to £147 million, the payment of debt charges commenced in 1992 and was rescheduled to end in 2013, with every adult paying an additional £25 annually in local tax (Seyd 1993). Table 7.3 illustrates that Sheffield's expenditure on sport had moved by the end of the 1980s to significantly above the national average, having trailed for most of the rest of the period. Although Table 7.4 suggests that Sheffield's expenditure reverted to below that of the national average in the 1990s, this is misleading in that the rescheduling of Sheffield's debt repayments and the ongoing revenue costs of running the new facilities are not taken into account in this budget heading because of the establishment of an independent trust to run the new facilities.

In political terms, the strategy also appears to have been problematic. Labour's votes locally diminished significantly against the national trend, and though it may be difficult to attribute this wholly to the Games issue, this was certainly a salient and hotly debated issue. A group calling itself the 'Stuff the Games Group' campaigned heavily locally against the subsidy during the staging of the Games and had political support within the Labour Party as well as from other local community and political groups.

Table 7.4 Expenditure on sport and recreation and on the arts excluding debt charges for Sheffield and for all metropolitan districts

	Indoor Sport and Recreation	Outdoor Sport and Recreation	Arts
1994/5			
Sheffield	8.12	9.96	4.76
All metropolitan districts	10.09	11.42	4.08
1998/9			
Sheffield	5.36	6.83	2.82
All metropolitan districts	8.32	14.16	4.14

While the Games were financially a disaster for the city, and politically a problem for the Labour Group controlling the city, they did leave a legacy of facilities which has allowed the attraction of a programme of events of international sporting significance (Gratton 1998; Kronos 1997). In addition, they had a positive effect on the environment, the sporting facilities in effect creating a sport and leisure 'corridor' through the Don Valley, the area of the city most affected by de-industrialisation. However, in terms of meeting the social needs of the local population, the Games legacy has been problematic. The management of the new facilities was placed by the local authority in the hands of a division of a City Trust, namely Sheffield International Venues Limited, established for this purpose. This Trust is, however, contracted by the local authority to meet certain standards of financial performance but has no significant social goals specified by contract. As a result of this, social goals have been de-prioritised and contractual standards of financial performance given prominence. The policy of centralising swimming provision in a large city centre facility of international competition standard has also radically affected those neighbourhoods which lost their swimming pool to permit this centralisation. As Taylor (2001) has shown, participation in swimming in the city has actually declined in the 1990s following the introduction of the new facility, against the national trend.

The overall outcome in terms of sport policy might be characterised therefore as a two-tier policy, with an increase in consumer rights for those who could afford to pay private sector or near private sector rates, with some lower level welfare rights (subsidised sports development) for others who do not have the financial resources to benefit from consumer choice.

Conclusion

Grenoble and Sheffield are cities with very different political, cultural and economic histories. Notwithstanding these differences, there are key and perhaps obvious similarities in the nature and direction of sports policy change, which can be characterised along four dimensions. In both cases, sports policy exhibits a shift:

1   from a concern with social and community development through sport (among other policy areas) to one of economic development and urban entrepreneurialism;
2   from a concern with participatory approaches to planning, to one of decision-making by political and business elites;
3   from decentralised policy making within the local authority to centralised decision-making; and
4   from an emphasis on sport for all to one on professional and/or elite sport.

The direction of policy change described here is consistent with features of a shift away from traditional, Fordist modes of social regulation. The provision of sport for all as part of the social wage delivered to the working population within the context of a welfare state has clearly been eroded and replaced by a concern to target the needs of the service class and of their employers and/or to generate revenue through sporting provision. However, if charges of reductionism are to be countered, changes in respect of local policy cannot simply be 'read off' from changes in the wider political economy, and variation in policy between cities does exist (Goodwin et al. 1993; Goodwin and Painter 1996). Indeed, we can assert that though similar tendencies may be observed elsewhere, Sheffield and Grenoble stand out as having been to the fore in promoting this type of sports policy change and cannot therefore be regarded as typical.

How then in Sheffield and Grenoble did the 'localised conditions of production and consumption, and local constellations of social forces and cultural practices' (Goodwin et al. 1993: p. 69), which are said to produce policy change, result in post-Fordist approaches to sports policy being fostered? In order to explain this, we would argue that account has to be taken of three sets of factors: the local political context, the institutional context and the structural context, as well as the activities of the significant policy actors in both cities. It is not necessary to explain similar policy outcomes as resulting from similar local contextual factors since the same outcome may be explained by different sets of contexts, but it is important to tease out the relationship between context, action and policy outcomes if one is to explain the emergence of a particular pattern of policy at any given point of time.

Local political context

There are clearly distinctive political histories in the two cities in the period under consideration. Grenoble was subject to the rule of two charismatic figures in the form of Dubedout and Carignon, of different party affiliations and ideological leanings. The shift from the 'socialist' approach of Dubedout's administration to the 'neo-liberal' approach of Carignon is marked and represents a clear break and is in part a reflection of what is seen as the growing failure of socialist political ideas to deal with the local consequences of the global recessions of the late 1970s and early 1980s. (Although the *Parti socialiste* had swept to power in 1981 in national elections, the failure of the Socialist government's attempts to employ Keynesian economics to 'spend its way out of recession' had damaged its credibility, thus Dubedout's task in the local elections was made all the more difficult.)

In contrast, Sheffield was continuously under the control of the Labour Party in the period concerned. Sheffield did experience the charismatic leadership of a national figure in the form of David Blunkett in the early 1980s, but leadership in the adoption of policies related to urban entrepreneurialism and the use of sport as tool of city marketing were a product of the period of control under the less well-known Clive Betts. Thus, while the electoral failure of the local socialist leadership of Dubedout in 1983, together with the business orientation and the powerful personality of Carignon, explains much of the shift in sports policy in Grenoble, one has to look beyond the local political context to explain policy change in Sheffield.

Institutional context

In relation to the institutional context of French local government, decentralisation introduced in 1982 was crucial in strengthening the role of local government in mediating and/or determining policy change. Indeed, even before 1982, Dubedout's forcefulness in developing local initiatives had allowed Grenoble in many ways to act as a forerunner to the approach promoted in the legislative changes, and decentralisation legislation further strengthened the hand of strong local leadership.

Ironically, in the British context, the autonomy of local government was being curtailed across the 1980s. Sheffield was prominent in its opposition to central government in this respect. Ironically, it is this very opposition and central government's subsequent refusal to provide financial support for Sheffield after it had committed to invest in the World Student Games, which left the city's leadership with relatively few options other than to commercialise existing provision to reduce costs and promote income.

The structural context

In terms of the structural location of the two cities within the national and global economies, there are again major contrasts. Grenoble had emerged in the 1960s as a *technopole*, host to a growing number of technologically sophisticated industries, while Sheffield was very much a traditional industrial city which was to deindustrialise rapidly in the 1980s. Both cities sought to position themselves as service centres with Sheffield in particular seeking to use sport to combat a negative industrial image. Grenoble in effect employed sport to complement its already strong association with an alpine sports environment. Thus, both cities approached the development of sports policy in the post-Fordist mode from very different perspectives, Grenoble because this was perceived as an appropriate fit with its existing image and location in the national and global economic structure and Sheffield because its city's politicians recognised the need to change dramatically its image if it was to change its structural location in economic terms.

Thus, although there are strong parallels in the development of sports policy in the two cities, their political culture and history and their institutional and structural settings are very different. Grenoble's adoption of a post-Fordist-related set of sports policies may be regarded as the product of the political espousal of a neo-liberal policy approach, within a newly defined, decentralised set of local political institutions designed to foster local autonomy and within a structural context in which the city was seeking to reinforce its image as an exciting place to live and work for the new service class. In essence, as a city with a post-industrial profile, Grenoble was a natural candidate for post-Fordist urban sports policy orientation. By contrast, Sheffield's political and institutional context was much less evidently one which promised such an outcome. Indeed, while in Grenoble, increased local political autonomy through decentralisation legislation fostered the new approach to sports policy via a neo-liberal mayor, the reduction of local political autonomy in Britain under Margaret Thatcher's governments (and in particular the curbing of local taxation powers which such legislation introduced) together with negative structural location of Sheffield in the national and global economic contexts left the city's Labour leadership with the notion that it had few options but to enter into the policy 'game' of seeking to attract inward investment through sport while reducing the local bill for such services by commercialising the operation of such services. The outcome of these very different sets of circumstances is one of equifinality. There is in both cases a 'structured coherence' (Goodwin et al. 1993; Harvey 1995) between the hardware (spectacular sporting facilities/events/sporting spectacle), organisational forms (commercialised, de-bureaucratised operations) and the dominant sets of social relations (increasingly market relations dominated) which characterise their sports policy systems and which systematically privilege market over social interests.

8 Discourses on modern sport and values in a non-Western context

A case study of Algeria

Mahfoud Amara and Ian Henry

Introduction

In the 1960s, Malek Bennabi described the reasons behind the crisis of the Arab and Islamic world in the following terms: '... instead of constructing a civilisation, we have sought to accumulate its products ... the outcome of Islamic renaissance has not, during the last fifty years, been a construction but rather an accumulation of materials' (Bennabi 1970: translation by the authors). The implication of Bennabi's words which are still applicable more than three decades later is that the real crisis in the contemporary Arab and Muslim world is not one of the material means but is first and foremost a crisis of ideas and concepts. The implication of this realisation is that there should be a recognition of a need today in the Arab and Muslim world to deconstruct and demystify the over-politicised and ideological discourses about all domains of society: sport, literature, cinema, music, religion, education, history, etc. In order to achieve this, a culture of dialogue and a culture of accepting differences of opinion need to be established. An aim of the study reported here, therefore, is to open a debate, by giving voice to a number of parties (politicians representing different political tendencies or projects for society, academics and sport administrators) to question and to express their views about a concept or a domain, which has been neglected in the academic field, that is, the place of sport in Arabo-Muslim, and specifically in Algerian, society. The study thus focuses on the discursive construction of policy in the range of language/value communities identified, constituting a (relatively rare) example of a Type IV approach to comparative policy analysis, 'defining discourse'.

It has become common place in recent years to refer to the 'crisis of modernity' in western societies. Such a claim marks the assumption that one can generalize about this crisis since it takes different forms in different western contexts and is subject to a variety of accounts or explanations. However, there is a general consensus that such a crisis is as much at the level of epistemology and ethics as at that of politics, economics and cultures. Thus, both Arabo-Muslim and western 'crises' are in a sense the product of the crumbling certainties of the old order and of modernity.

Academic meetings, debates and international conferences have been organised in different institutions to discuss the question of the 'appropriate' research paradigm for the study of non-western or ex-colonised societies in the age of 'globalisation', 'globalism' and/or 'Americanisation'. This has coincided with another crucial debate in philosophy and sociology linked to the problematic of whether the concept of modernity or that of postmodernity (in their various qualified characterisations) can better explain the features of globalisation. As sociologists, historians or philosophers consider the arguments for or against the proclaiming of a new postmodern era, one of the arguments put forward is that modernity as a philosophy and value system has reached its saturation point, and subsequently, a postmodern world view (through postmodern sociology or at least the sociology of postmodernism: Bauman 1997) is regarded as providing a more adequate account of the contemporary condition. The same is true in relation to concepts such as the 'other' and 'the periphery', where (imposed) post-colonial projects of 'developmentalism' (such as Thirdworldism, Ba'athism, Pan-Arabism, Nasserism) have exhausted themselves, or reached their limits, to be discarded and replaced by other political ideologies based on 'Islamism' or 'Islamised' modernity and/or local and regional (ethnic and cultural) identities. Such identities have emerged to challenge the (homogeneous) state's secular definition of the nationalism and modernisation project.

It should be noted that most of the concepts and approaches used to discuss globalisation, the new world order and 'Americanisation', as well as the impact that such processes have had on local cultures and national identities, are of western origin. In other words, they are the product of what Sayyid (1998) has termed the 'western master signifier'. They were developed by western thinkers with the initial aim of describing and explaining social phenomena that emerged in the West and as a result are related directly to the western historical experience or western historicity (Arkoun 2003). Theories and concepts such as modernity, nation state, liberalism and secularism may have different meanings in Arabo-Muslim cultural and linguistic accounts. Notwithstanding this, the same observation can also be made in relation to the West/the Occident, the supposed birth place of modernity and the 'Enlightenment project', an entity which is usually presented as homogenous, but where in fact conditions of modernity are understood and applied in a variety of ways (Lyotard 1984). It could be argued also that the existence of multiple understandings and uses of modernity are apparent in the discourse of western postmodernity, which can range from Lyotard's project of de-universalisation or de-occidentalisation of the western meta-narrative to that of Baudrillard's (1997) relativism (or scepticism).

To be inclusive of these multiple (western and non-western) narratives, the type of analysis applied in this chapter is that of 'self-critical pluralism' (Scheurich 1997), which adopts a similar line to that of the sociology of post-modernism promoted by Bauman (1987). According to Scheurich, all perspectives imply political arrangements and invariably exclude some groups, some voices, thus employing 'some sort' of social relativist or postmodernist perspective is necessary to explicitly acknowledge the inclusions and exclusions of one's own account. However, this should certainly not be done in a romanticised manner (Scheurich 1997: p. 40), for instance, relying on concepts such as a 'unitary and unified blackness' or a 'third-world identity' or locality (Featherstone 2005; Hall 1991). In addition, our discussion of the West and non-West in relation to globalisation processes, modernity and postmodernity, is not that of a stereotypical 'we' versus 'others' or 'Orientalist' versus 'Occidentalist'. Our different cultural backgrounds as authors[1] and our commitment to work together on projects such as this reflect such a decision.

Thus, the debates that this chapter seeks to initiate are those associated with three broad aims:

1   To examine modern sport from the perspective of a 'non-western' context (at least in terms of conceptualisation), applying 'local modernist' approaches to the study of modern sport (as a social phenomenon, a value system and form of management) with a particular emphasis on the project of the professionalisation of football in Algeria.

2   To position the debate on the study and discourse of modern sport in a 'non-western' milieu in relation to geo-political and temporal contexts which may contribute to the general understanding of multiple meanings expressed around modern sport in general, and professional sport in particular. The geo-political context is that of Algeria, an African, Arabo-Berber and Muslim country, whose Mediterranean location favours its close historical economic and cultural links with western Europe. The temporal context is that of 'late modernity' characterised by the crisis of the modernity project in the West (Giddens and Lash 1994) and the failure of the development project and post-colonial ideologies to achieve justice and progress in major Arab and Muslim countries (Akbar and Donnan 1994).

3   To consider the application of discourse analysis as a research method that can offer researchers in sport studies, with an interest in cross-cultural policy studies (in particular, 'western–non-western' studies), a reflexive set of tools that help to grasp more effectively the complexity of applying (dominant) western research paradigms and theories in the study of a social phenomenon in a 'non-western' context (i.e. modern sport in 'non-western' societies).

The nature and roles of sport in 'formerly colonised' nations

Before going on to discuss the specific case of discourses in contemporary Algeria, some introduction to the roles which sport can play in formerly colonized nations would be helpful. A 'globalist' approach seeks to explain the global diffusion of sport and the accompanying superseding of traditional games and promotion of national identities (Wright 1999). This approach undermines the degree of freedom for decision-making that nation states have in joining the global world of sport, particularly those located in the periphery. As Cantelon and Murray (1993) point out, a former colonial power which still maintains a certain cultural weight within the context of a global culture does not experience globalisation in the same fashion as former colonies may do:

'the experiences of sport at the level of the stadium, pool, gym or rink do vary from place to place and person to person', and thus 'to suggest a global sports culture as a one-way street towards greater homogenisation with no possibility of uniqueness or distinctiveness, would be a mistake'

Hence, to comprehend the globalisation of a cultural market such as sport, both global and local approaches need to be considered in equal manner, whether one is referring to the 'cultural core' (the major sources of global cultural diffusion) or to 'peripheral' countries, since in either case, reference to cultural standardization or homogenisation would be mistaken (Warnier 1999). Consumption (intercepting and then interpreting the products of cultural industries) represents a space for the production of cultural specificity. For this reason, studies of cultural consumption (including studies on the consumption of sport) are obliged to take into consideration the complex relations between global and local spaces (McDonald et al. 2001). These global and local sensitivities are evident in formerly colonised societies.

At the end of the struggle for independence (at least in political terms), western ideologies of socialism, liberalism, secularism and nation state all influenced the modernisation of the newly independent countries, where the appropriation of the colonial model of sport was accepted with little criticism or adaptation (Fates 1994). In these contexts, the appropriation of the dominant model of sport was seen as inevitable, taking into account the multiple uses of sport as an element for political, social and cultural recognition. The adoption of this 'universal' language (sport) was accumulated by the adhesion of newly independent countries, during the 1960s, to the homogeneous laws which regulate the functioning system of international sports movements and international federations. The latter was regarded as being an effective arena for future international treaties and conventions between North and South and East and West (Fates 1994: p. 37). Having said this, one can nevertheless argue that the adhesion of formerly colonised nations to the international sporting community, as Fates describes it, did not happen in a straightforward manner. The newly independent countries have also used international sporting events, and particularly the media coverage that such events can attract, as a space to express their regional political and ideological concerns (e.g. anti-imperialism and pan-Africanism), which has led sometimes to critical situations in the sports world (e.g. the struggle over the GANEFO Games in 1965, Black September at the Munich Olympics in 1972 and the boycott of the Olympic Games to denounce apartheid in South Africa in 1976).

The debate on modernity and modern sport in Algeria

As previously stated, in this chapter, we aim to discuss the meaning of the system of modern sport (which is argued to be the product of western rational thinking) in non-western societies. In relation to identifying a non-western society (and here we need to make the distinction between 'West' as geography and 'West' as a philosophical and political entity), our focus is on Algeria. It is a country which as a result of its geographical position and its history of colonisation (and decolonisation) is today torn between its fascination with the East, the centre of Islamic enlightenment, and its attraction to Europe, the centre of western progress. In other words, it reflects a core tension between its Berber-Arabo-Islamic identity on the one hand and European values on the other hand. The tension, indeed, is perhaps most clearly evident in the multilingual culture of Algeria – Francophone, Arabophone and Berberophone. This dual conception of Algerians concerning their identity and origins, situated between 'traditional' values (not in the sense of pre-modern but in the sense of what is perceived as authentic) and values of 'modernity' – defined by Malek Bennabi (1970) as the dichotomy between authenticity and efficiency, has resulted in a nationalist sensitivity that is a mixture of the (manipulated) culture of Islamic civilisation and the (imposed) European model of nation state and modernity.

Furthermore, this position of Algeria between East and West and North and South has given different meanings and dimensions to the reception of modern sport and its local transformation. Modern sport, which is considered to be the heritage of the French colonial presence in Algeria, has been developed throughout the modern history of Algeria for different purposes. While it was used by the colonial administration as a means of integration of the 'indigenous' population into the plural (ethnic and religious) and republican values of France, for the Algerian nationalist movement, sport was an arena for political resistance against colonial hegemony. The establishment of the FLN football team by the National Liberation Front [Front de Libération National (FLN) is the political party that led[2] the armed revolution against French colonialism) became an important symbol of the Algerian struggle for independence and was taken as a model for other nations to follow in the use of sport in symbolic resistance against colonialism (e.g. the Palestinian national football team).

In the early years of the post-independence era, driven by populist and (Islamic) socialist values, sport was seen by the FLN state as an important element in the political formation and mobilisation of the masses (students, workers, women) for nation state building. This period experienced a spreading of physical education and the practice of sport at school, at university and in the work place. Following the example of other Eastern socialist and communist countries, sport was utilised as an arena for political gigantism, characterised by the development of massive new sports facilities and the participation of Algeria in major regional games (Arab, African and Mediterranean Games) and international sporting events (the Olympic Games and international championships). Sport was thus recognised by the state as being an effective way to represent the Algerian (socialist) model of development.

Since the early days of political independence, Algeria's FLN-led socialist experiment has floundered and has finally been abandoned. In ideological terms, socialism as a political movement suffered a crisis of legitimacy with the fall of the Berlin Wall and the end of the Cold War, which signalled, for some authors at least, 'the end of history' and the victory of liberalism (Fukuyama 1992). This crisis of political legitimacy was also accompanied by a crisis of economic policy, with the state seeking ways of transferring responsibility for funding some policy areas away from the public purse. Sport became a candidate for such a policy change, and 'professionalisation' represented a means for introducing market forces to replace state subsidy. In cultural terms, the impact of growing media exposures and cultural flows fostered by satellite television also had an impact on local football culture and its predisposition to favour a 'professionalised' game. Thus, just as sport had been mobilised by colonial resistance, and the post-independence socialist government, so sport and the promotion of professionalisation in the contemporary context has become a vehicle for post-socialist political, cultural and economic values.

The definition of sport in Algeria in 'late modernity'

The dominant line in western literature argues that the emergence of modern sport in nineteenth-century Europe was associated with the advent of capitalism, industrialisation and urbanisation. Such forms of social organisation were linked to the institutionalisation and rationalisation of sports practices. Therefore, sport may also be characterised as part of the discourse on global diffusion of modernity which takes the West or the western philosophy of enlightenment as 'the master signifier' to define the meaning of modern sport. It should be noted, however, that discussing globalisation processes, which have led to the diffusion of modern sport, as unidirectional (i.e. flows from 'core' to 'periphery'), and as an exclusively western/Eurocentric project, require critical reappraisal. Notions of globalisation, as a form of homogeneous world system, or indeed 'globalism' (Hoogvelt 1997), when defined as the diffusion (or imposition) of western values of progress (ideologies of liberalism, modernity and the nation state), have been subject to severe criticism. This criticism is apparent both in the West and in other cultures. One of the arguments put forward is that there is no such thing as a unique, universal model of modernity and liberalism. These values are understood and applied differently within occidental and non-occidental contexts. Modern sport, which is the main subject of this chapter, is an example of this heterogeneity. As Said (2001: p. 380) has argued, 'Society and culture have been the heterogeneous product of heterogeneous people in an enormous variety of traditions and situations'. Sport is conceived differently even within the West, for example in Europe and the USA, where one can distinguish between a centralised, state-interventionist model of professional sport (e.g. France) and a market-driven (e.g. the UK) and 'controlled' liberalism (e.g. the USA). Modern sport may be seen today as evidence of the heterogeneity, pluralism and fragmentation of the world system rather than its standardisation.

Based on our earlier discussion of different applications of modernity and how this is reflected in sporting domains, the principle questions that we want to ask in relation to the focus of this chapter are as follows:

- How is modern sport understood in non-western (ex-colonised) nations, particularly in Arabo-Islamic countries, and in our case, in Algeria?
- Are we moving in the Arabo-Islamic societies, and particularly in Algeria, towards the 'assimilation' of western (liberal and neo-liberal) norms, as well as forms, of practice and management of modern sport?
- What definitions of modern sport are applicable to non-western societies? More importantly, do non-western nations (defined in the globalisation literature as the 'periphery') have the will, and resources to develop a role, in shaping modern sports?

Developing a research strategy and methods

To answer some of these questions, we adopt a constructivist approach, which stresses the need to look at 'reality' or phenomena, such as the professionalisation of sport in Algeria, as a social construct, framed by competing/interacting discourses. The 'professionalisation' of sport in Algeria is thus seen as shaped by the Algerian local (and internal) cultural, political and historical contexts, in relation to (external) global changes or challenges. Critical discourse analysis (CDA) was thus used in the study; we report here to analyse interviewees' conceptualisation of globalisation processes on the one hand and questions related to the formulation and implementation of the government's project for professional sport on the other. It should be noted that the development of sport, and more particularly the professionalisation of sport in Algeria, is studied not as a distinctive, specific (Arab, North African and 'Third World') case but rather as a social phenomenon illustrative of the local–global nexus.

To identify the different meaning systems of modern sport values in the Algerian context, 16 in-depth qualitative interviews[3] were conducted with representatives of the football community, the Algerian polity and civil society in Algeria, in June 2001 and June 2002 (Amara 2003). The interviews lasted for between 45 minutes and one hour in each case. These included representatives of three major political parties, namely the Movement of Society for Peace (MSP), Rally for Culture and Democracy (RCD) and FLN.[4] These three parties seek to promote different ideologies or projects for society that may be characterised in relation to their response towards globalisation (modernisation and westernisation) processes as falling into one of the following approaches: (a) assimilation (RCD) – adopting western modernity and laïcité (broadly a secular approach to politics); (b) integration (FLN) – incorporating 'difference', accepting some aspects of modernity but adapting them to the (Arabo-Islamic) specificities of the Algerian context; and (c) Islamic reformism (MSP) – reconciliation of Islam and modernity (rejection of aspects of modernity that are not consonant with an Islamic world view).

The other interviewees were academics, lecturers in political science, sociology and anthropology at the university of Algiers as well as sports administrators (representatives of clubs, the Algerian Olympic Academy, the Algerian Football Federation, National Football League, Ministry of Youth and Sport).[5]

These interviewees were asked about their conception of modern sport from both technical (organisational, managerial) and politico-ideological terms. We compared this with their views on whether an 'Algerian-specific', local application of modernity should be promoted. We also asked them about their views, as academics, politicians and sport administrators, in relation to the effect of globalisation processes on Algerian society's cultural identity and economy. In relation to sport, the focus in the interviews was on a specific mode of sporting management, that is, professional sport. Our aim was not to provide insight on the expression of politics and cultures as received through the discourse of sport. Rather, we sought to ascertain whether, in the detailed study of these particular interviewees, there was a relationship between concepts/perceptions evident in the domain of sport and in the domain of the more general economic, political and cultural concerns about globalization.

Professional sport was chosen for its strong link, at least in its contemporary form, with western modernity in general and its liberal ideology in particular. The constructs or key words that interview questions covered were related to the following:

- the features which constitute globalisation processes;
- the power of response to the challenges of globalisation;
- the Algerian position in the new world order;
- western domination of world football (values and institutions);
- commercialism and the values of professional sport; and
- Algerian cultural heritage and challenges of globalisation (and of the introduction of professional sport).

Those constructs were organised into two categories of questions, one related to globalisation issues and the other to questions linked to sport issues. This permitted a certain flexibility in asking questions and choosing those categories, which for any given interviewee, may need more focus than others, depending on the interviewee's familiarity with the concepts.

In relation to language, two versions of interview questions were designed, one in Arabic and one in French. Knowing the connotation that the language use in Algeria (Arabophone vs Francophone or Berberophone vs Arabophone)[6] can have on the perceptions and world views (on national identity, political ideology and culture) of both interviewee and interviewer,[7] it was left for the interviewees themselves to choose their own language of communication, Arabic or French or a mixture of Arabic and French. Some of the key words for this study such as globalisation and the West had to be adapted to the Algerian context and were replaced by concepts of 'Mondialisation' and 'Occident', and in Arabic by 'Awlama' and 'El-Gherb', respectively, more accessible to an Algerian audience, although they may express different meanings (positive or negative connotations) in Arabic, Anglo-Saxon and Francophone literatures.

The core issues addressed in the interviews are listed in Appendix 8.1 at the end of this chapter.

We should emphasise here the circumstances in which the interviews took place. It was between 2001 and 2002 that Algeria was slowly emerging from more than ten years of political violence. During this period, some 150,000 people lost their lives, and the country sustained major material and infrastructural damage to the estimated value of $30 billion. In addition to the 7,200 cases of disappearances, resulting from the actions of Algerian security forces and acknowledged by the Algerian government, there were as many as 10,000 cases of abduction by armed groups and over 100,000 people were displaced or forced to leave their homes. Millions of Algerians thus found themselves in a real state of distress and uncertainty about their future.

Even sport, which is the focus of our study, was not safe from this cycle of violence. Some well-known personalities within the sports' media and administrative fields, as well as ordinary football fans, became direct victims of the daily assassinations and bomb attacks. Examples of prominent football personalities who were victims of the bloodshed include, M. Haraigue, the president of the Algerian Football Federation, the President of Bourdj Mnaïl Football Club (East of Algeria) and 'Yamaha', a well-known football fan of the Belouazded Football Club (ex-CR Belcours) (Boudjedra 1999; Colonna 1999). The list of victims also included ten young supporters of USMA Algiers, who were killed while celebrating the success of their team in the 1997 Cup final. This happened in Bouzéreah, in the heart of Algiers, in one of the Algiers' most popular streets adjacent to 5 July Olympic Stadium. However, because all kinds of people have been the direct victims of this generalized violence, we cannot make any assumptions with regard to the political or ideological objectives behind the assassination of personalities within the domain of football. The reason for targeting them may simply be the popularity of the game and the media exposure that it attracts rather than a violent rejection of a Western cultural phenomenon.

It was hard under such conditions for the interviewer (the first-named author of this chapter) to ask interviewees about sport and the Algerian government's project for the professionalisation of sport. However, discussion about sport could be regarded, not as a form of escapism from the hard reality of violence in Algeria, but more as an attempt to search (for both the interviewer and the interviewees) to identify some signs of normalization and a break from the depressing daily news headlines.

Data collection and the approach to analysis

Prior to the conducting of interviews in Algeria, three pilot interviews were conducted with British and Algerian intellectuals in the UK (each of whom specialised in Algerian, francophone and post-colonial studies). The primary aim was to check the comprehension by, and reactions of the respondents to, the different questions asked particularly in relation to theories and concepts such as modernity, globalisation, multi-national, secularism or neo-liberalism. Interviews for both the pilot and the main interviews were recorded with digital recorder (with the permission of the interviewees). The selection and contacting of interviewees in Algeria were undertaken after the interview schedule had been evaluated and modified.

Further sources, namely press articles and official reports, were also used.[8] These were useful to identify the values as well as the goals and organisational strategy of the Algerian national sport (football) system. The cross-checking of data, resulting from different strategies and research tools, was utilised to clarify meanings and to check the 'repeatability' of observations or interpretations.

CDA was employed to analyse the interview transcripts. The aim of CDA is to 'unmask' ideologically permeated and often obscured structures of power, political control and dominance, as well as discriminatory inclusion and exclusion (group, gender, class) in language use, 'taking into account that discourse is structured by dominance, that every discourse is historically produced and interpreted (situated in time and space) and that dominance structures are legitimated by ideologies of powerful groups' (Wodak and Meyer 2001: p. 3). For the purpose of this chapter, the aims of the analysis were first to reveal/discover how the designation of 'self' (locality, Algerianity – an Arabo-Berber-Islamic and Mediterranean identity) and the 'other' (global forces, the West) to operate for Algerians from different intellectual, ideological or political backgrounds. The second and related concern was to understand the position of interviewees in relation to professional sport, which is identified in the literature predominantly as a global and western product. In other words, did the respondents regard sport as a defining feature of 'the other'?

CDA may be regarded here as facilitating a general research strategy of the deconstruction of sport in local modernity. This deconstruction attempts to reformulate or redefine globalisation and modern sport (including professional football), concepts that were arguably established in the West and based on a western history of modernity. This deconstruction provides a lens through which to view the homogeneity/heterogeneity and the dichotomy existing in the designation of interviewees of themselves (e.g. through their references to 'we', 'I' and 'our') and of 'others' (e.g. through their references to global forces, multinationals, the West, IMF, international sports organisations). Additionally, the approach aims to discover whether the interviewees' perceptions of 'we' and 'others' have/do not have an impact on their positions in relation to professional sports (practice and values), or by contrast, whether it is viewed as a 'neutral' field, relatively unaffected by local positioning in relation to the global order. Figures 8.1 and 8.2 illustrate the different horizontal and vertical levels of analysis.

Discourse analysis which focuses on studying discourse as text and talk in social practices allows us to analyse discursive strategies employed in different social environments (e.g. media, family, political institution), in order to establish multiple realities or remaking(s) of the world. The task of discourse analysis is not, therefore, to apply pre-existing categories and concepts (e.g. sport, modernity, local identity) to participants' talk but rather to identify the ways in which participants (themselves) produce, construct and employ concepts, arguments and meanings.

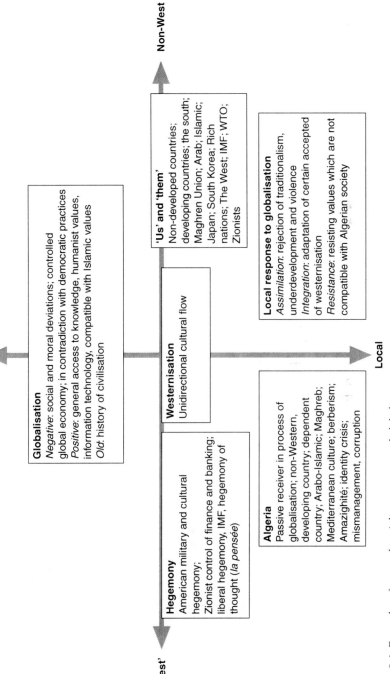

Global

Globalisation
Negative: social and moral deviations; controlled global economy; in contradiction with democratic practices
Positive: general access to knowledge, humanist values, information technology, compatible with Islamic values
Old: history of civilisation

'West'

Hegemony
American military and cultural hegemony;
Zionist control of finance and banking; liberal hegemony, IMF, hegemony of thought (*la pensée*)

Westernisation
Unidirectional cultural flow

Algeria
Passive receiver in process of globalisation; non-Western, developing country; dependent country; Arabo-Islamic; Maghreb; Mediterranean culture; berberism; Amazighité; identity crisis; mismanagement, corruption

Non-West

'Us' and 'them'
Non-developed countries; developing countries; the south; Maghren Union; Arab; Islamic; Japan; South Korea; Rich nations; The West; IMF; WTO; Zionists

Local response to globalisation
Assimilation: rejection of traditionalism, underdevelopment and violence
Integration: adaptation of certain accepted of westernisation
Resistance: resisting values which are not compatible with Algerian society

Local

Figure 8.1 Examples of respondents' discourses around globalisation.

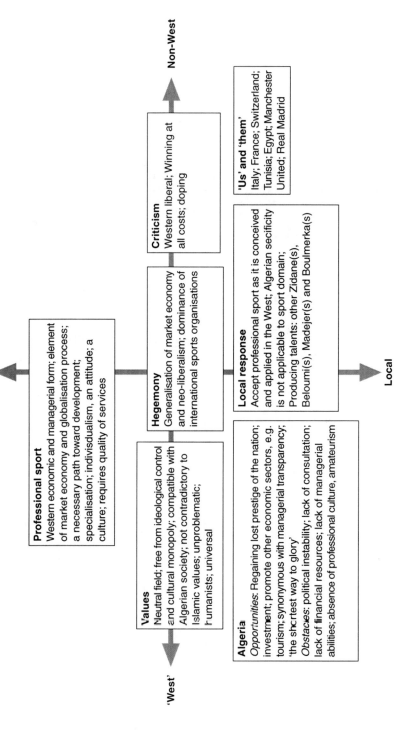

Figure 8.2 Examples of respondents' discourses around professional sport.

Accordingly, the aim is to go beyond content to see how discourse is used, consciously or unconsciously, to achieve particular functions and effects, that is, the way the world is socially constructed. This implies identifying multiple realities rather than a singular reality. Moreover, such an approach seeks to unmask structures of power, political control and dominance, which may be ideologically obscured given that the discourse we use usually serves to reinforce our interests, positions and privileges. Discourse analysis seeks to provide a (re)construction of the perceptions and attitudes of representatives of different political and ideological groups (e.g. strategies of assimilation, reformism and integration) that exist within Algerian national space. These attitudes and perceptions relate to their group feeling and solidarity, to the attribution to 'self', as well as towards 'others', members of out-groups. In other words, this reflects the construction of meaning of 'local singularity' in contrast to the global order and of local resistance (if such exists) towards global challenges.

The applied strategy of discourse analysis

The critical discourse analytic approach employed by Wodak *et al.* (2001) provided us with examples of the process of doing discourse analysis which we adapted to our purposes and which enabled us to attain a degree of rigour in our analysis of interviewee's discourse positions, not in a positivist sense but in terms of warrantability (soundness and trustworthiness) (Wood and Kroger 2000). The kind of discursive construction or 'analytical intervention' (Wodak and Meyer 2001: p. 8) served to detect different (plural or singular, heterogeneous/homogeneous) productions by respondents of local uniqueness or distinctiveness in adapting global cultural, economic and political forms (in our particular case, the professionalisation of sport). The discourse included the following justifications.

Justification of 'positive' forms of uniqueness and resistance

A strategy of differences between 'us' and 'them' described Wodak and Meyer (2001: p. 37) as a strategy of singularisation and differences that incorporate arguments concerning notions of national positive uniqueness (including 'we are superior to them'), in addition to notions of national independence and autonomy.

Arguments concerning external threats (global forces) and warnings (shared worries) about the loss of national autonomy or independence.

The will to unify/co-operate/feel and show solidarity to resist such external threats.

Resistance/rejection of an action, the consequences of which are depicted as negative for the country (e.g. western modernity, liberalism, secularism).

Negative uniqueness or neutrality

Extra-national dependence/external forces/force of facts (e.g. IMF, World Bank, FIFA).

Rejecting neutrality and negative singularisation/or isolation (e.g. hyper localism).

In the context of this study, the appreciation of these principles implied three stages or phases of analysis. The first stage of the analysis focused on understanding different interviewers' representation of local group feeling(s) or national identity(ies). In other words, what was the respondent's description of local distinctiveness? Was it nationalism based on western modernisation and a western perception of 'nation'? Or was it part of what Tahi (1992) describes as 'active-syncretic acculturation' that consists of selection and active application of suitable (western) extraneous cultural elements (in addition to Arab nationalism), an approach that adopts both the European system of nation state and the separation of religion from politics? Or was it based on Islam as the foundation of nationality for Muslims, which is superior to any other forms of association or any national commitment? Most importantly, do all respondents define locality in the same manner?

The second stage of the analysis emphasised the interviewees' views on globalisation: Did they perceive globalisation as an imposed, hegemonic, western and unidirectional project or in contrast as a universal movement in the elaboration of which countries from the periphery can participate? How could the relationship between the interviewees and globalisation be described? Was it a relationship based on resistance (total rejection of the hegemony of the West and multinationals), or was it based on integration and negotiation? How did respondents view the role of Algeria in the new world order?

In the last stage of the analysis, the orientation was to re-conceptualise the interviewees' perception of the professionalisation of sport in Algeria. How was the professionalisation of sport viewed or explained? Was it part of the globalisation process? What was the relationship of respondents to this project? Was it a relationship of resistance or total acceptance? Or was it perceived as being a neutral domain (part of universal culture) and therefore not under any ideological or political manipulation by global forces (such as international sports federations)?

Defining the discourses: results of the analysis

We provide next a summary of the main respondents' discourses in relation to globalisation challenges and the professionalisation of sport.

Globalisation in the interviewees' discourse

On the issue of local responses towards global forces, we can divide interviewees discourse into the following groupings:

Statements in favour of positive globalisation and resistant towards negative globalisation

This group comprises of the representative from Islamic reformism/the Movement for Peace and the political scientist. Both respondents acknowledged the benefit of positive globalisation in the progress of Algerian society and called for a rejection of:

- negative globalisation which represents a threat to the nation's sovereignty and was also seen as synonymous with social deviance, immorality and inequality between nations and
- radical resistance towards the West adopted by local groups (associated with violence and isolationism). Within this group, effective resistance was to be achieved through local and regional co-operation with, in particular, supporters of Arab identity and of Islamic solidarity but also through positive adaptation to the external environment without renouncing or diluting commitment to Algerian identity and also maintaining what the political scientist referred to as the 'minimum of institutional principles and values'.

It [globalisation] is bringing back the age of feudalism ... globalisation neglects the concept of democracy. From an Islamic perspective we strive for the development of human rights and freedom. Globalisation has come to take away those human rights, of sovereignty and ownership. Financially and economically, globalisation becomes a tool of oppression that prevents freedom of expression or choice .... More dangerously the country is facing terrorism and violence that has affected the principal (strongest) value of Algeria's nationalism and union, that is Islam. Causing deviation from and deforming its real message, resulting also in a regionalisation of the country
(Interview with respondent from Islamic reformism/Movement for Peace
June 2001)

The problems of Algerian society are different from those of British society ... in the mechanisms of development, consciousness and traditions.
(Interview with political scientist June 2001)

Statements in favour of positive globalisation and calling for a compromise or integration of global and local approaches

This group incorporates statements by the majority of respondents, namely the representative of the National Liberation Front, the Director of the Algerian Olympic Academy, the sociologist and the anthropologist. These respondents all agreed about the importance of positive globalisation for non-western, underdeveloped nations, in the acquisition of democracy, access to knowledge and human rights, and moreover, this was regarded as a necessary condition of development and progress. This group also agreed about the need for compromise and adaptation while dealing with global challenges which were seen as a threat to Algerian identity and sovereignty and which were strongly associated with social failings, family breakdown, corruption, materialism, sectarianism and individualism. However, not all members of this group agreed about the way to compromise or react towards the negative aspects of globalisation processes. The discourse regarding this point was ambiguous or inconsistent. On the one hand, the notion of compromise was expressed as an 'adapted' integration that needed to adjust to the ('unpredictable') parameters of globalisation. This is apparent in the following excerpt: '*We are obliged to compromise*. This compromise will include 50/50 or 30/70 *we cannot know*, because it is *hard to predict* the result of globalisation influences on young generations [more than others]' (interview with representative of the Party of National Liberation Front June 2001). On the other hand, the same concept was presented as a 'positive' resistance, which aimed to transform western products in line with local realities and the adaptation of past western experiences of integrating tradition and modernity. In the words of the sociologist, what has happened in Algerian society represents conflicts in the struggle to find solutions for a crisis and new conditions for development,

> Globalisation consists of *two movements or faces*: first *unification* or *unipolarism*. Technology and market economies have experienced a real boom after the decline of communism in the world, which played in the past the role of slowing down this historical movement and paid a high price for this position. The other face is *the emergence of population and cultures* as a result of conflicts … conflict in this case becomes the *engine for change*. This is *my view* about globalisation. It is *a contradictory, conflictual*, and *an ancient phenomenon* with new forms …. This conflictual movement is *the engine* of nations' emancipation … new forms that combine *tradition and modernity* … the question is how can we gather social forces, which include specific abilities, culture and civilisation, for development?
>
> (Interview with sociologist June 2001)

In both cases, resistance towards western hegemony and the western economic order can exist only in a virtual sense. It exists for the interviewees in theory but in practice is impossible to apply, due to the uneven position that globalisation has created between rich and poor countries and the internal challenges that the latter are facing. 'It is *hard* for any country *to affirm the existence of a cultural policy to resist* [this diffusion]. There may *exist a sort of resistance* but it is *very limited one*' (interview with representative of the Party of National Liberation Front June 2001).

Statements in favour of globalisation without reserve

This approach was reflected by the respondent from the RCD, representative of democratic/*laïque* political wing, who argued that the problem was not situated in values associated with globalisation, but at the local level, that is at the level of the government's representatives who are in charge of negotiating with international bodies. The 'positiveness' of the process for this respondent depended on the high level of adoption of globalisation conditions and the internal condition of the country, as well as the regime's policy towards culture and identity. This respondent recognised both the legitimacy of globalisation's contribution to progress and the enlightenment project, and regionalisation trends, particularly in relation to *Berberism*. Globalisation was thus not problematic but was regarded as a necessary condition of development and democracy. Terms such as resistance, rejection, opposition towards western values were absent in this discourse.

> The entire problem is situated in this issue [identity]. There is in Algeria a hybrid regime. A regime that refuses to recognise its identity and its origin. A large part of the population, which the constitution did not take into consideration, is rejected and not recognised. I am giving a political view regarding the recent events in the Kabylie region. The problem emerged after the 1980 riots in this region and the creation of the Berber movement. For a country to achieve stability socially and economically we need first to respect the person, the citizen, to respect his/her values and cultural identity. The cultural question needs to be resolved urgently …. It needs to be resolved as soon as possible in order to be able to resolve other problems.
>
> (Interview with representative of the Party of Rally for Culture and Democracy June 2001)

Professional sport in the discourse of the interviewees

The observations which emerge from our analysis of interviewees' discourse in relation to the distinctiveness of Algerian sporting culture reflect a general scepticism on the part of interviewees concerning any cultural exceptionalism or specificity of the Algerian case. This was the case both in relation to the position of Algeria in the new world order and in relation to the government's implementation of the plan to introduce professional football. The discourse of criticism directed towards aspects of western ideology (namely liberalism, individualism, secularism, or political and economic hegemony) under the form of Algerian nationalism and Islamic identity (particularly from a reformist point of view) existed alongside discourses of acceptance, assimilation and a notion of the 'passive outsider' on the part of individuals from other parts of the political spectrum. The question of the compatibility of professional football (and its liberal/neo-liberal) values with Algerian society and identities remained unasked or was not perceived as essential or a priority in the respondents' discourse. The responses of the political scientist and of the representative of the RCD Party reflect these tendencies.

> Globalisation is not only a case of space reduction between populations, it is about the attempt to expand and diffuse unidirectional principles, as reported by Fukuyama on ideological conflict and liberal hegemony.
>
> (Interview with political scientist June 2001)

There is no such thing as Algerian *spécificité*, players are human beings, they need to be free, to be well managed and respected too (respect plays an important role). In Algeria players are not respected ... we need to apply this model of professional sport 100% ... there will be no such thing as Algerian specificity at least in sport, because sport is a universal culture. In the domain of sport it would be a monumental mistake to consider Algerian specificity.

(Interview with respondent from the Rally for Culture and Democracy June 2001)

The principal engine is the economy and individualism that may take the form of group interest in developing sport practices .... There is also techno-logical development and capitalism. Other aspects related to specialisation, *spiritual needs, respect for the environment and religion.* The latter could be used to resolve identity problems.

(Interview with sociologist June 2001)

In the response of the interviewees, we find that the discourse of 'we', while talking about Algerian identity, or that of the reconstruction of the society's lost identity and integrity (referring to the political violence) was present, or explicitly referred to, while discussing educational, financial and cultural ques-tions. However, in the sport domain, the concept of Algerian identity was com-pletely rejected, put aside or was simply absent, and sport was treated by most respondents as a apolitical, non-ideological, universal and value-free system. In the same vein, professional football was conceived as a 'secular' domain that needed to be regulated, as with any other economic sector, by market rules and managerial, scientific, modern and rational standards, in which the values of the market economy (competitiveness and market forces) represent key facets.

I think there is a fundamental aspect, we have only to copy what others have done before us, 30 years ago and try to gain time. Of course we are not going to start from scratch, we have only to adopt what other countries have already achieved. If they took 20 or 30 years to achieve their actual level, we can save at least 20 years .... In other words 10 years trying to attain their level.

(Interview with representative of National Football League June 2002)

Because professional sport was explained as being an integral product of the globalisation process, it was therefore a 'natural' model for management, in which progress as well as other aspects of modernity in sport, namely economic profit and nation state building could be achieved.

the primary stage is to look for a model ... but Algeria is entering into mondialisation, and has just signed a partnership with the European Union ... Algeria will soon join the WTO, ... international rules which are going to be imposed on us, while we are preparing ourselves to apply them gradually ... we have to do it, or we are going to remain in an archaic system ... it is the same for industry.

(Interview with representative of the Algerian National Football League
June 2002)

One can argue that the transformation of football from amateurism to 'non-amateurism' (rather than to professionalism), to use the description employed by some respondents, or from the state's (étatique) legalistic model to that of a professional 'market' system[9] coincided with the transformation of Algerian society or, at least, of the state's political and economic ideology. This transition was from a system based on socialism, populism and the welfare state to one based on liberalism and a market economy. The latter was conceived as an essential condition of 'progress' which would facilitate the integration of Algeria into the new world order in political, economic, industrial and financial levels. This integration would follow a period of more than ten years of absence from the arena of international affairs, largely as a consequence of internal political violence. In addition, because of the perceived failure of twenty years of populism and socialism, the market economy was equated, at least at a psychological level, with democracy and freedom (Ellyas 1996).

The professionalisation of sport should not be linked to ideological criteria but to criteria of ability and stability, because it is concerned with human experiences that could be developed .... Professional sport is based on humanist values, changed but not directed by any ideology. Our party views sport as a beneficial sector if it is well planned.

(Interview with respondent from Islamic reformism/Movement for Peace
June 2001)

Professional values are compatible with Algeria in society, because it is a society open to the market economy. Why should sport be an exception? ... there is a logic of interest, whether with free movement of players, or recruitment/ or reduction of staff. Those are mechanisms resulting from this logic. Sport could not be excluded from the general frame of society.

(Interview with the director of the Algerian Olympic Academy June 2001)

Buying and selling players is in fact concerned with buying and selling talents and skills. This is acceptable in Islamic values .... Professionalism is synonymous with financial revenue. Transforming sport to a financial resource .... Professionalism is a criterion that can be used to evaluate the political, economic and social system and development of any country .... Professionalism is based on competition, which leads to technical development and which needs special equipment and infrastructures.

(Interview with the anthropologist June 2001)

In terms of professional football, the values of democracy and liberalism imply an opening up of the government project of professionalisation of sport to a national debate, where political parties, sponsors, clubs managers and players should participate, first in the revision of state's objectives in relation to national sport by giving priority to elite sports and second in the redefinition of the conditions for clubs to turn professional and to maximise their sources of revenue (specifically merchandising, sponsorship, media income and gate receipts).

Furthermore, it was argued that there should be a reconsideration of the sport's governing body's criteria concerning the distribution of broadcasting rights, which according to respondents should be based on performance rather than the old socialist values of equality and state dirigisme or that of Algerian collective 'solidarity'. This implies a revision of the state's role (i.e. a limitation of state power, horizontal subsidiarity and de-centralisation) and a reconsideration of the clubs' position in terms of decision-making (e.g. establishing the club presidents' association as a new 'positive' force). This is reflected in the following statements:

> It is for the clubs themselves to decide about prices of tickets [the most significant source of revenue for the clubs] ... the supporters of Real Madrid need to pay the price to watch Zinedine Zidane .... Supporters, unemployed or not, have to pay the ticket price and the clubs themselves should decide on the price.
>
> (Interview with the director of National Football teams June 2002)

> thus it is a domain that needs to be explored and put in place. Myself I think to reach this level we need first to organise ourselves [as clubs presidents] in an association ... which should serve as a positive force that could bring concrete benefits to football, in collaboration with the National League of Football .... In other words this association shouldn't have to interfere in the work of the National Football League ... but will constitute a proposing body ..., trying to defend all this and put in place mechanisms that enable us to protect the club image. It is the Clubs and the National Football League's task to establish more efficient means without affecting both clubs and the National League of Football.
>
> (Interview with president of USMA football club June 2002)

'Resistance' in the sense of rejecting, challenging or even transforming or re-adapting a professional football model to the Algerian context was not envisaged. The only form of 'resistance' expressed was the promotion of equal opportunities to allow 'Third World' countries to win and compete at international level, which could contribute to the regaining of international prestige and to the resolution of internal political, cultural and social crisis.

> Professionalism is not a choice .... Professional sport has imposed itself for one reason: the search for glory and the shortest route to achieve the best results. ... Therefore, it is not possible to be open in the domain of culture and the economy and not in sport. Professionalism is part of a global

change and ... countries, which have refused ... Superficially ... to adopt this form, in reality are obliged to apply it.

> (Interview with respondent from the Party of National Liberation Front June 2001)

Localisation of professional sport is problematic and hard to achieve in Algeria.

> (Interview with sociologist June 2001)

There are also some international pressures that impose on national systems adoption of external models. The FIFA regulations could be viewed as mechanisms that regulate sport activities, including sanctions that can be applied on countries which refuse to respect those regulations. Sometimes it results in a total ban on participation in international competitions.

> (Interview with political scientist June 2001)

We cannot create a model similar to Germany, but we can compete and win against Germany.

> (Interview with respondent from Islamic reformism/Movement for Peace June 2001)

we want this to be confrontation between equals. Openness to those universal dimensions in sport means openness to the world. Sport is an important phenomenon in the third millennium. I do not think that its establishment will be reduced to fulfil recreational needs. Sport is an important element in political plans ... small countries that succeed in marking their presence create a mobilisation at national level and consolidation of identity.

> (Interview with director of the Algerian Olympic Academy June 2001)

Concluding remarks

The fundamental question the above groups and categories of responses invite is why do interviewees accept professional sport, which is acknowledged as a western product with its values and mode of practice, virtually without reserve? In parallel with this, in the name of Algerian identity and Islamic principles, the same respondents (with different levels of intensity) expressed concerns about criticism and even resistance to globalisation, the values of which, according to the interviewees themselves, have the same (western) ideological and geo-political origin as professional sport. Some aspects of (negative) globalisation (namely individualism, secularism and materialism) were even presented in generic terms as a serious challenge to Algerian sovereignty, which is threatened by the hegemony of American and world banks (which were described by the representative of the Movement for Peace, for example, as being controlled by Zionist forces). The only respondents who showed consistency in their view about globalisation on the one hand and professional sport on the other were the representatives from the RCD and the political scientist. The former accepted both concepts and processes of globalisation and professionalisation, which he regarded as being essential conditions for development and progress and thus important elements for modernity for Algerian society. The latter expressed concerns when talking about the results of imposing both global values and professional sports on other non-western cultures, which in his view may be the cause of future conflicts or clashes between cultures.

Our analysis of interviewees' remarks shows that the discourse of criticism directed towards aspects of western ideology, or political and economic (banking) hegemony, under the aegis of Algerian nationalism, and Islamic identity (particularly from a reformist point of view), existed alongside a discourse of acceptance, assimilation and the notion of Algeria being a passive outsider in the global order. These tendencies were in relation to both the globalisation processes and the professionalisation project for football. The question of compatibility or incompatibility of professional (liberal/neo-liberal) values in football with Algerian societal values and identities remained unasked or was not perceived as essential or a priority in the respondents' discourse. One of the reasons that the sports domain was conceived by interviewees, consciously or otherwise, as a neutral field (neutral in the sense of being low in political salience, non-ideological and a relatively value-free system) related to the anticipation of the national prestige that the adoption of professional sport could bring. From our understanding of respondents' positions, this objective may be seen as more important than any other concerns associated with local distinctiveness. If this is the case, the question we may ask is to what extent is the endeavour for national prestige a function of the previous ten years of political instability and violence which has affected the image of Algeria in the international scene?

The local Algerian context was presented as a negative function which stood in stark contrast to the situation in other developed nations which had enjoyed success (such as France or Spain). This negative view of the Algerian sporting context was evident at all levels, whether in relation to the application of the professional system or in respect of creativity, modernisation, sense of organisation and managerial culture in football. In Algeria, sport in general, and football for our case study, was still managed, at least in the interviewees' terms, according to regionalist (intra-Algerian) considerations, a pragmatic and improvised approach. An example of such a unilateral approach was the decision to suspend the relegation system in the league for two years.[10] This decision was taken, according to respondents, as a top-down (state) imposed decision and was described as illustrating an 'unscientific' (archaic, outdated, traditional) approach. For the respondents, the crisis of the current national football system was simply a reflection of Algerian society's multiple and compound crisis, with clubs operating without the economic means to be professional and with too much central intervention.

> I can talk a little bit about Tunisia. The Tunisians started applying professionalism which involves only four well known clubs maximum; Esperance

de Tunis, Etoile Sahel, Club Africain, Sfax .... *Those are clubs...*I had the chance to visit Tunisia ... *Esperance de Tunis has all the means to become professional* ... a professional club.

(Interview with representative of Ministry of Sport and Youth June 2002: emphasis added)

It is the clubs' and the National Football League's task to establish more efficient means without affecting both clubs and the National Football League ...the National Football League's role is to establish a calendar, designating matches, and that is all .... There are other subjects that we need to discuss .... *I think that quite soon*, we are going to discuss TV rights and issues of clubs' image ... sports products.

(Interview with president of USMA football club June 2002: emphasis added)

Professional sport is conceived as a 'secular' domain that needs to be regulated just like any other economic sector by the market, with managerial and scientific (up-to-date and rational) standards, where the values of the market economy (liberalism and generation of profit) are among its most important facets. Thus, accepting the application of 'professional' football both as reflecting a set of values and as a mode of organisation will require a redefinition of the state's objectives in relation to national sport. This would mean giving priority to elite sports, sometimes to the detriment of mass sport (e.g. in the use of facilities). It would also require, in terms of the football business, a redefining of the conditions which clubs should meet if they are to turn professional, maximising other sources of revenue (merchandising, sponsoring, gate receipts) and requiring a reconsideration of the National Football League criteria for the distribution of broadcasting rights. This implies a revision of the state's role (e.g. limiting state power, fostering horizontal subsidiarity and decentralisation) and a reconsideration of the clubs' position in terms of decision-making so that they might represent a new 'positive' force, within the national football structure.

Furthermore, the success of professional sport will depend on favourable economic, cultural and social conditions, as well as on good governance based on rational and scientific measures (an appropriate juridical system), and will require a better (controlled) use of existing funds for the development of football.

Distribution of revenues has to be based on performance rather than equality ... the role of the National Football League is to be the judge, resolving different conflicts within the league.... We cannot talk about balance or equity between clubs...it is the market economy that regularises professional football and not the Ministry of Youth and Sport (whose role is linked mainly to ethical issues such as doping).

(Interview with director of National Football teams June 2002: emphasis added)

The position of Algeria, defined by respondents, as a country of the periphery (at least in the world of football), leaves the Algerian football authorities 'no alternative' but to follow the path of professionalisation of sport, already adopted by other nations, including neighbouring Arab, Islamic and African countries. This approach is advocated without asking questions about the positive or negative impact that such a project may have on the future of football. In other words, respondents accept the position of Algeria as both 'participant' (in the football system) and 'outsider' (in the sense of having to accept certain conditions or types of approach), thus accepting both the positive and negative sides of *mondialisation* (e.g. a decrease in the capacity to defend national interests and the growth of hyper consumerism).

For the respondents, the issue in relation to professionalisation is not whether the system is compatible with Algerian societal and cultural contexts, its traditions and belief systems, but rather whether appropriate discussions have taken place.

> the lack of state subsidy. Can we talk about state subsidy in professional sport? This should be the responsibility of clubs' presidents. Today some clubs, which cannot afford to travel, are threatening to stop competing before the end of the season, because they do not have enough money. This is not professional sport.
>
> (Interview with representative from the Party for Culture and Democracy
> June 2002)

> Every time that a Minister of Youth and Sport is changed, a new President of the Federation is nominated. Every time that the coach of the national team is dismissed a new formation is called. There is instability in the mind of national sport managers. ... Algeria lacks efficient (professional) sport administrators, planned strategy in building professional schools, and links between sports clubs and companies. Therefore the application of professional sport could elevate the level of sport practice and performance for both genders, in order that other Zidane(s), will emerge in the future .... We need a new vision and strategy able to assimilate potential like Morcelis, Madjers, Hassibas. These are models in expressing Algerian abilities in competing.
>
> (Interview with respondent from Islamic reformism/Movement for Peace
> June 2001)

> *We are thinking about professionalism* without taking into account human means and abilities ... *we need real management and experience in directing enterprises* [business oriented] that could bring a plus [like Manchester United or Real Madrid].
>
> (The director of the Algerian Olympic Academy: emphasis added)

Research implications

Finally, we would underline that the aim of this study was neither to evaluate policy (the government project for professional sport) nor to generalise the empirical study results, suggesting an applicable model for professional football in Algeria (in the Maghreb or in the Arab and Islamic world), which would take into consideration the uniqueness of that region of the world as an alternative to western model(s). The contribution of the research was, we hope, to raise questions that had not been addressed before, at least in the Algerian context. Such questions relate to Algerian identity and particularism (or spécificité), which link on the one hand, modernity, postmodernity and globalisation theories, approaches and debates to Algerian history, society, polity and geography and link on the other hand the discussion on globalisation and localisation, within the Algerian context, to sport in general and football in particular, looking at a specific ideology or mode of management and practice in sport, which is 'professionalism'.

For this reason, we have chosen a constructivist rather than positivist/modernist way of both addressing and analysing the research questions. The approach was based on deconstruction and reconstruction of certain presumed realities 'out there' that we tend (as Algerian, or western policy analysts, sociologists, historians, Francophone or Arabophone) to take for granted. The research problematised, for those concerned with the Algerian context, the existence 'out there' of a common, a uniform and a homogeneous understanding of Algerian (we versus others) 'locality', 'identity', 'history', 'geography', 'ideology' and society. In relation to our case study, a shared conceptualisation of the meaning of 'professional football' within the academic, political and sports community was similarly problematised. The use of discourse analysis to interpret the language use allows us to glimpse interviewees' interests, world views and argumentation strategies and has, we would argue, helped us to gain a certain flexibility, critical subjectivity and self-reflexivity, which traditional methods would fail to capture.

Appendix 8.1: the interview schedule

A. *Globalisation issues*

Algeria is developing politically, economically and culturally in a globalised context. By globalisation I mean that the world is experiencing increasingly rapid and extensive flows of finance, technology, ideas/values, people, media, etc.

- Do countries from the world's economic core and transnational corporations use this process of globalisation to extend their economic, political and cultural influences (or control)? How?
- Is national sovereignty to be regarded as under threat, due to the increased

external pressure coming from above (multinationals, supra-national organisations) transforming the nationstate into a relatively powerless agent?

- Do you see globalisation as simply another form of US dominance, or do you think that new forms of global and local politics, economics and cultures are emerging?
- What tools do people or nations in non-Western countries have at their disposal to embrace, adapt to and/or resist globalisation?
- It is said that the neo-liberal (market economy) model of society is spreading throughout the globe. In resistance to this some groups advocate total rejection and the adoption of locally specific cultural and political forms. Is there any other model of development that Algerian society could adopt which is a compromise between total acceptance of neo-liberalism, and total rejection of the West?

B. Sport issues

The Algerian government's plan for professional sport has been developed over recent years.

- What have been the major influences
  a) in promoting the drive to have a professional league?
  b) in shaping the kind of system adopted?
- Is the Algerian model of professional sport unique, i.e. a wholly locally developed system?
- Is it a system 'borrowed from' or adapted from the model of professional sport in other countries?
- Why do you think the state developed the professional sport system at this point in time?
- What do you (or your party) think about modernist and Western values in professional sport (consumerism, free movement of players, roles of agents, etc.)?
- Can the values associated with professional sport in the West be applied to Algerian society? Do you think that professional sport in Algeria is an assimilation of the Western model of professional sport (in terms of its values and organisation)?
- Are we able to build a local model of professional sport compatible with the Algerian context and its values?
- Will the development of sport result in the meeting of commercial needs rather than social needs (sports participation, health)?
- Do you consider it is important to preserve

  a) local art?
  b) local cultural forms?
  c) local sport forms?
  d) if so why? And how?

Part III

Interculturalism in policy analysis

Methodological pluralism and ethical discourse

9 Bridging research traditions and world views

Universalisation versus generalisation in the case for gender equity

Ian Henry

There is a classic distinction made in the policy analysis literature between analysis *for* policy (i.e. contributing more or less directly to the policy process) and analysis *of* policy (critical analysis of what governments do or do not do in a given policy area). Chapters 4 and 6 of this book (representing Types I and II approaches) are more closely associated with analysis for policy (indeed both draw on commissioned work) while Chapters 5, 7 and 8 are more clearly characterised as examples of analysis of policy (and represent Types II–IV). This distribution across Types I–IV is no surprise of course since analysis for policy reflects the kinds of research commissioned by policy makers and tends to be more often associated with empirical if not empiricist/positivist approaches and, though less often, with ideational, rich description, with the use of ideal types as models and (if any) with explicit reference to the theoretical context, tending to focus on a middle range theoretical frame. Much has been made in policy rhetoric in recent years of the injunction for 'evidence-based practice', and this has probably intensified the emphasis on Types I and II approaches in analysis for policy, and in particular empiricist, positivist evidence.

These four paradigmatic positions (positivist, interpretivist/ideational, critical/neo-realist and postmodernist) are often presented as 'hermeneutically sealed' off from one another, that is, that their ontological and epistemological premises are mutually incompatible. Thus, if ontological and epistemological positions are explicitly acknowledged (and of course they all too rarely are), then the embracing of 'quantitative', evidence garnered from positivist approaches, might seem to be inconsistent with Types III and IV approaches, and for the purist even Type II. Indeed, Marsh and Furlong (2002) point out that ontological positions are 'more like a skin than a jacket' and therefore cannot be chopped and changed simply at the whim of the researcher. However, some policy actors and academics do range across the methodologies, or at least the methods, identified to some degree (as the author's involvement in the range of studies reported in this book illustrates). Is this then a critical inconsistency of approach? Of course, there may be a certain amount of theoretical pragmatism especially where ontology and epistemology remain implicit concerns. However, mixing of method is also explicitly justified from a range of perspectives. Thus, I want to answer this question of methodological relativity in two ways: first with an argument in principle about the flexibility of method implied by a particular ontological and epistemological position, that of critical realism; and subsequently with an example of the application of mixed methods in a particular comparative sports policy example. This will subsequently take us on to consider the ethical dimension of particular perspectives.

Critical realism and methodological pluralism

To begin with the argument in principle, let us consider some fairly well worn ground in simplified terms. Postmodern critiques of scientific objectivity have undermined confidence in the Modernist notion of the establishing of universal truths. Even in the physical world, it is not possible to refer, in an 'absolute' manner, to the speed and direction in which a particular object is travelling without some initial agreement on what is going to be assumed to be the 'static' point from which one can measure speed and direction of travel. In the social world also, there is a need of some consensus on, for example, the point from which one measures, on what counts in terms of units of measurement and how such measurement tasks are to be undertaken. Thus, universally true claims cannot be made about social and physical phenomena, since the premises of arguments cannot be regarded as 'universally true' (true for all persons for all time) or 'universally held' (true by all persons for all time). However, though *universal* claims cannot be made, *generalisable* claims may be. In order to make such general claims in the physical world (e.g. lead is heavier than water), or in the social world (e.g. patriarchal structures reduce women's access to positions of power), we need to develop agreed premises for the argument promoted.

Let us take, for example, the premises of the critical realist position, associated with Bhaskar (1975, 1979, 1989). Bhaskar's characterisation of science argues that the quest for scientific knowledge or explanation starts with an uncontroversial description of some phenomenon p (note that this is not an incontrovertible statement – the former being socially agreed as generally accepted, rather than the latter 'undeniable').

> The question is then asked, 'What must be the case for p to be possible?' ... An example from social life might be: 'Jane is a student.' For anyone to be a student there must be teachers, bodies of knowledge to be taught and learned, educational institutions to define the roles of teacher and student and so on. Since Jane is a student, the necessary conditions of possibility for someone to be a student must be satisfied, and so for example we can conclude that educational institutions exist.
>
> (Benton and Craib 2001: pp. 122–3)

How we conclude that such phenomena are associated with p is partly by the observation of a pattern (with the caveats that such observations may not always be accurate and that observations are not theory-neutral) and subsequently by asking the question 'What underlying structure or mechanism would, if it existed, explain this pattern?' Subsequently, the scientist goes on to ask, 'If the existence of this underlying mechanism, structure or tendency was assumed, what further effects would we expect to observe?' Finally, the scientist will search for evidence of these anticipated observations actually existing under appropriate conditions.

Of course, in many of the natural sciences, we can seek, especially through experimental controls, to separate out intervening variables, in order to isolate those in which we are particularly interested and thus demonstrate their particular effects. The laboratory experiment is a closed system. However, in the social sciences where we operate with open systems and cannot isolate variables, we are restricted to seeking to explain the existence of mechanisms or tendencies by identifying critical instances. Thus, for example, claims about the influence of patriarchal mechanisms might be evaluated by reference to the observation of organisations/social contexts in which women rather than men exercise power.

Bhaskar's analysis implies that there are three levels of reality:

- the **real** (mechanisms, powers, tendencies or deep structures which the natural and social sciences seek to identify);
- the **actual** (sequences of events which may be produced under experimental conditions or are *in principle* observable under certain conditions in the social world);
- the **empirical** (observed events).

For critical realists, social theory is analogous to natural science in seeking to explain the first of these dimensions, the *real*. It might, for example, seek to explain the nature and impact of patriarchal structures, positing that to explain the gender disadvantage observed at the *empirical* level, a set of patriarchal structures would have to exist (even if these structures cannot be directly observed). At the level of the *actual*, social theorists might argue that in certain circumstances (an ideal typical, wholly 'female' environment), one might expect to observe particular non-patriarchal processes at work. This level is in principle observable even if in practice finding contexts which incorporate such an environment proves to be impossible or impractical. Observation at the third level, the empirical, is used to inductively construct ideal types and/or structures from which to subsequently explain further empirical observations.

The nature of the critical realist account thus accommodates methodological pluralism. Empirical research (rather than empiricist/positivist research) is valued in the sense of providing base level or confirmatory data, and theorising provides explanatory frameworks (identifying 'real' linkages between structures or mechanisms and social phenomena). The identification of ideal types provides approximations to the 'actual' (e.g. phenomena which would be observed under specific conditions).

In the above discussion, we took as a starting point the question 'What must the world be like for *p* to be the case?' This in effect refers to what Bhaskar terms the intransitive dimension of science. However, he also recognises that science is a social practice, and the above question is supplemented with the question of 'What must scientists be like for them to be able to investigate phenomenon p, in other words what must scientists be like for science (natural or social) to be possible?' This latter question relates to what Bhaskar terms the transitive dimension. Whereas enquiry in the intransitive dimension for Bhaskar can only take place when there are agreed uncontroversial statements such as 'p is the case', the investigation of this intransitive dimension implies that certain transitive conditions of science are met. In other words that science is a social practice, the existence of which presupposes the institutions of scientific communications and criticism (Bhaskar 1998).

I have two principal difficulties with Bhaskar's account. The first stems from this distinction of the transitive and the intransitive. As we noted earlier, the intransitive starts with an uncontroversial description of p. However, this is not absolute or incontrovertible as a description, but one which is actually socially agreed. In fact (to use Wittgenstein's terminology), p is likely to be described differently in different 'language games'. This is bound up with the issue that statements are not theory-neutral. If we consider the case discussed earlier, the statement 'Jane is a student' is not theory-neutral, since already it implies the existence of some educational process or system. To provide an example from observation of the 'natural' world, the Western scientifically trained observer may describe the sunrise in one way and the 'primitive' sun worshipper in a very different way. Finding a common description of this phenomenon p (the sunrise) may thus prove impossible. Discourse analysis of course provides a way of establishing which particular types of description (and types of analysis such as 'science' and what counts as science) are dominant or become dominant. Thus, in a 'traditional' critical realist account, discursive construction of what is regarded as 'intransitive' is inadmissible. I would argue instead here for regarding what Bhaskar describes as intransitive, or uncontroversial, as representing a *consensus* within a particular language community (e.g. social science language community) as to what to take as a fixed point or shared premise for the development of an explanation. This leaves room for the investigation of how such consensus is reached, using, for example, discourse analysis techniques. Type IV studies allow us to deconstruct the way in which phenomenon p has been conceptualised, and to identify, for example, whose interests are promoted by this type of conceptualisation. The treatment of professionalisation of sport in Algeria in the previous chapter provides an example of such a deconstruction.

The second difficulty with critical realist accounts relates to appeals to causality in discussion of deep structures. If we take language as an example – the use of the English language by a variety of users over an extended period of time has produced a social practice (language) with its own structures (e.g. grammatical structures, meaning systems). Learning these structures or how to use the language correctly does not mean that I have to be able to describe grammatical rules (propositional knowledge), but I can demonstrate my awareness of how to use the structures (acquaintance knowledge of grammatical rules) by my proper use of the language. The language system thus *enables* me to say certain things (and may *constrain* me in terms of what I cannot say). However, it does not *cause* me to speak as I do. Thus, I would argue that it makes no sense to talk of causal necessity in the social world even in the context of Bhaskar's appeal to the concept of an open system where causality is 'masked'. Agents choose to behave in particular ways given the variety of options open by virtue of the access to the resources for action provided by the structures within which they are implicated.

This brief discussion of critical realism allows us to recast the key features of the argument in ways which reflect the potential for methodological pluralism. Thus, adapting the description applied in Marsh and Stoker (2002) and illustrating the argument in parentheses by reference to gender disadvantage and patriarchal structures:

- the world exists independently of our knowledge of it (we may be unaware of patriarchal structures, but they may nevertheless impact on our behaviour);
- there are 'structures' in the world that we cannot directly observe (we cannot directly observe patriarchal structures, but we can infer their existence);
- actors discursive knowledge regarding 'reality' has a construction effect on the outcomes of social interrelations (as discursive agents we can, for example, raise awareness of the nature of gender disadvantage and what might be taken as legitimate measures to counter it);
- structures constrain and enable action rather than determine outcomes, and therefore, structures may be modified by individual action (patriarchal structures do not require men or women to act in certain ways but do provide or deny access to resources for behaviour);
- social science involves the study of reflexive agents who may construct, deconstruct and reconstruct structures (policy makers would thus also be reflexive agents who can seek to change the structural context, for example, modifying patriarchal structures);
- finally, as language users, we can, as members of a language community, seek to modify the terms in which a phenomenon is cast, and thus the basic consensus/premise on which an explanation is built (as language users, we may promote anti-feminist discourse which identifies the differences between genders as 'natural' or biologically based, and thus not amenable to change, thus limiting the policy agenda).

This last point is particularly relevant when considering comparative analysis since policy problems may be conceptualised very differently in different language communities/national policy systems/policy communities, etc.

Religious world views and gender equity in Olympic sports leadership: a case study in mixed methods

Earlier in this chapter, we raised the question of whether adopting approaches which ranged across different types of comparative method implied a critical inconsistency. We have addressed this in the above discussion, but we move on now to aspects of a case study of the use of mixed methods. This was a study undertaken in partnership with the IOC (Henry *et al.* 2004). Our aim here is partly to use this example as a vehicle for discussion of the application of mixed methods, and partly to lead us on to a discussion of the ethical dimension of comparative and intercultural research, since research requires some consensus not simply at the level of ontology and epistemology but also along ethical dimensions, concerning what constitutes a 'desirable' or acceptable set of outcomes.

The study of *Women and Leadership in the Olympic Movement* was an evaluation of the introduction of targets by the IOC in terms of women's involvement in executive decision-making in Olympic bodies. Specifically, the study sought to identify the factors relating to the achievement of the target of having women as at least 10 per cent of NOC Executive Committee members by December 2001 and at least 20 per cent by December 2005. The methods involved a questionnaire sent to all Secretary Generals of National Olympic Committees and to all female members of NOC Executives, together with interviews conducted with approximately one in eight of all Secretary Generals ($n = 24$) and of all women NOC Executive Committee Members ($n = 30$).[1] The use of mixed methods here allowed us to investigate aspects of the current situation in each of the NOCs (quantitative and qualitative questionnaire responses) as well as the discursive construction of the problem, its 'causes' and potential policy solutions among male and female interviewees. For the purposes of the current discussion, commentary will be restricted to the issue of religious world views and gender equity and specifically to the representation of Muslim women in NOC Executive Committees.

Specifically in this discussion, we will address three issues:

1 (inter)relationships between cultures, and in particular the problems deriving from treatment of cultures as essentially incompatible;
2 deconstructing Western perspectives relating to the place of non-Western women in a global movement;
3 the establishing of a consensus on the ethical dimension and the place of discourse ethics in achieving intercultural understanding.

(a) Treating cultures as incompatible – the dangers of the Huntington thesis

Huntington (1996: pp. 26–7), in his description of the 'world of civilisations post-1990', characterises the world as constituted by nine civilisational blocks,

Western, Latin American, African, Islamic, Sinic, Hindu, Orthodox, Buddhist and Japanese. These blocks, he argues, embrace value positions which are in many instances incompatible and not amenable to negotiation. This is supported by the claim that most of the world's conflicts exist in the 'fault lines' where the different cultures abut one another. However, though Huntington describes these 'civilisational blocks' in fairly monolithic terms, there is in fact enormous diversity of views in any 'civilisational block'. Thus, as Tibi (2001) argues, the building of consensus will sometimes be easier between groups *within different* 'civilisational blocks' than between groups within a given civilisational grouping. For example, consensus in Western societies about the approach to gender equity will continue to be difficult to achieve because of the problems of incorporating anti-feminist opinion which views gender differences implicitly or explicitly as a product of biological difference. By contrast, building some level of consensus between feminists in Chinese, Muslim or Hindu civilisational blocks (despite difficulties) is likely to be more straightforward as, for example, the United Nations World Conferences on Women have demonstrated. Here, programmes of action have been agreed despite the considerable heterogeneity of world views represented at these Conferences (United Nations 1995).

Thus, Huntington's model of separate cultures is not helpful. Indeed, the implications of his approach to culture, at least as interpreted by some commentators, and the 'monocentric diffusion' model of culture propounded by Francis Fukuyama (1992) which recognises no standard of civilisation other than that of the West (Kim and Hodges 2005) suggest that since cultural value systems are effectively mutually exclusive in this kind of context, the only way in which the West can ultimately defend its values will be by force. This is a dangerous conclusion and one which has been used by some commentators to legitimate action beyond international law.

(b) Deconstructing Western perspectives on gender equity in a global sporting organisation

In addressing the issue of religion and world view, one is likely to meet the claim that religious world views are invariably 'traditionalist' and 'conservative' and thus militate against women adopting an equal position in respect of sports administration and executive decision-making. The example which most readily springs to the Western (non-Muslim) mind is that of Muslim practices. While the data for this study, for example, show that women's representation on NOC Executive Committees is lower on average in the countries which are members of the Organisation of the Islamic Conference (7.9 per cent compared with an overall average of all countries of 12.9 per cent), to explain this by reference to religion rather than by reference to local cultures is problematic. There are perhaps two principal objections to the 'religion-blaming' strategy. The first is that in the context of the present study, it is not only Muslim societies which manifest gender inequality. When such gender inequality is present in Western societies, academic analyses tend to explain this by reference to the concept of patriarchy, but when it is present in Muslim societies, it tends to be explained by Western commentators by reference to religious practice. Such an argument applies double standards and leaves proponents open to the charge of Orientalism (Said 1991; Volpp 2001; Winter 2001).

It is important in this context to differentiate between 'religiosity' (the customs and practices associated with a group practising a particular religion) as opposed to religious beliefs, the fundamental tenets of a religious group. The norms and practices (religiosity) may vary from one group to another within the same religious grouping, even where fundamental beliefs are shared. There is a lively debate within Muslim feminist literature about the distinction between 'revealed truth' in the form of the Q'ran and the Hadith on the one hand and *ijtihad* and the opinions of (male) religious scholars on the other (Stowasser 1998). Muslim feminists and feminist commentators such as Fatima Mernissi (Mernissi 1985; Mernissi and Lakeland 1991), Haleh Afshar (1998), Azza Karam (1998) and Therese Saliba *et al.* (2002) show how, for many, it is not Islam but certain male interpretations of Islam, which promulgate gender subordination.

The second fallacious aspect of the argument is that it assumes there is some uniformity of approach to women's roles within and between Muslim societies. This simply is not the case. The differences between the societies of some of the Gulf States and those, for example, of North Africa or Turkey are considerable, as reflected in the differing roles played by women in these societies (Haddad 1998), but also studies such as Afshar (1998), Karam (1998) and Al-Ali (2000) show how, even in 'conservative' contexts (Iran and Egypt, respectively), different forms of feminism are evident, warning against a simplistic notion of a single unitary perspective on the appropriate roles for women in wider society. This is reflected also in our own study in which two countries (Iran and Gambia) which are members of the Organisation of the Islamic Conference exhibited levels of female membership of NOC Executives which were more than double the average for all countries.

A diversity of interpretation was also very evident in our qualitative data, in relation to the issue of women's sporting dress, in the responses of three of our four female Muslim interviewees. Of these three interviewees, one is from a North African state, the second from an Asian country and the third is from the Middle East. Our respondent from North Africa had been a world figure in her sport, and had experienced no problem in wearing the athletic clothing of the era, with the only criterion of concern being to allow freedom of movement to maximise performance.

> No I have never had any opposition. I had millions of letters of support when I won which surprised me. Not even one letter of criticism. And I even had letters, let's say, from Saudi Arabia from all the Gulf States, all of North Africa. It was incredible millions of letters, thousands and I am still keeping them. I have never had any negative thoughts from anyone concerning my attire. And I surprised the international media when they saw

me and they said – 'Oh, she is a [nationality], and a Muslim – where is her veil?' and I think when you have a strong belief it is in your heart it is not in your look. ... And even now the race I organise you see a large range of different categories of women, those who are veiled, those who are unveiled, and it's interesting.

(Interview 22, Africa)

By contrast, the Asian interviewee had actively considered whether the wearing of athletic apparel contravened religious requirements to maintain modesty and had in fact sought the advice of a central religious authority.

A lot of Non-Muslims also asked me ... and I think that, quite often the Muslim women themselves and even the Muslim men also do not understand the Shariah or the Islamic Law, ... as I said in netball, our girls wear short skirts because that is more convenient, but I did also ask, because I was a bit worried, whether what the girls are doing could be wrong for them in Islam, for them and for me, because I had been with them. I did ask some of the persons who are knowledgeable in Islam, [names Islamic scholar], before he became the religious advisor to the Prime Minister, he was a lecturer at [a local university] before, he said 'the most important thing is what is your intention, if your intention is to wear your brief costume so that you can play better and the idea is to win, so that Muslim women could win, then it is otherwise permissible, but, if you wear the short skirts and all that, and the idea is to show off your beautiful legs and all that then of course it is not permissible, it is haram. Now if the men come and watch and they have say, dirty things on their minds, that is their problem, that is their sins, not yours'. So I was quite happy, so what we do is, we tell our girls, they wear the skirt when they are playing and when they are in the arena The moment they go out of the arena, they put on their track bottom

(Interview 21, Asia)

The third Muslim woman to be interviewed was well known for her very public espousal of separate sports competition for women, performing a leading role in promoting the Islamic Countries Women Sports Federation and the Islamic Countries Women's Sports Games. These games held three times since their inauguration in 1993 in Iran and provide Muslim women with the opportunity to participate in international competition by holding events in an all-female environment. For this interviewee, there could be no compromise on the issue of wearing of modest covering for the body in public, and separate competition therefore offers the only possibility for Muslim women's participation.

Translator: After 1989 when she was involved in the NOC as Vice-President, she thought that a women's organisation was necessary and so she founded the organisation for women. The main reason for this was due to the problem of [her country's] women and their clothes during sporting

activities. There was a gap between the Islamic countries and other areas of
the world in sport. She was given support through the Olympic Committee.
She had to travel to Kuwait and Mr. Samaranch was there and he gave her
support, inviting her to be present in the decision for a women's organisation.

(Interview 15, Asia)

Thus, the positions adopted on this issue are by no means uniform. Such variety
lends support to the criticism of positions adopted by commentators such as
Huntington (1996) who seek to portray civilisations in terms of monolithic
ideologies. Critics such as Bassam Tibi (2001) have underlined the heterogeneous nature of religiosity in Muslim populations, and such heterogeneity is
clearly exemplified by our interviewees.

Azza Karam (1998) outlines three ideal typical feminisms in the context of
Egyptian society (while acknowledging that the label 'feminist' may not be one
which is readily accepted by some groups of Muslim women despite their
common concern to enhance the lives of women). The first of Karam's types is
that of Islamist feminism which she identifies with 'Islamist women ... who are
aware of a particular oppression of women, they actively seek to rectify this
oppression by recourse to Islamic principles' (Karam 1998: p. 9). Karam's
second type of feminism is Muslim feminism, which incorporates women who
draw on both human rights and religious discourse but who privilege the latter.
They

> also use the Islamic sources like the Q'ran and the Sunna ... but their aim
> is to show that the discourse of equality between men and women is valid
> within Islam. [they] ... steer a middle course between interpretations of
> socio-political and cultural realities according to Islam and a human rights
> discourse. [for these women] a feminism which does not justify itself within
> Islam is bound to be rejected by the rest of society.
>
> (Karam 1998: p. 11)

The third type of feminism is termed secular feminism which relates to those
who ground their discourse outside the realm of any religion, whether Christian
or Muslim, placing it instead, within the international human rights discourse.
Here, religion is respected as a private matter for the individual. While we
would not claim that the respondents we cite could be fitted to the categories
outlined here, one might suggest that the positions adopted by our three respondents reflect aspects of this typology with the Middle Eastern respondent reflecting aspects of Karam's Islamist feminism, the Asian respondent the traditional
'Muslim feminism' and the North African respondent secular (Muslim) feminism. The point is that each such type is associated with the addressing of gender
inequities, even though how such inequities are conceived will depend on the
particular world view of the individual concerned.

The issue of IOC support for separate competition for women in the form promoted by the Islamic Countries Women's Sports Games was an issue which was raised in the interviews with the male Secretary Generals, and there was an interestingly heterogeneous response. Respondents tended to adopt one of the four following positions:

1   the enthusiastic adoption of the initiative as a good end in its own right;
2   outright opposition;
3   promotion or at least acceptance of this initiative as providing the only possible form of participation in international competition for some women from Islamic countries;
4   acceptance of the initiative as the first step to full integration.

The very existence of this range of responses highlights the difficulty of establishing consensus on how to proceed in such matters. This brings us back to the fundamental question of the line a transnational body such as the IOC might adopt in relation to the promotion of equity in widely varying cultural contexts. If we choose Huntington's line, we can expect not to be able to reach a consensus but to have to impose a view on the wider world (Figure 9.1)

(c) Discourse ethics and the establishing of moral consensus

In the foregoing discussion, it is clear that in terms of comparative research there are more than simply ontological and epistemological issues at stake. We not only have to consider issues of what is (ontological issues), and how we know about what is (epistemological issues), there is also an ethical dimension (questions about what should be) incorporated in our research agenda. In our project, for example, the issue of gender equity is a core *ethical* concern. Just as postmodern critiques have undermined universal claims in the ontological and epistemological domains, so universalism in the moral domain has been subject to the same critique. We need therefore to consider how to establish ethical consensus, since without this shared ethical basis for policy (establishing what it

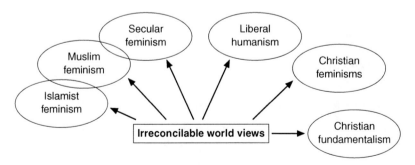

Figure 9.1 Incompatible cultures: the implications of Huntington's 'Clash of Civilisations Model'.

ought to achieve), we will not be in a position to evaluate outcomes (what it has achieved).

How then do we go about establishing a general agreement of what is right or wrong, what rights individuals should enjoy and how therefore differences can be resolved without recourse to force or violence of one party on another? We live in a world of diverse cultures, norms, values and social practices, so how can we establish a moral basis for action across a wide range of cultural sub-systems? An answer to this question is in part to be found in moral philosophy.

I want to develop an answer to this question by outlining a simplified (and selective) typology of developments in thinking about ethics. I will refer briefly to four approaches to identifying ethical response to such moral dilemmas, and will do so against a background of the shift from pre-modern/traditional approaches to ethics, through rational modernity, and postmodern ethics, to the ethics of the postmodern.

Pre-modern, traditional religious ethics

The first set of approaches is that associated with what one might term 'traditional religious universalism' where universal moral judgements are 'revealed' usually by analogy, example or prescription in divine texts (Schockenhoff 2003). The problem with this type of approach is that ultimately one has to subscribe to the particular religious authority if one is to accept the system of ethics proposed.

Modernist ethics

The second set of ethical approaches is what might be described as 'modernist approaches', by which we mean the rational application of universal principles based either on inductive logic in the shape of utilitarian ethics (basing judgements on a single universal principle, that of the greatest happiness of the greatest number) (Rodgers 2003) or on deductive logic – Kant's rationalist categorical imperative to act only by rules one would wish to be universally applied (Abdullah 2000; Kerstein 2002). Difficulties here relate, in terms of utilitarianism, in its various forms to problems of calculating (in principle and in practice) what constitutes the greatest happiness of the greatest number and, in relation to the Kantian position, the difficulty of finding imperatives which should never be broken.

Postmodern ethics

The third approach is that of 'situational ethics' in which absolute standards are rejected in favour of the requirements of a particular situation. Thus, moral judgements or standards used may vary from one situation to another and may even contradict one another (Robertson *et al.* 2002). This view of ethics is subject to the critique of moral relativism and is in stark contrast to the moral universalism of both modernist and traditional religious types cited above.

Ethics of the postmodern

The final strategy is what we will term here 'negotiated consensus'. By this, we imply the development, within limits, of a consensus between groups about what constitutes morally defensible behaviour. Such an approach would be akin to Habermas's (1990) concept of communicative rationality, the bridging of different 'language games' about morality, evident within different world views which he promotes within the framework of discourse ethics.

However, unlike Habermas (who argues that through communicative action we can arrive at *universal* norms), we would wish to argue that through such discourse one can arrive at *general* norms (norms which can be generalised across different groups when the premises of what constitute public morality are formally negotiated and agreed). Such an approach steers a course to avoid both universalism and relativism. It suggests that while one cannot identify moral judgements which will be true in all places, at all times, for all people, this does not mean that one has to accept that anything goes and that no general moral claims can be made. Nevertheless, such claims have to be founded on negotiated principles.

If we take Habermas's own statement of his position:

> Under the pragmatic presuppositions of an inclusive and non-coercive rational discourse among free and equal participants, everyone is required to take the perspective of everyone else, and thus project herself into the understandings of self and world of all others; from this interlocking of perspectives there emerges an ideally extended we-perspective from which all can test in common whether they wish to make a controversial norm the basis of their shared practice; and this should include mutual criticism of the appropriateness of the languages in terms of which situations and needs are interpreted. In the course of successfully taken abstractions, the core of generalisable interests can then emerge step by step.

Thus, the recognition of three principles here is core. First, that the development of generalised norms is predicated upon a discourse in which the premises on which any argument will be based are agreed. Such a discourse will incorporate principles such as reciprocity of respect and understanding. Second, that such generalised norms are just that, 'generalised', rather than universal Third, that the moral positions taken up by individuals or groups from within particular civilisational blocks will not be homogeneous and thus moral discourses will incorporate members of different 'civilisational blocks' (to borrow Huntington's terminology) but will not incorporate all from any given such block. It does not make sense therefore to generalise about Christian morality, Hindu morality or Muslim morality, since there will be commonalties between and differences within such groups. Thus, the process of moral leadership in respect of women's role in governance is one which requires consensus building through discourse construction rather than through universalistic assertion of the dominance of one world view. Figure 9.2 seeks to illustrate this situation, recognising that consensus has limits and that some groups will almost invariably stand outside the consensus achieved but that consensus is an ongoing project constructer upon mutual respect and dialogue.

The point about rehearsing these strategies is that while the IOC's adoption of targets without sanctions has been criticised by some commentators as naïve, one reading at least suggests that this could form part of a more sophisticated strategy more likely to achieve significant change in the longer term than the imposition of Western 'universal' values. Such an approach is reflected in the comments of one of our respondents:

> we are trying to find a title for our next conference because we are trying to bring men and women together … when you put too much pressure, specifically in certain countries where taboos and customs are very strong, you might even take away the men's team and I think you should try to work slowly but surely. … So that is why I am telling you that other countries [from certain regions] tell you [that you] don't need to duplicate the occidental system, otherwise it will not work in our own system. … You have to understand us.
>
> (Interview 22, Africa)

Conclusions

In Chapter 1 of this book, we identified three claims which we sought to challenge. The first was that globalisation had so diminished the significance of the nation state that nation state-based analyses of policy were no longer essential. This argument was addressed in Chapter 1, but the significance of the nation

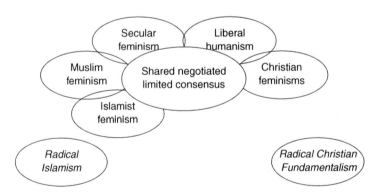

Figure 9.2 The building of consensus – a form of discursive ethics.

state-based level of analysis (and of other levels) is evidenced in the range of case study materials discussed throughout. The second claim which we have sought to dismiss related to the ontological and epistemological critique posed by the postmodernist assault on universality. The development of our positioning relation to this critique is introduced in Chapter 2, illustrated in the case study material, and our resolution to such challenges explicitly addressed in this chapter.

The final claim we have sought to challenge relates to the argument that Western and non-Western values are incompatible. This purported 'incompatibility' is not simply a matter of ontology and epistemology but also importantly a question of ethical standpoint. In our increasingly culturally heterogeneous world, this particular dimension is of increasing importance. It has thus been a core element running through our argument, that all three dimensions (ontological, epistemological and ethical) require some prior consensus on what to take as the point of departure, the given premises of any analysis or prescription, if we are to engage in cross-cultural or intercultural dialogue. It is not necessary to argue that we all see the world in the same way, but it is essential, if we are to engage in shared reflection, explanation and evaluation, to establish the nature and limits of our shared premises.

Notes

1 Globalisation, governance and policy

1 While the term 'UK' as used here is appropriate to the discussion of much which follows, some of the policy arrangements alluded to relate only to England. With the Labour Government's introduction of devolution particularly for Scotland, Wales and Northern Ireland, policy specificities are increasingly important.

3 Evaluating alternative theoretical perspectives on sports policy

1 The IOC's own Web pages identify the Athens Session as the 58th Session under its pages on Olympic Solidarity (www.olympic.org/uk/organisation/commissions/solidarity/history_uk.asp), but as the 59th Session elsewhere (www.olympic-museum.de/iocsession/iocsessions60.htm).
2 This reference to the dissolution of the Committee is puzzling since the IOC's account of the development of Olympic Solidarity describes a seamless progression from the Committee for International Olympic Aid. The Committee became a Commission in 1967 and subsequently in 1972 was renamed the Olympic Solidarity Commission adopting the term from the committee of that name established by the PGA of NOCs.

5 Political clientelism and sports policy systems – case studies of Greece and Taiwan

1 The value of the Taiwan dollar stood at US$1 = NT$32.5.
2 The allegations described here were public, in that they were reported in the media as the subsequent commentary indicates. However, since the case was in process at the time of writing, the individual is not named in this passage.
3 This three-level argument is one we originally developed in relation to the Greek context, Henry, I. P. and Pantelis Nassis. 1999. 'Political clientelism and sports policy in greece'. *International Review for the Sociology of Sport* 34:43–58, but which we contend is equally relevant to this present comparative study.

6 Multiculturalism, interculturalism, assimilation and sports policy in Europe

1 The research partners are acknowledged by name in the preface to the report Amara, M., D. Aquilina, I. Henry, and M. Taylor. 2004. *Sport and multiculturalism*. European Commission: DG Education and Culture, Brussels. The opinions presented in this chapter are, however, those of the authors and do not represent the views of the European Commission or any other party.
2 To this end, we engaged with core partners at the German Sports University in

Cologne (Prof. Karen Petry and Michael Groll); The Jozef Pilsudski Academy of Physical Education in Warsaw (Dr Jolanta Zysko); and Institut National des sports et d'éducation physique (INSEP) in Paris (Claude Legrand and Denis Musso) whose significant contribution to the study we are pleased to acknowledge.

7 Sports and social regulation in the city: the cases of Grenoble and Sheffield

1 The Sheffield analysis draws on material collected for two other studies by one of the authors in conjunction with Juan Paramio-Salcines (Henry and Paramio-Salcines 1999) and with David Denyer (unpublished study of *The development of potential partnerships in sport*, commissioned by Sport and Recreation Department, Sheffield, 1999). Acknowledgement of the contribution of these two colleagues in conducting interviews and discussion of analysis is gratefully recorded.
2 The *Office Municipal des Sports* is an association formally constituted by the law of 1901, which is an umbrella organisation with representatives of clubs affiliated to competitive sports federations.

8 Discourses on modern sport and values in a non-Western context: a case study of Algeria

1 This chapter is the product of a discourse between East and West, both in its substantive content and the issues it addresses and in terms of the nature of its authorship.
2 The FLN had imposed itself as the sole political force, which could represent the Algerian population. The other political parties, the supporters of integration or assimilation of Algeria into the French republic, had only one choice, to side with the FLN in its struggle for independence, or against the FLN, and thus against the independence of Algeria from France. Harbi, M. 2002. 'Le poids de l'histoire et la violence vint à l'Algérie'. *Le Monde Diplomatique* July: 1–15.
3 The paper draws on Amara, M. 2003. 'Global sport and local modernity: the case of "professionalisation" of football in Algeria'. Unpublished PhD Thesis, Loughborough University.
4 The president of the High Political Commission of the MSP, a representative of the RCD group in the Algerian Parliament and a representative of the FLN group in the Algerian Parliament.
5 These included the president of the National Football League, the directors of Algerian national teams, the president of USMA football Club, the director of the Algerian Olympic Academy and a representative of the Directorate General of Sport at the Ministry of Youth and Sport.
6 It is worth noting the linguistic association, in terms of rhetoric in the Algerian discourse, of Arabic as a language with notions 'purity and authenticity' and 'nationalism and historical legitimacy' and of French with 'modernity and democracy'.
7 The use of English helped us to avoid in a way the complexity of applying discourse analysis to Arabic and French language responses knowing the ideological (politicised meanings) connotations that language uses have within the Algerian media, educational, political and cultural contexts. Nevertheless, it should be acknowledged that the use of English imposed a new challenge, with the application of English (the language of globalisation and information technology) to the study and understanding of the Algerian (glocal) context.
8 Ministère de la Jeunesse et des Sports: *Programme d'action prospectif* (March 1994); *Assises Nationales sur Le Sport* (1993) and *Assises Nationales sur Le Sport: Les Actes* (1993).
9 The system also went through an intermediate stage, that of *le model de l'entreprise*, where each club was under the tutelage of the public company that it represents.

Bouchet, P. and M. Kaach. 2002. 'Le développement du sport dans les pays Africains francophones: mythe ou réalité?' in *Paper presented at the Colloque international de management du sport: le sport comme vecteur de développement économique et social.* Rabat-Salé, Maroc; and Chehat, F. 1993. *Le livre d'or du sport Algérien.* Alger: ANEP.

10 The first professional season 1999–2000 was played with no relegation system, following a decision made by *le Groupement professionnel* (GPF), the body initially in charge of professional football. This created a league without any real incentive to compete for most professional clubs.

9 Bridging research traditions and world views: universalisation versus generalisation in the case for gender equity

1 Questionnaires were distributed in English and French, and responses were returned in English, French, Spanish and Russian. The interviews were conducted by a multicultural, multilingual team (in English, French, Spanish, Arabic, Malay and Maltese). Interviews with the 24 male Secretary Generals were undertaken by the author with Dr Mansour Al-Tauqi. Interviews with the female NOC Executive Members were conducted by a range of interviewers including the author, Dawn Aquilina, Wirdati Radzi, Dr Emma Rich, Dr Chris Shelton, Dr Eleni Theodoraki and Dr Anita White.

References

Abdullah, M. Amin. 2000. *Kant and Ghazali: the idea of universality of ethical norms.* Frankfurt: Landeck.

Afshar, Haleh. 1998. *Islam and feminisms: an Iranian case-study.* New York: St. Martin's Press.

Aglietta, M. 1998. 'Capitalism at the turn of the century: regulation theory and the challenge of social change'. *New Left Review* 41–90.

Aitchison, C. 1997. 'A decade of compulsory competitive tendering in UK sport and leisure services: some feminist reflections'. *Leisure Studies* 16:85–106.

Akbar, A. and H. Donnan. 1994. *Islam, globalisation and postmodernity.* London: Routledge.

Al-Ali, Nadje Sadig. 2000. *Secularism, gender, and the state in the Middle East: the Egyptian women's movement.* Cambridge and New York: Cambridge University Press.

Al-Tauqi, M. 1993. 'Olympic solidarity: global order and the diffusion of modern sport between 1961 and 1980'. PhD thesis, School of Sport and Exercise Sciences, Loughborough University.

Allen, J. 1992. 'Post-industrialism and post-Fordism'. Pp. 169–220 in *Modernity and its futures*, edited by S. Hall, D. Held and T. McGrew. Cambridge: Polity/Open University Press.

Altheide, D. 1996. *Qualitative media analysis.* London: Sage.

Amara, M. 2003. 'Global sport and local modernity: the case of professionalisation' of football in Algeria'. Unpublished PhD thesis, Institute of Sport and Leisure Policy, School of Sport and Exercise Sciences, Loughborough University.

Amara, Mahfoud and Ian Henry. 2004. 'Between globalization and local modernity: the diffusion and modernization of football in Algeria'. *Soccer and Society* 5:1–26.

Amara, M., D. Aquilina, E. Argent, M. Betzer-Tayar, Fred Coalter, I. Henry and J. Taylor. 2005. *The roles of sport and education in the social inclusion of asylum seekers and refugees: an evaluation of policy and practice in the UK.* Loughborough: Institute of Sport and Leisure Policy, Loughborough University and Stirling University.

Amara, M., D. Aquilina, I. Henry and M. Taylor. 2004. *Sport and multiculturalism.* Brussels: European Commission: DG Education and Culture.

Amara, M., I.P. Henry, J. Liang, and K. Uchiumi. 2005. 'The governance of professional soccer: five case studies – Algeria, China, England, France and Japan'. *European Journal of Sports Sciences* 5:189–206.

Andreff, W., with J.F. Bourg, B. Halba and J.F. Nys. 1995. *Les enjeux économiques du sport en Europe: financement et impact économique.* Paris: Editions Dalloz.

Andrew, C. and M. Goldsmith. 1998. 'From local government to local governance – and beyond?' *International Political Science Review* 19:101–17.

Appadurai, A. 1990. 'Disjuncture and difference in the global cultural economy'. In *Global culture: nationalism, globalization and modernity*, edited by M. Featherstone. London: Sage.

Ardagh, J. 1990. *France today*. London: Penguin.

Arkoun, M. 2003. 'Rethinking Islam'. *The Annals of the American Academy* 588:18–39.

Arnaud, L. 1999a. 'Ethnic minorities and sports policy in Birmingham and Lyon'. PhD thesis, UFRAPS, Université Claude Bernard, Lyon.

——. 1999b. *Politiques sportives et minorites ethniques*. Paris: L'Harmattan.

Arnaut, J.L. 2006. 'Independent European Sport Review 2006'. (www.independentsportreview.com).

Audit Commission. 1989. *Sport for whom? Clarifying the local authority role in sport and recreation*. London: HMSO.

Avrillier, R. and P. Descamps. 1995. *Le système Carignon*. Paris: La Découverte.

Bakke, E. 1995. 'Towards a European identity?' *Tidsskrift for Samfunnsforskning* 36:467–494.

Bale, J. and J. Sang. 1996. *Kenyan running: movement culture, geography and global change*. London: Frank Cass.

Ball, Amanda, Jane Broadbent and Cynthia Moore. 2002. 'Local government-best value and the control of local government: challenges and contradictions'. *Public Money & Management* 22:9.

Banks, T. 1998. 'The European Union and sport: speech by the Minister for Sport to the European Parliamentary Sports Intergroup'. Unpublished paper. European Parliament, Brussels.

Barlow, J. 1995. 'The politics of urban-growth – boosterism and nimbyism in European boom regions'. *International Journal of Urban and Regional Research* 19:129–44.

Barnett, J.R. 1999. 'Hollowing out the state? Some observations on the restructuring of hospital services in New Zealand'. *Area* 31:259–70.

Baudrillard, Jean. 1997. *The consumer society: myths and structures*. Translated by G. Ritzer. London: Sage Publications.

Bauman, Z. 1987. *Legislators and interpreters*. Cambridge: Polity.

——. 1997. *Globalization: the human consequences*. Cambridge: Polity.

Bell, D. 1960. *The end of ideology: the exhaustion of political ideas in the fifties*. Glencoe: The Free Press.

Bellamy, R. and A. Warleigh. 1998. 'From an ethics of integration to an ethics of participation: citizenship and the future of the European Union'. *Millennium: Journal of International Studies* 27:447–70.

Benington, J. 1987. 'Sheffield – working it out, an outline employment plan for Sheffield – Sheffield-City-Council'. *Local Government Studies* 13:103–4.

Bennabi, M. 1970. *Le probleme des idees dans le monde musulman*. Cairo: Dar El Fikr.

Benton, T. and I. Craib. 2001. *Philosophy of social science: the philosophical foundations of social thought*. Basingstoke: Palgrave.

Benzerti, K. 2002. 'Olympism in Africa'. Retrieved 23 May 2003 (www.sport.gov.gr/2/24/243/2431/24312/e243123.html).

Bergeaud, P. 1980. 'La municipalité et les clubs grenoblois (2): "Renforcer la vie associative" '. P. 22 in *Le dauphiné libéré*. Grenoble.

Bernoux, P. 1985. *La sociologie des organisations*. Paris: Le Seuil.

Betterton, R. and S. Blanchard. 1992. *Made in Sheffield: towards a cultural plan for*

Sheffield in the 1990s. Sheffield: Sheffield City Council, Sheffield Hallam University, Yorkshire and Humberside Arts Board.

Bhaskar, Roy. 1975. *A realist theory of science*. York: Alma.

———. 1979. *The possibility of naturalism: a philosophical critique of the contemporary human sciences*. Atlantic Highlands, NJ: Humanities Press.

———. 1989. *Reclaiming reality: a critical introduction to contemporary philosophy*. London; New York: Verso.

———. 1998. 'Philosophy and scientific realism'. Pp. 16–47 in *Critical realism: essential readings*, edited by M. Archer, R. Bhaskar, A. Collier, T. Lawson and A. Norrie. London: Routledge.

Billingham, A. 1996. *Broadcasting of sport: a discussion paper*. Strasbourg: European Parliament Sports Intergroup.

Black, C. 1992. 'Conservatism and the paradox of Europe'. Pp. 54–74 in *Reshaping Europe in the twenty-first century*. New York: St Martins Press.

Bobbio, N. 1997. *Left and right*. Cambridge: Polity.

Bonzy, D., M. Durbet and B. Podico. 1988. *Grenoble. Portrait de ville avec lendemains*. Grenoble: Didier Richard.

Bosco, J. 1992. 'Taiwan factions: guanxi, patronage, and the state in local politics'. *Ethnology* XXXI:157–84.

Boswell, C. 2003. *European migration policies in flux: changing patterns of inclusion and exclusion*. Oxford: Blackwell.

Bouchet, P. and M. Kaach. 2002. 'Le développement du sport dans les pays Africains francophones: mythe ou réalité?' in *Paper presented at the Colloque international de management du sport: le sport comme vecteur de développement économique et social*. Rabat-Salé, Maroc.

Boudjedra, R. 1999. *La vie à l'endroit*. Paris: Lgf.

Bousetta, H. and B. Marechal. 2003. 'L'islam et les musulmans en Belgique: enjeux locaux et cadres de réflexions globaux'. Retrieved 21 May 2007 (www.kbs-frb.be/files/db/fr/PUB_1414_Islam_et_musulmans_en_Belgique.pdf).

Bovaird, Tony and Arie Halachmi. 2001. 'Learning from international approaches to best value'. *Policy and Politics* 29:451.

Bowker, M. 1997. 'Nationalism and the fall of the USSR'. Pp. 238–254 in *The limits of globalization*, edited by A. Scott. London: Routledge.

Boyer, R. 1986. *La theorie de la regulation: un analyse critique*. Paris: Editions de la Decouverte.

———. 2005. 'How and why capitalisms differ'. *Economy and Society* 34:509–57.

Boyle, M. and G. Hughes. 1994. 'The politics of urban entrepreneurialism in Glasgow'. *Geoforum* 25:453–470.

Brademas, J.D. 1988. 'Public leisure service delivery systems in Greece'. *World Leisure and Recreation* (Summer).

Bramham, P., I. Henry, H. Mommaas and H. van der Poel. 1993. 'Leisure policy: supranational issues in Europe'. In *Leisure policies in Europe*, edited by P. Bramham, I. Henry, H. Mommaas, and H. van der Poel. Wallingford, Oxon: CAB International.

British Broadcasting Corporation. 1999. 'Football: how healing has opened football's wounds'. Retrieved 2004 (http://news.bbc.co.uk/1/hi/sport/football/177584.stm).

Brohm, J.M. 1978. *Sport: a prison of measured time*. London: Ink Links.

Brown, D.A., E.P. Moon and J.A. Robinson. 1998. 'Taiwan's 1998 local elections'. *Asian Survey* xxxviii:569–584.

Bruneteau, B. 1998. 'Le 'mythe de Grenoble' des années 1960 et 1970. Un usage politique de la modernité'. *Vingtième siècle* 58:111–26.

Busch, A. 2000. 'Unpacking the globalization debate: approaches, evidence and data'. In *Demystifying globalization*, edited by C. Hay and D. Marsh. Basingstoke: Palgrave.

Cai, S.Y. 1998. 'The complete file of the black and the gold (in Chinese)'. Congressional Workshop of Legislator Cai Shi-Yuan, Taipei.

Caillois, R. 1961. *Man, play and games*. New York: Free Press of Glencoe.

Calmes, B. 2004. 'Is Iraq back in time for the Olympics?' Retrieved 29 June 2004 (www.sinomania.com/CHINANEWS/Is_Iraq_Back.htm).

Cantelon, H. and S. Murray. 1993. 'Globalization and sport: structure and agency, the need for greater clarity'. *Leisure and society* 16:275–91.

Casanova, P.G. 1996. 'Globalism, neoliberalism, and democracy'. *Social justice* 23:39–48.

Caubet, P. 1993. 'L'anneau de vitesse olympique de Grenoble'. Mémoire de maîtrise thesis, STAPS, Université J. Fourier, Grenoble.

Centre for Leisure and Tourism Studies. 1992. *The nationwide impact of CCT in the leisure services*. London: University of North London.

——. 1993. *National information survey on CCT*. London: University of North London.

Centre for Leisure Research. 1993. *Sport and leisure management: compulsory competitive tendering; National Information Survey Report*. London: Sports Council.

Chalip, L. 1996. 'Critical policy analysis – the illustrative case of New Zealand Sport Policy Development'. *Journal of Sport Management* 10:310–24.

Chamakos, T. 1994. *Heavy sports* (in Greek). Proposal to the 1994 PASOK National Congress for Sport, Athens.

Chang, Y.T., Y.H. Chu and F. Tsai. 2005. 'Confucianism and democratic values in three Chinese societies'. *Issues & Studies* 41:1–33.

Chao, L.Y. 2000. 'The 14th proceeding of Education and Culture Committee in the Legislative Yuan' (in Chinese). *The Parliamentary Debate* 89(1), 33–91.

Chehat, F. 1993. *Le livre d'or du sport Algérien*. Alger: ANEP.

Chen, T.H. 1999. A comparative study of American and Taiwanese baseball development: a media-centered perspective, Taipei: National Taiwan University.

Cheng, P.P. 1988. 'Political clientelism in Japan — the case of "S"'. Asian Survey 28, 471–483.

China News. 1997. 'Going. Going. Gone?' Taipei, 14 February, p. 8.

China Times. 2001. 'The 2001 Baseball World Cup in Taipei' (in Chinese). Taipei, 13 July, p. 6.

China Post, The. 2001. 'Farmers Association head held over vote-buying'. Taipei, 27 April 2001. Online: http://th.gio.gov.tw/show.cfm?news_id=8390.

Christopherson, S. 1994. 'The fortress city: privatized spaces, consumer citizenship'. Pp. 409–27 in *Post-Fordism: a reader*, edited by A. Amin. Oxford: Blackwell.

Chu, Y.H. 1992. *Crafting democracy in Taiwan* (in Chinese). Taipei: Institute for National Policy Research.

Chu, Y.H. and J.W. Lin. 2001. 'Political development in the 20th century Taiwan: state-building, regime transformation and the construction of national identity'. Pp. 102–29 in *Taiwan in the twentieth century: a retrospective view*, edited by R.L. Edmonds and S.M. Goldstein. Cambridge: Cambridge University Press.

Chun, A. 2000. 'Democracy as hegemony, globalization as indigenization, or the "culture" in Taiwanese national politics'. *Journal of Asian and African Studies* 35:7–27.

CIPFA. 1976. *Leisure and recreation statistics 1976–7 estimates*. London: Chartered Institute of Public Finance and Accountancy.

——. 1982. *Leisure and recreation statistics 1982–3 estimates*. London: Chartered Institute of Public Finance and Accountancy.

——. 1984. *Leisure and recreation statistics 1984–5 estimates*. London: Chartered Institute of Public Finance and Accountancy.

——. 1988. *Leisure and recreation statistics 1988–9 estimates*. London: Chartered Institute of Public Finance and Accountancy.

——. 1990. *Leisure and recreation statistics 1990–91 estimates*. London: Chartered Institute of Public Finance and Accountancy.

——. 1992. *Leisure and recreation statistics 1992–3 estimates*. London: Chartered Institute of Public Finance and Accountancy.

——. 1993a. *Leisure and recreation statistics 1992–3 estimates*. London: Chartered Institute of Public Finance and Accountancy.

——. 1993b. *Leisure and recreation statistics 1993–4 estimates*. London: Chartered Institute of Public Finance and Accountancy.

——. 1994a. *Leisure and recreation statistics 1993–4 estimates*. London: Chartered Institute of Public Finance and Accountancy.

——. 1994b. *Leisure and recreation statistics 1994–5 estimates*. London: Chartered Institute of Public Finance and Accountancy.

——. 1995a. *Leisure and recreation statistics 1994–5 estimates*. London: Chartered Institute of Public Finance and Accountancy.

——. 1995b. *Leisure and recreation statistics 1995–6 estimates*. London: Chartered Institute of Public Finance and Accountancy.

——. 1996a. *Leisure and recreation statistics 1996–7 estimates*. London: Chartered Institute of Public Finance and Accountancy.

——. 1996b. *Leisure and recreation statistics 1995–6 estimates*. London: Chartered Institute of Public Finance and Accountancy.

——. 1997a. *Leisure and recreation statistics 1997–8 estimates*. Croydon: Chartered Institute of Public Finance and Accountancy.

——. 1997b. *Leisure and recreation statistics 1996–7 estimates*. Croydon: Chartered Institute of Public Finance and Accountancy.

——. 1997c. *Leisure and recreation statistics 1997–8 estimates*. London: Chartered Institute of Public Finance and Accountancy.

——. 1998a. *Leisure and recreation estimates special tabulations by RDAs*. Croydon: Chartered Institute of Public Finance and Accountancy.

——. 1998b. *Leisure and recreation statistics 1998–9 estimates*. London: Chartered Institute of Public Finance and Accountancy.

——. 1999. *Leisure and recreation statistics 1999–2000 estimates*. London: Chartered Institute of Public Finance and Accountancy.

Clogg, R. 1987. *Parties and elections in Greece: the search for legitimacy*. London: C. Hirst & Co.

Clumpner, R.A. 1994. '21st century success in international competition'. Pp. 353–63 in *Sport in the global village*, edited by R.C. Wilcox. Morgantown, WV: Fitness Information Technology.

Coalter, F. 1990. 'The politics of professionalism: consumers or citizens?' *Leisure Studies* 9:107–120.

——. 1995a. 'Compulsory competitive tendering for sport and leisure management: a lost opportunity'. *Managing Leisure: An International Journal* 1:3–15.

——. 1995b. 'The impact of social class and education on sports participation: some evidence from the general household survey'. In *Leisure and social stratification*, edited by K. Roberts. Brighton: Leisure Studies Association.

Cochrane, A., J. Peck, and A. Tickell. 1996. 'Manchester plays games: exploring the local politics of globalisation'. *Urban Studies* 33:1319–36.

Collins, Michael F. 2002. *Sport and social exclusion*. London: Routledge.

Collins, M.F., with I.P. Henry and B.M. Houlihan. 1999. *Research report: sport and social exclusion*. London: Department of Culture, Media and Sport.

Colonna, V. 1999. *Yamaha d'Alger*. Paris: TRISTRAM.

Comptroller and Auditor General. 2005. *UK sport: supporting elite athletes*. London: National Audit Office.

Critcher, C. 1991. 'Sporting civic pride: Sheffield and the World Student Games of 1991'. In *Leisure in the 1990s: rolling back the welfare state*, Conference papers no. 46, edited by C. Knox and J. Sugden. Brighton: Leisure Studies Association.

Darby, P. 1997. *Sport, politics and international relations: Africa place in the Federation Internationale de Football Association (FIFA's) global order*. Coleraine: University of Ulster.

——. 2002. *Africa, football, and FIFA: politics, colonialism, and resistance*. London; Portland, OR: F. Cass.

Darke, R. 1992. 'Gambling on sport: Sheffield's regeneration strategy for the 90s'. Unpublished paper. Sheffield University.

Davaki, K. and E. Mossialos. 2005. 'Plus ca change: health sector reforms in Greece'. *Journal of Health Politics Policy and Law* 30:143–67.

Davies, I.R.L. and G.G. Corbett. 1997. 'A cross-cultural study of colour grouping: evidence for weak linguistic relativity'. *British Journal of Psychology* 88:493–517.

Deakin, N. and J. Edwards. 1993. *The enterprise culture and the inner city*. London: Routledge.

dellaSala, V. 1997. 'Hollowing out and hardening the state: European integration and the Italian economy'. *West European Politics* 20:14–33.

Department of National Heritage. 1995a. *The British Academy of Sport: a consultation paper*. London: Department of National Heritage.

Department of National Heritage. 1995b. *Sport: raising the game*. London: Department of National Heritage.

Descartes, R. 1881. *The method, meditations, and selections from the principles of Descartes*. Translated by J. Veitch. London: William Blackwood.

Diamandouros, N. 1983. 'Greek political culture in transition'. In *Greece in the 1980s*, edited by R. Clogg. Basingstoke: Macmillan.

Digaetano, A. and J.S. Klemanski. 1993. 'Urban regime capacity – a comparison of Birmingham, England, and Detroit, Michigan'. *Journal of Urban Affairs* 15:367–84.

Dine, P. 1997. 'Peasants into sportsmen: modern games and the construction of French national identity'. In *The symbolism of sport in France*, edited by P. Dine and I. Henry. Stirling: University of Stirling.

Donaghu, M.T. and R. Barff. 1990. 'Nike just did it – international subcontracting and flexibility in athletic footwear production'. *Regional Studies* 24:537–52.

Downs, A. 1972. 'Up and down with ecology: the issue attention cycle'. *Public Interest* 28:38–50.

Dubedout, H. 1971. 'Editorial'. P. 5 in *Le sport à Grenoble*, edited by Ville de Grenoble. Grenoble: Plaquette Municipale.

——. 1975a. 'La politique sportive municipale ne changera pas'. P. 15 in *Le dauphiné libéré*. Grenoble.

——. 1975b. 'Sport de masse. Sport d'élite? Faux problème. Rendre le sport accessible à tous'. P. 16 in *Le dauphiné libéré*. Grenoble.

Dulac, C. 1998. 'Stratégies d'adaptation des politiques locales à la pression des lobbies sportifs'. *Annales de recherche* 79:78–89.

——. 1999. 'Ordre sportif local et stratégie d'acteurs. Evolution des relations Municipalité-OMS à Grenoble, à propos du sport d'élite durant la période 1983–95'. *Science et motricité* 35:46–56.

Dunleavy, P. 1980. *Urban political analysis*. London: Macmillan.

Durkheim, Emile. 1952. *Suicide: a study in sociology*. London: Routledge & Kegan Paul.

——. 1982. *The rules of sociological method and selected texts on sociology and its method*. Basingstoke: Macmillan.

Ehrenberg, A. 1988. 'The age of heroism – sport, business, and the fighting spirit in contemporary-France'. *Cahiers Internationaux De Sociologie* 85:197–224.

Ellyas, A. 1996. 'Les perspectives d'avenir pour les jeunes déplomés'. In *Algérie, comprendre la crise*, edited by G. Manceron. Alger: Interventions.

English Sports Council. 1999. *Best value: case studies*. London: Sport England.

——. 2000. *Best value: performance measurement for local authority sports halls and pools*. London: Sport England.

Espagnac, R. 1971. 'Les moyens d'une politique sportive'. P. 7 in *Le sport à Grenoble*, edited by Ville de Grenoble. Grenoble: Plaquette Municipale.

Esteves, A., Fonseca, M.L. and Malheiros, J. 2003. 'Portugal'. In *EU and US approaches to the management of immigration* edited by J. Niessen, Y. Schibel and R. Magoni. Brussels: Migration Policy Group.

Etzioni, A. 1993. *The spirit of community: rights, responsibilities and the communitarian agenda*. London: HarperCollins.

Europa. 2003. 'Draft Treaty establishing a Constitution for Europe'. (http://europa.eu.int/futurum/constitution/part3/title3/chapter5/section4/index_en.htm).

European Commission. 2003. *Standard Summary Project Fiche: improved access to health care for the Roma minority in the Slovak Republic*. Brussels: European Commission.

European Tour Operators Association. 2006. *Olympic report*. London: ETOA.

Farnham, D. and S. Horton. 1993. 'The new public service managerialism: an assessment'. Pp. 237–54 in *Managing the new public services*, edited by D. Farnham and S. Horton. London: Macmillan.

Fates, Y. 1994. *Sport et Tiers Monde, pratiques corporelle*. Paris: Presses University of France.

Featherstone, K. 2005. 'Introduction: "modernisation" and the structural constraints of Greek politics'. *West European Politics* 28:223–41.

Featherstone, M. 1995. *Undoing culture: globalization, postmodernism and identity*. London: Sage.

Federation Internationale de Football Association. 2002. '2002 FIFA World Cup™ TV coverage'. Retrieved 29 June 2004 (www.fifa.com/en/marketing/newmedia/ index/0,1347,10,00.html).

Foley, P. 1991. 'The impact of the World Student Games on Sheffield'. *Environment and Planning C-Government & Policy* 9:65–78.

Foucault, M. 1972. *The archaeology of knowledge*. London: Tavistock.

——. 1986. 'Disciplinary power and subjection'. Pp. 229–42 in *Power*, edited by S. Lukes. Oxford: Blackwell.

Frappat, P. 1979. *Grenoble, le mythe blessé*. Paris: Alain Moreau.

Friedberg, E. 1993. *Le pouvoir et la règle*. Paris: Le Seuil.

Fu, H. 1987. 'The mutation and reconstruction of the constructional structure'. *National Taiwan University Law Review* 16:1–32.

Fujita, K. 2003. 'Neo-industrial Tokyo: urban development and globalisation in Japan's state-centred developmental capitalism'. *Urban Studies* 40:249–81.

Fukuyama, F. 1992. *The end of history and the last man.*

——. 1993. *The end of history?* London: Institute of Economic Affairs.

Gamble, A. 1988. *The free economy and the strong state: the politics of Thatcherism.* London: Macmillan.

Garnham, N. 1983. 'Concepts of culture, cultural policy and the cultural industries'. In *Cultural industries and cultural policy in London conference.* London: Riverside Studios.

Giddens, A. 1990. *The consequences of modernity.* Cambridge: Polity Press.

Giddens, A. and S. Lash. 1994. *Reflexive modernisation.* Cambridge: Polity Press.

Gold, Thomas, Doug Guthrie and David Wank. 2002. *Social connections in China: institutions, culture, and the changing nature of guanxi.* Cambridge: Cambridge University Press.

Göle, N. 1997. 'Modernité locale'. Pp. 40–9 in *Post colonialism, decentrement, déplacement, dissemination*, edited by M. Khelladi. Paris: Débale, revue international semestriel.

Goodbody, J. 1991. 'Soviet sports empire crumbles'. *Times.*

Goodwin, M. and J. Painter. 1996. 'Local governance, the crises of Fordism and the changing geographies of regulation'. *Transactions of the Institute of British Geographers* 21:635–648.

Goodwin, M., S. Duncan and S. Halford. 1993. 'Regulation theory, the local state and the transition of urban politics'. *Environment and Planning D: Society and Space* 11:67–88.

Gratton, C. 1998. 'Economic impact of major sports events: lessons from the study of six world and European championships'. In *Sport in the city*, edited by C. Gratton and I. Henry. London: Routledge.

——. 1999. *COMPASS 1999: a project seeking the coordinated monitoring of participation in sports in Europe.* London: UK Sport and Italian Olympic Committee.

Gratton, C. and I. Henry. 2001. *Sport in the city: the role of sport in economic and social regeneration.* London: Routledge.

Greater London Enterprise Board. nd. *Altered images: towards a strategy for London's cultural industries.* London: Greater London Enterprise Board.

Green, E., S. Hebron, and D. Woodward. 1990. *Women's leisure, what leisure?* Basingstoke: Macmillan.

Green, M. 2004. 'Power, policy and political priorities: elite sport development in Canada and the United Kingdom'. *Sociology of Sport Journal* 21:376–96.

Green, M. and Houlihan, B. 2005. Elite sport development: policy learning and political priorities. London: Routledge.

Guardian. 2002. 'Soccer sorcery as Cameroon outwit Mali'. (http://football.guardian.co.uk/africannationscup/story/0,5764,646841,00.html).

Gunes-Ayata, A. 1994. 'Clientelism: premodern, modern, postmodern'. Pp. 19–28 in *Democracy, clientelism, and civil society*, edited by L. Roniger and A. Gunes-Ayata. Boulder, CO: Lynne Rienner.

Guttmann, A. 1978. *From ritual to record. The nature of modern sports.* New York: Columbia University Press.

——. 1994. *Games and empires modern sports and cultural imperialism.* New York: Columbia University Press.

Gyford, John. 1985. *The politics of local socialism*. London: Allen & Unwin.

Habermas, Jurgen. 1990. *Moral consciousness and communicative action*. Cambridge, MA: MIT Press.

Haddad, Y.Y. 1998. 'Islam and gender: dilemmas in the changing Arab world'. Pp. 3–29 in *Islam, gender and social change*, edited by Y.Y. Haddad and J. Esposito. Oxford: Oxford University Press.

Hall, S. 1991. 'The local and the global: globalization and ethnicity'. Pp. 19–40 in *Culture, globalization and the world-system*, edited by D. King. London: Macmillan.

Hallin, D.C. and S. Papathanassopoulos. 2002. 'Political clientelism and the media: southern Europe and Latin America in comparative perspective'. *Media Culture & Society* 24:175–95.

Hambleton, R. 1988. 'Consumerism, decentralization and local democracy'. *Public Administration* 66:125–47.

Hambleton, R., P. Hoggett and F. Tolan. 1989. 'The decentralization of public-services – a research agenda'. *Local Government Studies* 15:39–56.

Harbi, M. 2002. 'Le poids de l'histoire et la violence vint à l'Algérie'. *Le Monde Diplomatique* July:1–15.

Harding, A. 1991. 'The rise of urban-growth coalitions, UK-style'. *Environment and Planning C-Government & Policy* 9:295–317.

——. 1994. 'Urban regimes and growth machines – toward a cross-national research agenda'. *Urban Affairs Quarterly* 29:356–82.

Harding, A. and P. Le Galès. 1997. 'Globalization, urban change and urban policies in Britain and France'. P.p 181–201 in *The limits of globalization*, edited by A. Scott. London: Routledge.

Hardtmautner, G. 1995. 'How does one become a good European – the British-press and European integration'. *Discourse & Society* 6:177–205.

Hargreaves, J. 1992. 'Sport and socialism in Britain'. *Sociology of Sport Journal* 9:131–53.

Harvey, D. 1987. 'Flexible accumulation through urbanization: reflections on "post-modernism" in the American city'. *Antipode* 19:260–86.

——. 1989. *The condition of postmodernity*. Oxford: Basil Blackwell.

——. 1995. *The urbanisation of capital*. Oxford: Blackwell.

Hay, C. 1997. 'Blaijorism: towards a one-vision polity?' *PQ* 68:372–8.

Hay, C. and D. Marsh. 2000. *Demystifying globalization*. Basingstoke: Palgrave.

Haynes, M. and K. Pinnock. 1998. 'Towards a deeper and wider European Union'. *Economic and Political Weekly* 33:415–30.

Heeg, S., B. Klagge and J. Ossenbrugge. 2003. 'Metropolitan cooperation in Europe: theoretical issues and perspectives for urban networking'. *European Planning Studies* 11:139–53.

Henry, I. 1993. *The politics of leisure policy*. London: Macmillan.

——. 1997. 'The politics of sport and symbolism in the city: a case study of the Lyon conurbation'. *Managing Leisure* 2:65–81.

——. 2001a. *The politics of leisure policy*. London: Palgrave.

——. 2001b. 'Postmodernism and power in urban policy: implications for sport and cultural policy in the city'. *European Sport Management Quarterly* 1:5–20.

Henry, I. and P. Bramham. 1986. 'Leisure, the local state and social order'. *Leisure Studies* 5:189–209.

Henry, I. and P.C. Lee. 2004. 'Governance and ethics'. In *The business of sport management*, edited by J. Beech and S. Chadwick. London: Pearson.

Henry, I. and N. Matthews. 1998. 'Sport policy and the European Union: the post-Maastricht agenda'. *Managing Leisure: An International Journal* 4:1–19.

Henry, I.P. and Pantelis Nassis. 1999. 'Political clientelism and sports policy in Greece'. *International Review for the Sociology of Sport* 34:43–58.

Henry, I. and J. Paramio Salcines. 1999a. 'Sport and the analysis of symbolic regimes: an illustrative case study of the city of Sheffield'. *Urban Affairs Review* 34:641–66.

——. 1999b. 'Sport and the analysis of symbolic regimes: a case study of the city of Sheffield'. *Urban Affairs Review* 34:641–66.

Henry, I. and J.L. Paramio-Salcines. 1999. 'Sport and the analysis of symbolic regimes: a case study of the city of Sheffield'. *Journal of Planning Literature* 14.

Henry, I. and K. Uchiumi. 2001. 'Political ideology, modernity and sports policy: a comparative analysis of sports policy in Britain and Japan'. *Hitotsubashi Journal of Social Sciences* 33:161–85.

Henry, I., W. Radzi, E. Rich, C. Shelton, E. Theodoraki and A. White. 2004. *Women, leadership and the Olympic movement.* Loughborough: Institute of Sport and Leisure Policy, Loughborough University & the International Olympic Committee.

Hill, J.H. and B. Mannheim. 1992. 'Language and world-view'. *Annual Review of Anthropology* 21:381–406.

Hirst, P. and G. Thompson. 1995. 'Globalization and the future of the nation-state'. *Economy and Society* 24:408–42.

Hix, S. 1996. 'The Transnational Party Federations' Union'. In *Political parties and the European Union*, edited by J. Gaffney.

Ho, M.S. 2003. 'Democratization and autonomous unionism in Taiwan: the case of petrochemical workers'. *Issues & Studies* 39:105–35.

Hood, S.J. 1996a. 'Political change in Taiwan: the rise of Kuomintang factions'. *Asian Survey* XXXV:468–82.

——. 1996b. *The Kuomintang and the democratization of Taiwan.* Boulder, CO: Westview.

Hoogvelt, A. 1997. *Globalisation and the postcolonial world.* Basingstoke: Macmillan.

Houlihan, B. 1997. *Sport, policy, and politics: a comparative analysis.* London: Routledge.

——. 2003. 'Sport and globalisation'. Pp. 345–363 in *Sport and society*, edited by B. Houlihan. London: Sage.

Hsieh, J.F.S. 2000. 'East Asian culture and democratic transition, with special reference to the case of Taiwan'. *Journal of Asian and African Studies* 35:29–42.

Huang, Y.P. 1997. Crime and bribe storm of Taiwanese professional baseball (in Chinese). Taipei: Shui Yung.

Hubbard, P. 1996. 'Urban design and city regeneration – social representations of entrepreneurial landscapes'. *Urban Studies* 33:1441–61.

Human Rights Watch. 2002. 'World Report 2002: Czech Republic'. Retrieved 6 August 2004 (www.hrw.org/wr2k2/europe8.html).

Huntington, S. 1996. *The clash of civilizations.* London: Simon & Schuster.

Hyman, Richard. 2001. 'European integration and industrial relations: a case of variable geometry?' *Antipode* 33:468.

Iglicka, K., Kaźmierkiewicz, P. and Mazur-Rafal, M. 2003. 'Poland'. In *EU and US approaches to the management of immigration*, edited by J. Niessen, Y. Schibel and R. Magoni. Brussels: Migration Policy Group.

Jessop, B. 1990. *State theory: putting capitalist states in their place.* Oxford: Polity Press.

——. 1995. 'The regulation approach, governance and post-Fordism – alternative perspectives on economic and political-change'. *Economy and Society* 24:307–33.

John, P. and A. Cole. 2000. 'When do institutions, policy sectors, and cities matter? Comparing networks of local policy makers in Britain and France'. *Comparative Political Studies* 33:248–68.

Joly, J. 1985. 'L'urbanisme et la politique urbaine'. Pp. 83–92 in *Grenoble et son agglomération*, edited by J. Joly. Paris: La Documentation Française.

Jonas, A.E.G. 1992. 'A place for politics in urban theory – the organization and strategies of urban coalitions'. *Urban Geography* 13:280–90.

Jones, H. 1989. *The economic impact and importance of sport: a European study*. Strasbourg: Council of Europe.

Jones, M. 1998. 'Restructuring the local state: economic governance or social regulation?' *Political Geography* 17:959–88.

Kantor, P., H.V. Savitch and S.V. Haddock. 1997. 'The political economy of urban regimes – a comparative perspective'. *Urban Affairs Review* 32:348–77.

Kao, Y.S. 1996. 'The social order and security is ruined by the criminal force' (in Chinese). *The Parliamentary Debate* 85:2310–11.

Karam, Azza M. 1998. *Women, Islamisms and the state: contemporary feminisms in Egypt*. Basingstoke: Palgrave.

Karambelias, G. 1989. *State and society after the restoration of democracy (1974–88)* (in Greek). Athens: Exantas.

Kastoryano, Riva. 2002. *Negotiating identities: states and immigrants in France and Germany*. Princeton, NJ: Princeton University Press.

Kau, M.Y.M. 1996. 'The power structure in Taiwan's political economy'. *Asian Survey* XXXVI:287–305.

Kazakos, P. 1990. 'Financial policy and elections: state control of the economy in Greece: 1979–1989'. In *Elections and parties in the 1980s* (in Greek), edited by C. Lyrintzis and I. Nikolakopoulos. Athens: Themelio.

Keil, R. 1998. 'Globalization makes states: perspectives of local governance in the age of the world city'. *Review of International Political Economy* 5:616–46.

Kennedy, B. 2000. 'Gangsters and good manners'. *Taipei Times* (www.taipeitimes.com/News/edit/archives/2000/08/14/47748).

Kerstein, Samuel J. 2002. *Kant's search for the supreme principle of morality*. Cambridge and New York: Cambridge University Press.

Kim, M. and H.J. Hodges. 2005. 'On Huntington's civilizational paradigm: a reappraisal'. *Issues & Studies* 41:217–48.

Kipfer, S. and R. Keil. 2002. 'Toronto Inc? Planning the competitive city in the new Toronto'. *Antipode* 34:227–64.

Kitschelt, H. 2000. 'Linkages between citizens and politicians in democratic polities'. *Comparative Political Studies* 33:845–79.

Klein, A. 1991. 'Sport and culture as contested terrain: Americanisation in the Caribbean'. *Sociology of Sport Journal* 8:79–85.

König, Karin and Bernhard Perchinig. 2003. 'Austria'. In *EU and US approaches to the management of immigration*, edited by J. Niessen, Y. Schibel and R. Magoni. Brussels: Migration Policy Group.

Kováts, András, Pál Nyíri and Judit Tóth. 2003. 'Hungary'. In *EU and US approaches to the management of immigration*, edited by J. Niessen, Y. Schibel and R. Magoni. Brussels: Migration Policy Group.

Krich, J. 2002. 'A shy 24-year-old slugger holds the pride of his diplomatically isolated island in his strong hands', *The Asian Wall Street Journal* 8 March, pp. 8–10.

Kronos. 1997. *The economic impact of events staged in Sheffield 1990–1997*. Sheffield:

Kronos on behalf of Destination Sheffield, Sheffield City Council's Events Unit and Sheffield International Venues Ltd.

Kuo, C.T. 2000. 'Taiwan's distorted democracy in comparative perspective'. *African and Asia Studies* 35:85–111.

Kurer, O. 1993. 'Clientelism, corruption, and the allocation of resources'. *Public Choice* 77:259–273.

Kurth, J. 1993. 'A tale of four countries: parallel politics in southern Europe, 1815–1990'. In *Mediterranean paradoxes: the politics and social structure of southern Europe*, edited by J. Kurth and J. Petras. Oxford: Berg.

Laabs, J. 1998. 'Nike gives Indonesian workers a raise'. *Workforce* 77:15–16.

Labour Party. 1997. *Labour's sporting nation*. London: Labour Party.

Lamassoure, Alain. 2003. 'After the convention: toward a European constitution'. *Commentaire* 26:603.

Lammer, Thomas. 2003. 'The future of Europe: a conception of Europe and a constitution'. *WeltTrends* 40.

Krich, J. 2002. 'A shy 24-year-old slugger holds the pride of his diplomatically isolated island in his strong hands', *The Asian Wall Street Journal* 8 March, pp. 8–10.

Lane, J.-E. 1995. *The public sector: concepts, models and approaches*. London: Sage.

Lawless, P. 1990. 'Regeneration in Sheffield: from radical intervention to partnership'. In *Leaderships and urban regeneration*, edited by D. Judd and M. Parkinson. London: Sage.

Leach, S., J. Stewart and K. Walsh. 1994. *The changing organisation and management of local government*. London: Macmillan.

Lee, C.H. 1996. 'The government should do something for professional baseball' (in Chinese). *The Parliamentary Debate* 85:284–5.

Lee, Kuo Yen. 2003. 'Sports industry and human resource management: case study of Taiwan Professional Baseball's Gambling Scandal' (in Chinese). Master dissertation thesis, Taipei Physical Education College, Taipei.

Lee, P.C. 2005. *The governance of professional baseball in Taiwan*. Loughborough: School of Sport and Exercise Sciences, Loughborough University.

Leitner, H. and M. Garner. 1993. 'The limits of local initiatives – a reassessment of urban entrepreneurialism for urban-development'. *Urban Geography* 14:57–77.

Levine, M.A. 1994. 'The transformation of urban-politics in France – the roots of growth politics and urban regimes'. *Urban Affairs Quarterly* 29:383–410.

Lia, T.H., R. Myers and W. Wei. 1991. *A tragic beginning: the Taiwan uprising of February 28, 1947*. Stanford: Stanford University Press.

Liang, S.L. 1993. 'Social development, power and the formation of sports culture: an analysis of Taiwanese Baseball Society, History, and Culture, 1895–1990' (in Chinese). Master dissertation thesis, National Chengchi University, taipei.

Lin, C.Y. 2001. 'Chen uses baseball tournament to attack the KMT'. Retrieved 15 August 2003 (www.taipeitimes.com/News/local/archives/2001/11/08/110600).

———. 2003. 'Taiwan sport: the interrelationship between sport and politics through three successive political regimes using baseball as an example'. PhD Thesis, Brighton University, Brighton.

Lithuanian Community in Latvia. 2004. 'Latvian Lithuanians'. Retrieved 2004 (www.lithuania.lt/IMI/i_en.jsp?nr=lietuviai_pasaulyje_latvija).

Liu, H.Y. 2003. *State, sport and politics: sport policy in Republic of China/Taiwan 1973–2002, through a strategic relations approach*. Loughborough: Loughborough University.

Liu, K.T. 2001a. 'Yen's conviction a good beginning'. Retrieved 28 February 2004 (www.taipeitimes.com/News/edit/archives/2001/09/11/102469).

——. 2001b. 'Time to take action on "black gold" '. *Taipei Times* (www.taipeitimes.com/News/edit/archives/2001/03/06/76400).

Lucy, J.A. 1997. 'Linguistic relativity'. *Annual Review of Anthropology* 26:291–312.

Lykovardi, Kalliopi and Eleni Petroula. 2003. 'Greece'. In *EU and US approaches to the management of immigration*, edited by J. Niessen, Y. Schibel, and R. Magoni. Brussels: Migration Policy Group.

Lyotard, Jean-François. 1984. *The postmodern condition: a report on knowledge*. Translated by G. Bennington and B. Massumi. Manchester: Manchester University Press.

Lyrintzis, C. 1989. 'PASOK in power: the loss of the third road to socialism'. In *Southern European socialism*, edited by T. Gallagher and A.M. Williams. Manchester: Manchester University Press.

MacCormick, N. 1997. 'Democracy, subsidiarity, and citizenship in the "European commonwealth" '. *Law and Philosophy* 16:331–56.

McDonald, M., T. Mihara and J. Hong. 2001. 'Japanese spectator industry: cultural changes creating new opportunities'. *European Sport Management Quarterly* 1:39–60.

McElvoy, A. 1994. 'Going for gold'. *Times*.

McKay, J. 1994. 'Masculine hegemony, the state and the incorporation of gender equity discourse – the case of Australian sport'. *Australian Journal of Political Science* 29:82–95.

Maffesoli, Michel. 1996. *The time of the tribes: the decline of individualism in mass society*. London: Sage.

Maguire, J. 1993a. 'Globalisation: sport and national identities: "the empire strikes back"?' *Loisir et societe* 16:293–322.

——. 1993b. 'Globalization, sport development, and the media/sport production complex'. *Sport Science Review* 2:29–47.

——. 1994. 'Preliminary observations of globalisation and the migration of sport labour'. *Sociological Review* 42:452–80.

——. 1995. 'Sportization processes: emergence, diffusion and globalization'. *Schweizerische Zeitschrift fur Soziologie* 21:577–96.

——. 1999. *Global sport: identities, societies, civilizations*. Oxford: Polity.

Manesis, A. 1986. 'The development of political constitutions in Greece'. In *Greece in a process of development* (in Greek), edited by A. Manesis. Athens: Exantas.

Mann, M. 1997. 'Has globalization ended the rise and rise of the nation-state?' *Review of International Political Economy* 4:472–96.

Marsh, D. and G. Stoker. 2002. *Theory and methods in political science*. Hampshire: Palgrave Macmillan.

Marsh, D. and P. Furlong. 2002. 'A skin not a jacket: ontology and epistemology in political science'. In *Theory and methods in political science*, edited by D. Marsh and G. Stoker. Basingstoke: Palgrave.

Marshall, C. 2000. 'Policy discourse analysis: negotiating gender equity'. *Journal of Education Policy* 15:125–56.

Maus, Didier. 2003. 'Regarding the European constitution: words and substance'. *Revue Politique et Parlimentaire* 105:32.

Mayer, M. 1994. 'Post-Fordist city politics'. Pp. 316–37 in *Post-Fordism: a reader*, edited by A. Amin. Oxford: Blackwell.

Mernissi, F. 1985. *Beyond the veil: male-female dynamics in a modern Muslim society*. London: Al Saqi Books.

Mernissi, F. and M. Lakeland. 1991. *The veil and the male elite: a feminist interpretation of women's rights in Islam.* Reading, MA and Wokingham: Addison-Wesley.

Middleton, M. 1991. *Cities in transition.* London: Michael Joseph.

Miller, David. 2000. *Citizenship and national identity.* Cambridge: Polity.

Mingione, E. 1994. 'Life strategies and social economies in the postfordist age'. *International Journal of Urban and Regional Research* 18:24–45.

Modood, T. 2005. 'Remaking multiculturalism after 7/7'. *Open Democracy.* Online: www.opendemocracy.net/conflict-terrorism/multiculturalism_2879.jsp.

Morris, L. 1997. 'Globalization, migration and the nation-state: the path to a post-national Europe?' *British Journal of Sociology* 48:192–209.

Morris, P.E., S. Morrow and P.M. Spink. 1996. 'EC law and professional football: Bosman and its implications'. *Modern Law Review* 59:893–918.

Nassis, P. 1994. 'Strategic relations theory and the development of sports policy in Greece 1980–93'. PhD thesis, Department of Physical Education, Sports Science and Recreation Management, Loughborough University, Loughborough.

Nazareno, M., S. Stokes and V. Brusco. 2006. 'Interest and electoral dangers of public expenditure in Argentina'. *Desarrollo Economico-Revista De Ciencias Sociales* 46:63–88.

Negus, K. 1993. 'Global harmonies and local discords – transnational policies and practices in the European Recording Industry'. *European Journal of Communication* 8:295–316.

Neumann, I.B. 1998. 'European identity, EU expansion, and the integration/exclusion nexus'. *Alternatives-Social Transformation and Humane Governance* 23:397–416.

Niessen, J. 2000. *Diversity and cohesion: new challenges for the integration of immigrants and minorities.* Strasbourg: Council of Europe: Directorate General III – Social Cohesion, Directorate of Social Affairs and Health.

Oakley, B. and M. Green. 2001. 'The production of Olympic champions: international perspectives on elite sport development system'. *European Journal for Sport Management* 8:83–124.

Paley, W. 1807. *Natural theology: or, evidences of the existence and attributes of the deity, collected from the appearances of nature.* London: Printed for R. Faulder and Son.

Pan, W.K. 1996. 'Issues of the penetration of gangsters in the professional baseball' (in Chinese). *The Parliamentary Debate* 85:2461–2.

Papatheodorou, F. and D. Machin. 2003. 'The umbilical cord that was never cut – the post-dictatorial intimacy between the political elite and the mass media in Greece and Spain'. *European Journal of Communication* 18:31–54.

Parent, J.-F. 1982. *Grenoble. Deux siècles d'urbanisation.* Grenoble: Presses Universitaires de Grenoble.

Parker, M. 1997. 'Organizations and citizenship'. *Organization* 4:75–92.

Patterson, A. and P.L. Pinch. 1995. 'Hollowing out the local state – compulsory competitive tendering and the restructuring of British public-sector services'. *Environment and Planning A* 27:1437–61.

Peck, J. and A. Tickell. 1995. 'The social regulation of uneven development – regulatory deficit, England south east, and the collapse of Thatcherism'. *Environment and Planning A* 27:15–40.

Peck, J. and M. Jones. 1995. 'Training and enterprise councils – Schumpeterian workfare state, or what'. *Environment and Planning A* 27:1361–96.

Peck, J.A. and A. Tickell. 1992. 'Local modes of social regulation? Regulation theory, Thatcherism and uneven development'. *Geoforum* 23:347.

Peppard, Victor and James Riordan. 1993. *Playing politics: Soviet sport diplomacy to 1992.* Greenwich, CT; London: JAI Press.

Perlmutter, H. 1991. 'On the rocky road to the first global civilisation'. *Human Relations* 44:898–906.

Petmesidou, M. 1996. 'Social protection in Greece: a brief glimpse of a welfare state'. *Social Policy & Administration* 30:324–47.

Petras, J., E. Raptis, and S. Sarafopoulos. 1993. 'Greek socialism: the patrimonial state revisited'. In *Mediterranean paradoxes: the politics and social structure of southern Europe*, edited by J. Kurth and J. Petras. Oxford: Berg.

Piattoni, S. 2001. 'Clientelism in historical and comparative perspective'. Pp. 1–30 in *Clientelism, interests and democratic representation: the European experience in historical and comparative perspective*, edited by S. Piattoni. Cambridge: Cambridge University Press.

Pierson, C. 1991. *Beyond the welfare state? the new political economy of welfare.* Cambridge: Polity Press.

Platzer, Hans-Wolfgang. 2002. 'Europeanization and transnationalization of labor relations in the EU'. *Internationale Politik und Gesellschaft* 2.

Pratchett, Lawrence. 2002. 'Local government: from modernisation to consolidation'. *Parliamentary Affairs* 55:331.

Prebisch, R. 1998. 'Dependence, development and interdependence'. In *The state of development economics: progress and perspectives*, edited by G. Ranis and T. Schultz. London: Blackwell.

Prelypchan, E. 2000. 'Candidates seek divine intervention'. *Taipei Times* (www.taipeitimes.com/News/front/archives/2000/02/06/22908).

Preston, P. 2000. *Understanding modern Japan.* London: Sage.

Quilley, S. 2000. 'Manchester first: from municipal socialism to the entrepreneurial city'. *International Journal of Urban and Regional Research* 24:601–15.

Ravenscroft, N. 1993. 'Public leisure provision and the good citizen'. *Leisure Studies* 12:33–44.

——. 1994. 'Leisure policy in the new Europe: the UK Department of National Heritage as a model of development and integration'. *European Urban and Regional Studies* 1:131–42.

Reaves, J.A. 2002. *Taking in a game: a history of baseball in Asia.* Lincoln, OR; London: University of Nebraska Press.

Rhodes, R.A.W. 1996. 'The new governance: governing without government'. *Political Studies* 44:652–67.

Rhodes, M. and B. vanApeldoorn. 1998. 'Capital unbound? The transformation of European corporate governance'. *Journal of European Public Policy* 5:406–27.

Ribeaud, S. 1973. 'Entretien avec M. R. Espagnac adjont aux sports'. P. 10 in *Le dauphiné libéré*. Grenoble.

Richardson, T. and O.B. Jensen. 2003. 'Linking discourse and space: towards a cultural sociology of space in analysing spatial policy discourses'. *Urban Studies* 40:7–22.

Robertson, R. 1992. *Globalization: social theory and global culture.* London: Sage.

Robertson, C.J., W.F. Crittenden, M.K. Brady and J.J. Hoffman. 2002. 'Situational ethics across borders: a multicultural examination'. *Journal of Business Ethics* 38:327–38.

Roche, M. 1992. 'Problems of rationality and democracy in mega-event planning: a study of Sheffield's World Student Games 1991'. In *Leisure and new citizenship, the VIIIth European Leisure and Recreation Association Congress*, edited by J. Gonzalez and R. San Salvador. Bilbao, Spain: Universidad de Deusto.

——. 1998. *Sport, popular culture and identity*. Aachen: Meyer and Meyer.

Rodgers, B. 1978. *Rationalising sports policies: sport in its social context: international comparisons*. Strasbourg: Council of Europe.

Rodgers, Jim. 2003. *Reason, conflict and power: modern political and social thought from 1688 to the present*. Lanham, MD: University Press of America.

Roniger, L. 2004. 'Political clientelism, democracy, and market economy'. *Comparative Politics* 36:353–75.

Roniger, L. and Gunes-Ayata, A. 1994. *Democracy, clientelism, and civil society*. Boulder, CO: Lynne Rienner.

Rosenau, J. 1989. *Interdependence and conflict in world politics*. Lexington: D.C. Heath.

Roy, D. 2003. *Taiwan: a political history*. New York: Cornell University Press.

Said, E. 1991. *Orientalism: western conceptions of the Orient*. London: Penguin.

——. 2001. *Reflections on exile: and other literary and cultural essays*. London: Granta Books.

Said, Edward W. 1994. *Culture and imperialism*. New York: Vintage Books.

——. 1997. *Covering Islam: how the media and the experts determine how we see the rest of the world*. New York: Vintage Books.

Saliba, Therese, Carolyn Allen, and Judith A. Howard. 2002. *Gender, politics, and Islam*. Chicago: University of Chicago Press.

Sardar, Z. 1998. *Postmodernism and the other: the new imperialism of western culture*. London: Pluto Press.

Sardar, Ziauddin. 1999. *Orientalism*. Buckingham: Open University Press.

Sartori, G. 1991. 'Comparing and miscomparing'. *Journal of Theoretical Politics* 3:243–257.

Sayyid, S.B. 1998. *A fundamental fear: eurocentrism and the emergence of Islamism*. London: ZED Books Limited.

Scheurich, J. 1997. *Research method in the postmodern*. London: Falmer Press.

Schmidt, V. 1990. *Democratising France*. Cambridge: Cambridge University Press.

Schockenhoff, Eberhard. 2003. *Natural law & human dignity: universal ethics in an historical world*. Washington, DC: Catholic University of America Press.

Schram, S.F. 1993. 'Postmodern policy analysis – discourse and identity in welfare policy'. *Policy Sciences* 26:249–270.

Seary, W. 1992. *Brussels in focus: EC access for sport*. London: Sports Council.

Seppanen, P. 1989. 'Competitive sport and sport success in Olympic games: acrosscultural analysis of value systems'. *International Review for the Sociology of Sport* 24:275–282.

Seyd, P. 1990. 'Radical Sheffield – from socialism to entrepreneurialism'. *Political Studies* 38:335–344.

——. 1993. 'The political management of decline 1973–1993'. In *The history of the city of Sheffield 1843–1993. Politics*, vol. 1, edited by C. Binfield. Sheffield: Sheffield Academic Press.

Shaw, M. 1997. 'The state of globalization: towards a theory of state transformation'. *Review of International Political Economy* 4:497–513.

Sheffield City Council. 1983. *Employment and environmental plan for the Lower Don Valley*. Sheffield: Department of Employment and Economic Development, Sheffield City Council.

Sheffield City Council Recreation Department. 1984. *Leisure challenge: a prospect for the Lower Don Valley*. Sheffield: Sheffield City Council.

Sheffield Economic Regeneration Committee. nd. *Sheffield 2000: the development strategy*. Sheffield: Sheffield City Council.

Shefner, J. 2001. 'Coalitions and clientelism in Mexico'. *Theory and Society* 30:593–628.

Shore, C. 1993. 'Inventing the Peoples Europe – critical approaches to European-community cultural policy'. *Man* 28:779–800.

——. 1996. 'Transcending the nation-state? The European Commission and the (re)-discovery of Europe'. *Journal of Historical Sociology* 9:473–96.

Sie, S. 1978. 'Sport and politics: the case of the Asian Games and GANEFO'. Pp. 279–96 in *Sport and international relations*, edited by B. Lowe *et al.* Champaign, IL: Stipes.

Silvestro, M. and A. Silvestro. 1996. 'The Bosman decision and sports in the European union (Le sport dans l'union europeenne et l'arret bosman). *Revue du marche commun* 1996: 489–92.

Sklair, L. 1991. *Sociology of the global system.* Brighton: Harvester Wheatsheaf.

Smith, A.D. 1992. 'National identity and the idea of European unity'. *International Affairs* 68:55–76.

Smith, M.J. 1998. 'Reconceptualizing the British state: theoretical and empirical challenges to central government'. *Public Administration* 76:45–72.

Solinger, Dorothy. 2006. 'The nexus of democratization: guanxi and governance in Taiwan and the PRC'. Center for the Study of Democracy, University of California, Irvine (http://repositories.cdlib.org/csd/06-13).

Sotiropoulos, D.A. 1994. 'Bureaucrats and politicians: a case study of the determinants of perceptions of conflict and patronage in the Greek bureaucracy under PASOK rule, 1981–1989'. *British Journal of Sociology* 45:349–66.

——. 2004. 'Southern European public bureaucracies in comparative perspective'. *West European Politics* 27:405–22.

Sports Industries Research Centre. 2003. *European sporting success: a study of the development of medal winning elites in five European countries.* London: UK Sport.

Stevenson, N. 1997. 'Globalization, national cultures and cultural citizenship'. *Sociological Quarterly* 38:41–66.

Stoddart, B. 1988a. 'Caribbean cricket – the role of sport in emerging small-nation politics'. *International Journal* 43:618–42.

——. 1988b. 'Sport, cultural imperialism, and colonial response in the British empire'. *Comparative Studies in Society and History.*

Stoker, G. 1991. *The politics of local government.* London: Macmillan.

Stoker, G. and K. Mossberger. 1994. 'Urban regime theory in comparative perspective'. *Environment and Planning C-Government and Policy* 12:195–212.

Stone, C. 1989. *Regime politics: governing Atlanta, 1946–1988.* Lawrence: University Press of Kansas.

Stone, C.N. 1993. 'Urban regimes and the capacity to govern – a political-economy approach'. *Journal of Urban Affairs* 15:1–28.

Stowasser, B. 1998. 'Gender issues and contemporary Quran interpretation'. Pp. 30–44 in *Islam, gender and social change*, edited by Y.Y. Haddad and J. Esposito. Oxford: Oxford University Press.

Strange, I. 1993. 'Public-private partnership and the politics of economic regeneration policy in Sheffield, c.1985–1991'. PhD thesis, Department of Politics, University of Sheffield, Sheffield.

——. 1995. *Directing the show? Business leaders, local partnerships and economic regeneration in Sheffield.* Leeds: Centre for Urban Development and Environmental Management, Leeds Metropolitan University.

Sturcke, J. 2006. 'Straw: I'd rather no one wore veils'. *Guardian unlimited.* Online. Available: http://politics.guardian.co.uk/homeaffairs/story/O,,1889173,00.html.

Su, W.S. 1998. *Professional baseball culture of Taiwan* (in Chinese). Master dissertation, Taipei: National Taiwan Normal University.

Szalai, Alexander. 1972. *The use of time.* The Hague: Mouton.

Tahi, S. 1992. 'The arduous democratisation process in Algeria'. *Modern African Studies* 30:397–421.

Taipei Times. 2000. 'From "black gold" into fool's gold'.

——. 2001a. 'Kaohsiung County strikes OUT'. Taipei, 13 July 2001. Online: http://th.gio.gov.tw/show.cfm?news_id=9721.

——. 2001b. 'Ma Irate Baseball Tournament'. Taipei, 12 July 2001. Online: http://th.gio.gov.tw/show.cfm?news_id=9690.

——. 2003. 'Editorial: the deep wells of black gold'. Retrieved 14 February 2004 (www.taipeitimes.com/News/edit/archives/2003/10/19/2003072527).

Taiwan Daily News. 2003. 'The gambling scandal and Hsiao Teng-Shih' (in Chinese). Taipei: Taiwan Daily News.

Taiwan News. 2004. 'Taiwan's chance to set agenda'. (http://etaiwannews.com/Editorial/2004/04/23/1082687268.htm).

Tam, H. 1998. Communitarianism: a new agenda for politics and citizenship. Basingstoke: Macmillan.

Taylor, J. 1990. 'Sheffield leisure services: compelled to compete and 'capped' into contraction. Crisis or catalyst for leisure policy in the City?' In *Leisure, culture and the political economy of the city conference.* Halkida, Greece: Unpublished.

Taylor, P. 2000. 'Izations of the world: Americanization, westernization and globalization'. Pp. 49–70 in *Demystifying globalization,* edited by C. Hay and D. Marsh. Basingstoke: Palgrave.

Taylor, Peter. 2001. 'Sports facility development and the role of forecasting: a retrospective on swimming in Sheffield'. Pp. 214–26 in *Sport in the city: the role of sport in economic and social regeneration,* edited by C. Gratton and I. Henry. London: Routledge.

Taylor-Gooby, P. 1991. 'Welfare state regimes and welfare citizenship'. *Journal of European Social Policy* 1:93–105.

Terskinas, Arturas. 2002. 'Minority politics, mass media and civil society in Lithuania, Latvia and Poland'. Retrieved 4 August 2004 (www.policy.hu/tereskinas/Research2002.html).

Theodoraki, E. 1999. 'The making of the UK Sports Institute'. *Managing Leisure: An International Journal* 4:187–200.

Thoma, J.E. and L. Chalip. 1996. *Sport governance in the global community.* Morgantown: Fitness Information Technology.

Tibi, Bassam. 2001. *Islam between culture and politics.* Houndmills, Basingstoke, Hampshire; New York: Palgrave.

Tickell, A. and J. Peck. 1995. 'Social regulation *after*-Fordism: regulation theory, neoliberalism, and their global-local nexus'. *Economy and Society* 24:357–86.

Tomlinson, A. 2001. 'Inside the Olympic industry: power, politics and activism'. *Sociological Research Online* 6:U165–U167.

Treasury, H.M. 2006. *Public expenditure statistical analyses 2006.* London: H.M. Treasury.

Tsai, Tai Heng. 2003. 'The study of the development of professional baseball in Taiwan (in Chinese)'. Master dissertation tThesis, National Pington Teacher College, Pington.

Tzanatos, Z. 1986. *Socialism in Greece*. London: Gower.

United Nations. 1995. *Report of the Fourth World Conference on women*. New York: United Nations Department for Policy Coordination and Sustainable Development.

——. 2006. 'World migrant stock: the 2005 revision population database'. (http://esa.un.org/migration/index.asp?panel=1).

Urbain, M.P. 1996. '[The Bosman affair] L'affaire Bosman'. *Revue du travail* 78–82.

Veblen, Thorstein. 1912. *The theory of the leisure class*. New York: Macmillan.

Vergopoulos, K. 1986. 'Economic crisis and modernisation in Greece and southern Europe'. In *Greece in a process of development* (in Greek), edited by A. Manesis. Athens: Exantas.

Volpp, L. 2001. 'Feminism versus multiculturalism'. *Columbia Law Review* 101:1181–218.

Wagner, E.A. 1990. 'Sport in Asia and Africa, Americanisation or Mundialisation?' *Sociology of Sport Journal* 7: 309–402.

Wallerstein, I. 1983. *Historical capitalism*. London: Verso.

Wang, Fang. 1994. 'The political economy of authoritarian clientelism in Taiwan'. In *Democracy, clientelism, and civil society*, edited by L. Roniger and A. Gunes-Ayata.

Warnier, J. 1999. *La Mondialisation de la culture*. Paris: La Découverte.

Weidenbaum, Murray and Samuel Hughes. 1996. *Inside the bamboo network: how expatriate Chinese entrepreneurs are creating a new economic superpower in Asia*. New York: Free Press.

Wilding, P. 1992. 'The British welfare state – Thatcherism's enduring legacy'. *Policy and Politics* 20:201–12.

Wilson, J. 1999. 'Baseball in Taiwan'. In *Total baseball*, edited by J. Thorn, P. Palmer, M. Gershman, M. Silverman, S. Lahman and G. Spira. New York: Total Sports.

——. 2002. 'Baseball player at center of betting scandal resurfaces', Taipei: *Taipei Times*, 9 May 2002. Online: www.taipeitimes.com/News/sport/archives/2002/05/09/135326.

Winter, B. 2001. 'Fundamental misunderstandings: issues in feminist approaches to Islamism'. *Journal of Women's History* 13:9–41.

Wodak, R. and M. Meyer. 2001. *Methods of critical discourse analysis*. London: Sage.

Wodak, R., R. Cillia, M. Reisigl and K. Liebhart. 1999. *The discursive construction of national identity*. Edinburgh: Edinburgh University Press.

Wood, A. 1996. 'Analyzing the politics of local economic-development – making sense of cross-national convergence'. *Urban Studies* 33:1281–95.

——. 1998. 'Making sense of urban entrepreneurialism'. *Scottish Geographical Magazine* 114:120–3.

Wood, L. and R. Kroger. 2000. *Doing discourse analysis: methods for studying action in talk and text*. London: Sage.

Wright, G. 1999. 'The impact of globalisation'. *New Political Economy* 4:268–272.

Wu, C.L. 2001a. 'Taiwan's local factions and American political machines in comparative perspective'. *China Report* 37:51–71.

——. 2001b. 'The transformation of the Kuomintang's candidate selection system'. *Party Politics* 7:103–18.

——. 2003. 'Local factions and the Kuomintang in Taiwan's electoral politics'. *International Relations of the Asia Pacific* 3:89–111.

Yang, J. 2001. 'Lien says KMT must reflect on losses'. *Taiwan News* (http://etaiwannews.com/Taiwan/2001/12/02/1007226763.htm).

Yang, Mayfair Mei-hui. 2002. 'The resilience of *guanxi* and its new deployments: a critique of some new *guanxi* scholarship'. *The China Quarterly* 170:459–76.

Yen, C.F. 2000. 'The 14th proceeding of Education and Culture Committee in the Legislative Yuan: issues of bidding for 2001 Baseball World Cup' (in Chinese). *The Parliamentary Debate* 89(1), 33–91.

Zaagman, R. 1999. *Conflict prevention in the Baltic states: The OSCE high commissioner on national minorities in Estonia, Latvia and Lithuania.* Flensburg: European Centre for Minority Issues.

Zimmer, K. 2005. 'Clientelism in the neo-patrimonial state – strategies for securing regional power in Ukraine'. *Osteuropa* 55:59.

Index